Winningest

The Bill Muncey Chronicles

First Edition 8-18-12

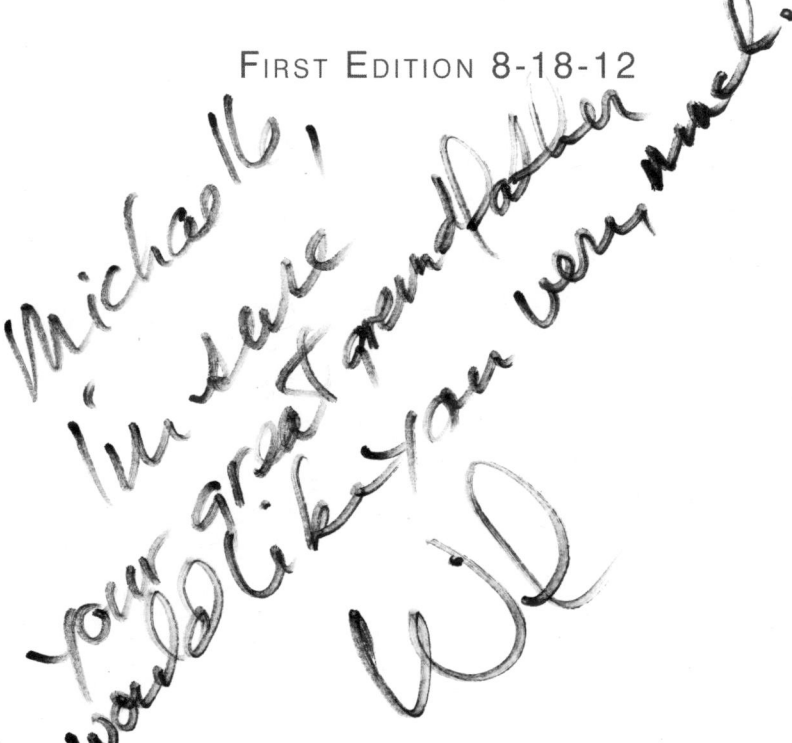

Cover photo by Alyce Dreewes

Dedication
This book is dedicated to my father's
favorite crew chief
and one of his dearest friends:

David Ernst Seefeldt

A champion if there ever was one.

THE INTRODUCTION

William Edward Muncey

November 12th, 1928 to October 18th, 1981

Winningest Open Cockpit Driver in the history of
Unlimited Hydroplane racing with 62 career wins including:

Eight Gold Cups
Seven Indiana Governor's Cups
Six President's Cups
Six Kentucky Governor's Cups
Five Champion Spark Plug Trophies
Four UIM World Championships

Seven time National High Point Champion Driver
(1960-61-62-72-76-78-79).

Note: The enclosed cockpit was developed within a year of his fatal accident which occurred while leading in the final heat of the World Championship in Acapulco, Mexico. With the safety of that technology it was still thirty years before his win record was broken.

The Bill Muncey Chronicles

Table of Contents

Raymond's Ride	Chapter One	1
Bogie Lake	Chapter Two	11
Pheasant Hunting	Chapter Three	21
Big Break	Chapter Four	25
Raven Hair	Chapter Five	41
Oranges	Chapter Six	47
The Army Years	Chapter Seven	55
Every Way But Straight	Chapter Eight	63
A Dumb Idea	Chapter Nine	77
Nobody Called Him Billy	Chapter Ten	87
He Had to Wrestle	Chapter Eleven	103
These Boats Turn	Chapter Twelve	111
The Mile	Chapter Thirteen	131
A Simple Tulip	Chapter Fourteen	153
Ice Cream	Chapter Fifteen	159
Testing	Chapter Sixteen	165
In The Saddle	Chapter Seventeen	175
The Legacy (unfinished)	Chapter Eighteen	195
Acknowledgement		199

CHAPTER ONE

Raymond's Ride

Detroit in the thirties was hardly prosperous for anyone. Ed Muncey was dedicated and determined but the resources within the Midwestern industrial community were stringent at best. Winter represented a chill that lingered with the snow that stayed on the ground and dictated a way of life that revolved around mittens and restrictive overly padded winter coats. Bill Muncey's parents, Ed and Esther, did their best to insulate their two boys from the stark realities of a nationwide depression and managed to maintain a substantial level of success. Nevertheless, tight finances encouraged the two brothers to find their own fun. The cost of a babysitter was out of the question so usually anything that Bill did involved bringing his little brother, Raymond, along with him.

The fact that the age difference spanned six years made the task easier for Bill. Two reasons contributed to this conclusion; Bill was substantially bigger and more authoritative in the presence of his little brother and Raymond sincerely adored his big brother. At twelve years of age, Bill represented all the best in Raymond's local heroes. From Tom Swift to Hopalong Cassidy, Raymond projected all the virtues of the stories Bill read to him onto his bigger brother. Bill could not only do no wrong, he could do all the "fun stuff." Bill's uncanny aptitude for music on the family piano was just one example of pastimes and adventures out of Raymond's reach. After all, he was only six.

The fact that Raymond regularly inherited Bill's hand-me-downs had a curious way of making him feel more like his older brother. The snug and down-filled fit of his coats created a double sense of security, almost as if they still contained some kind of magic aura that would protect and enable him. Raymond admired Bill's bent toward daredevil activities such as his recent ride in a boat powered by an outboard engine. Although Bill took Raymond swimming in the summers at Bogie Lake, Raymond knew better than to consider aquatic adventures unchaperoned. His older brother was his staunch benefactor and he returned this support and consideration with unquestioned obedience and loyalty.

Bill reciprocated with a depth of care and concern that only exists within the bond of brothers. The age difference dissipated any tendency toward competition between the two. Raymond was his ward and he took his mothers wishes and the responsibility as Raymond's older brother very seriously.

"Go outside and play with your brother," his mother Esther would say. "Stay out of trouble but don't leave him behind. You and your brother are a team." Nevertheless, trouble was not very far away.

One day the two of them were up on the roof of their one story house tasked with the responsibility of sweeping the leaves off. It was not a particularly complicated or sophisticated job. Their father, Ed, was down on the ground gathering up the sweepings and piling them in the back yard in order to burn them. In this part of America during the fall, it was an annual ritual of all the families in the neighborhood to gather up their leaves the weekend before Thanksgiving and burn them. The aroma permeated the streets and alleys with a thick but pleasant seasonal signal of the imminent holidays and the promise of cold mornings accompanied by cups of hot chocolate cupped between eager fingers - a communal sensory rite of tribal passage binding neighbors together that has disappeared with the decades.

Both brothers had been given strict instructions to stay away from the edge and the gutters.

"Sweep the leaves into small piles and let your brother Bill sweep them over the edge," Ed had said.

At first, it had been pretty interesting, making little calico colored piles tumble down the slope into a cascading flurry of leaves and stems that spread out on the lawn below. However, the novelty soon wore off. Ed had worked his way along the side of the home and away from where the boys were working. The sun was drying the leaves into a cooperative state, the process of which was visually embellished by the fact that wisps of vapor could be seen wafting into the midmorning air off the sloped roof. The boys found themselves with time on their hands waiting for their father to return. Perhaps they could do something more constructive with the time. Bill reasoned that they could get in a quick game of cowboys and Indians during the interim. Although Raymond had never played it before, he had surely seen it played around the neighborhood. It wasn't hard to explain and if he caught on quickly, he could be a

CHAPTER ONE

new player on Bill's team when he played with the other kids.

"OK, Raymond. " Bill always called him by his full name. "Let's play cowboys and Indians. You've seen me playing it around the neighborhood?"

Raymond nodded his confirmation, barely containing his enthusiasm for being included in such an important activity for the first time.

"Okay then. Here are the rules. I will be the Indian and you are the cowboy. You use your pointing fingers for guns and I will make believe a bow and arrow by putting my left fist out in front of me and pulling back an imaginary string with my right hand. If I can open my right hand before you point your finger at me that means that I got you and you have to fall down dead. Okay? "

Raymond could barely check his excitement. Although he only just recently turned six, he could understand the full implication of this initiation into neighborhood games. If he did this well, he could be part of the neighborhood clan. He would be entitled to share in the adventures and fun stuff that the Egan brothers and other big boys did. This was very important and he was determined to do it well. He nodded in agreement indicating his understanding and consent.

"I will count to ten with my eyes closed and you go find place to hide. One, two, three..."

Raymond bolted off to find a proper place of concealment. Unfortunately for Raymond, this was in the days before satellites, television antennas, or dish networks. In other words, there weren't a lot of places to hide on a roof. There was, however, a chimney. Raymond's heart pounded as he waddled as fast as he could in his over padded snowsuit to the opposite side of the chimney. It was a lot of work in the confining clothes because Esther did not want her youngest catching a cold. As he swung around the chimney's corner, he crouched into what he thought was a clever position in order to catch his breath without the breath plume in the cold air giving away his position. He seemed to recall how the Hardy Boys had caught a villain in one of their stories by seeing the bad guy's breath. Raymond was very pleased with how things were going. He promptly hopped around the next chimney corner intent on catching his brother in his finger gun sights.

Bill was standing right in front of him with his left hand forward in a fist and as Raymond watched, he saw Bill pull his right fist back and open it, launching the fictional arrow.

Although Raymond was disappointed that he had been shot "dead" so soon in the game, he also understood that a big part of game etiquette involved how well you could "die." Every kid had his own style and he had appreciated the extra groan and slump that the Egan brothers exhibited when he observed them from afar. He was determined to impress his big brother with his own unique style.

Raymond dropped like a bag of wet cement. The bag of cement which was wrapped in winter overalls, a jacket, and mittens rolled very much like a log off of the roof. Uttering, "You got me," as he reached the gutter seemed almost poetic in retrospect. Bill could only stare with his eyebrows up and his jaw open as his little brother rolled over the edge of the roof muttering something as he disappeared. Although it was only eight feet to the ground, it seemed that Raymond fell for an eternity before a soft thud was heard. And then, the longest silence of Bill's life followed. He had really killed his little brother!

A flood of emotions overcame Bill as he ran to the edge to look down. Somehow he already knew precisely where his father was if help was needed. Horror settled in the pit of his stomach as he realized the certainty of Raymond's demise. He was convinced that help wasn't going to be needed but if it was, he had to admit with further trepidation that he had no idea what you did with a broken little brother. Mom would know, but that determination also had its own dark side. This was big. This was real trouble.

As Bill looked down at the motionless Raymond spread eagle in a pile of leaves, he became aware of a strange sound that reached his disbelieving ears. It was kind of a whimper accompanied by a sniffle. With a start, he recalled Raymond nursing a cold and that Raymond would have to be alive to make a sound like that. With a mixture of dread and relief that overshadowed concern for his own well-being, Bill leaped down on to the ground beside Raymond.

"Jeepers, Raymond, are you O.K.?" Bill asked with tone of surprise and concern in his voice.

Raymond was trying very hard to be brave so that his big brother didn't think that he was a crybaby.

"Yeah, I didn't mean to fall off of the house, though. Do you think that Mom will be sore?" Raymond asked.

"Why do you have to tell Mom?" Bill asked, knowing that it would be big trouble and probably his old man's belt if either found out. Quickly doing the math and factoring how much time he may have before Dad came back around the corner for the very pile of leaves that Raymond was lying on, Bill made an executive decision.

"I'll let you have those cat's eye marbles and one of my steelies if you don't tell Mom." Bill offered. "I know you want them and I was kinda thinking of giving 'em to you anyhow. How about that?" he asked.

Choking back a small sob and cutting short a sniffle, Raymond said, "I guess that would be swell."

Bill pulled him up off the leaves and brushed off his back. He knew that Raymond was crummy at keeping secrets.

Raymond told Esther in spite of the bribe. But after all, Bill thought, he was only six.

Soon after the arrow incident, the December snows arrived in earnest. Snow stayed on the ground and compacted with ice into a slippery soupy swill on the streets that was a bane to truck driving Teamsters and an annual joy to anyone 12 or under.

While Raymond was in the house on West McKinley Street playing with his new marbles, Bill played with other kids in the neighborhood this time of year pursuing their favorite pastime. While a truck swished and slid down the ice packed road at a reduced speed, the neighborhood daredevil contingent would individually run up behind a passing truck and grab onto its tailgate while firmly planting their booted soles on the slickened pavement and enjoying a citified version of snow skiing. Based primarily on the dare system which is the coin of the realm for children under 12, each participant would dare the other to prolong the duration of the ride. On a rare occasion, the dare could be nullified by a driver stopping his vehicle and running the daree off down the road but usually the task was performed with great enthusiasm and aplomb. Of course, if the participants abbreviated the ride short of the determined distance and such an act was witnessed they would be anointed with the title " Shirley Temple", or some other derogatory caste bestowed by the darer until the next participant failed. This was somewhat confusing considering this was a coed activity. Nevertheless, such a timid title was to be firmly avoided at all costs and Bill was a competitive boy.

The sub-freezing temperatures had persisted into the afternoon. Street skiing conditions were excellent. The daily newspaper truck was due to rumble past the house in about twenty minutes and Bill was anxious to get outside. Although he had gotten his homework done and was therefore allowed to pursue less constructive activities, Esther had not returned from teaching her piano lessons and Bill was still tasked with supervising his little brother. Raymond had never participated in street skiing before and considering his size and age would not be today. Still Bill supposed Raymond was interested because he would see him peek out the window when he was outside with the other neighborhood kids. Maybe he could just bring him outside and watch after him while he kept an eye out for the paper delivery truck. Although all the details about his plan were a little foggy, Bill was certain his mother would be home soon and the issue would take care of itself. Esther was totally unaware of this recent street skiing fad and Bill wasn't anxious to tell her about it or have Raymond share his observations.

Making sure that his little brother was properly bundled in a double parka and his little hands were mittened together with a string through the sleeve so he couldn't lose one, the pair shuffled outside into the crisp, cold afternoon. The sun had been out just long enough to create a soft icing of slush over the compact snow and ice compressed onto the street in front of the Muncey house.

"Ideal conditions," Bill thought.

The pair sat down on the brick stoop that was attached to the front of their house and common to the homes of the period.

"When do you think it will come? " Raymond asked with a mixture of awe and anticipation.

This particular feat that his brother and the other "big boys" did was impressive. He thought the trucks were large, loud, smelly, and heavy. A lot of scary stuff. He had watched his big brother run up behind one before and grab the back bumper with both hands, his legs wide apart for balance. His boots pointed straight ahead. Paired roostertails arching out behind his heels exaggerated the force of his feet plowing through the slush. He recalled and was practically amazed to see a big smile on Bill's face. It looked terrifying to Raymond.

"The newspaper truck doesn't come back this way until it's

Chapter One

heading back to town empty," Bill said. "There may be some other truck that comes along, but I prefer the paper truck because its bumper is higher," Bill said with a voice of experience and authority. "It's easier to keep your balance, "he added.

Although he hadn't thought it out very far, Raymond secretly hoped that the truck would come before his Mom came home. She didn't approve of some of the games that the neighborhood kids played represented by the shrieks and yelling currently going on across the street and somehow he knew she wouldn't think much of this. She certainly wouldn't want him out in this cold any longer than necessary and would take him inside. As it turned out, that would have been a really good idea.

As though on cue in a Hitchcock movie, the local newspaper delivery truck lumbered around the corner and down the block. Rocking back and forth with its canvas top slapping the sides of the box frame, the two brothers stood up in unison as it drew nearer. Bill's pulse quickened and Raymond turned expectantly to see what his brother was going to do. He could see the level of concentration rising on his brother's face and could tell he was calculating the speed with which the truck was approaching.

"Raymond," Bill said. "How would you like to ride on the back of the paper truck?"

Raymond was already aware that the tailgate was commonly down and that it would be a relatively simple matter for his brother to set him on the back edge of the bed. Although the truck definitely represented a scary presence, Raymond could visualize his brother being right there beside him holding onto the bumper. All he would have to do was sit there.

"That would be pretty keeno." Raymond said using a term of approval that he had heard the big boys use. "Can you teach me how to street ski?" he asked, realizing that he was pushing his luck.

"We are just going to have time to do this one trip before Mom gets home, Raymond, " Bill said. " But you can learn a lot by watching me from the back of the truck. It's pretty easy once you get the hang of it. You'll see! "

With that said, Bill tugged Raymond up off of the step by his puffy coat sleeve and hurried down the walk to the street's curb.

"Time's a wastin," Bill added.

Fortunately, the driver's attention was drawn to a snowball fight across the street as he neared the Muncey house. Battle lines had been drawn between two opposing snowmen and the neighborhood was fully engaged. As the truck rolled by, Bill picked his little brother up by the waist and stepped behind the back of the vehicle. Almost as if it were a dance, he turned Raymond in the air as he lifted him and planted him squarely on the back edge of the bed of the truck. Any apprehension that might have shown on Raymond's face disappeared as soon as he felt planted on the bed.

Bill promptly grabbed hold of the bumper while spreading his feet apart being careful to keep his toes pointed forward. This was the tricky part of the ride because turning your feet sideways could cause you to trip or lose your balance.

Once his stance was established, Bill leaned back and proceeded to 'ski' over the ice-coated asphalt. Looking straight ahead and up at Raymond, he couldn't help but notice the excitement and admiration on his brothers face. This was an experience that he hadn't anticipated and overall the whole ride was going very well. Keeping his legs straight and his shoulders back helped him maintain the proper posture. The driver was apparently oblivious to their presence so nothing was going to curtail their adventure prior to reaching the end of the block, at which point the truck would turn back toward down town.

As the two brothers looked at each other with substantial smiles on their faces, it occurred to Bill that this was one of those defining moments that brothers sometimes share, a whole lot of private fun that they would remember and talk about for years.

It also occurred to him that he should start considering his 'dismount'. This usually involved a voluntary but gentle bounce or push-off from the bumper while being careful to keep the shoulders straight in order to maintain balance. As long as Bill kept his head up, he could usually coast to a non-eventful stop near the cement curb at the end of the street. A storm drain was approaching that he often used as a launch point. With a handful of seconds left, he looked up at Raymond's smiling face and began to realize that there was one factor of this ride that he hadn't fully thought out. A question began to present itself that wasn't accompanied by an immediate and satisfactory answer. If Bill reached up to grab Raymond around the waist, Bill's speed would slow down and start distancing him from the back of the paper truck. The standard release actually required him to push away from the truck. How was he going to grab Raymond? Looking up at his little brother, Bill realized that Raymond didn't have the slightest idea this problem existed. Moreover, there wasn't time to discuss it.

Salt is a remarkable substance. Inert and granulated, it can accomplish a lot of tasks with minimal effort. Deposits discovered under the community of Detroit years before had been mined to help the growing city control the impact of icy roads on the city's traffic. Coupled with some heat from the afternoon sun, it becomes liquefied and can substantially accelerate the melting process on the street, exposing the pavement below. The runoff from this process had created a bare patch near the storm drain and brought Bill the answer to his dilemma. It wasn't the answer he wanted but it was definite and immediate. The resulting traction sent him sprawling forward and onto his chest. Now spread eagle face down on the street, Bill began to spin gently in a circle. He could hear the truck powering away as he came around full circle and looked up at the tailgate. Raymond's eyes were as wide open as his mouth. Bill could tell that the expression was dedicated solely to witnessing Bill's own circumstances and that little Raymond had not yet considered his own impending personal consequences. The truck slowed slightly for a right turn and Raymond grabbed the side of the truck securely. The last expression Bill saw on Raymond's face during his ride was one of innocent distraction. Looking at the new sights, beyond his one-block limit imposed by Ed and Esther, was an interesting experience at the moment and not alarming in the least. The truck would not have occasion to stop and would barely slow down until it arrived at the paper's terminal in downtown Detroit.

Meanwhile, Bill's spin continued until he came to an unceremonious stop facing back down the street. Looking up, he noticed his Mom backing into their driveway a block away. He was doubtful that he would avoid Ed's belt his time.

The Detroit Street Skiers (Raymond and Bill Muncey)

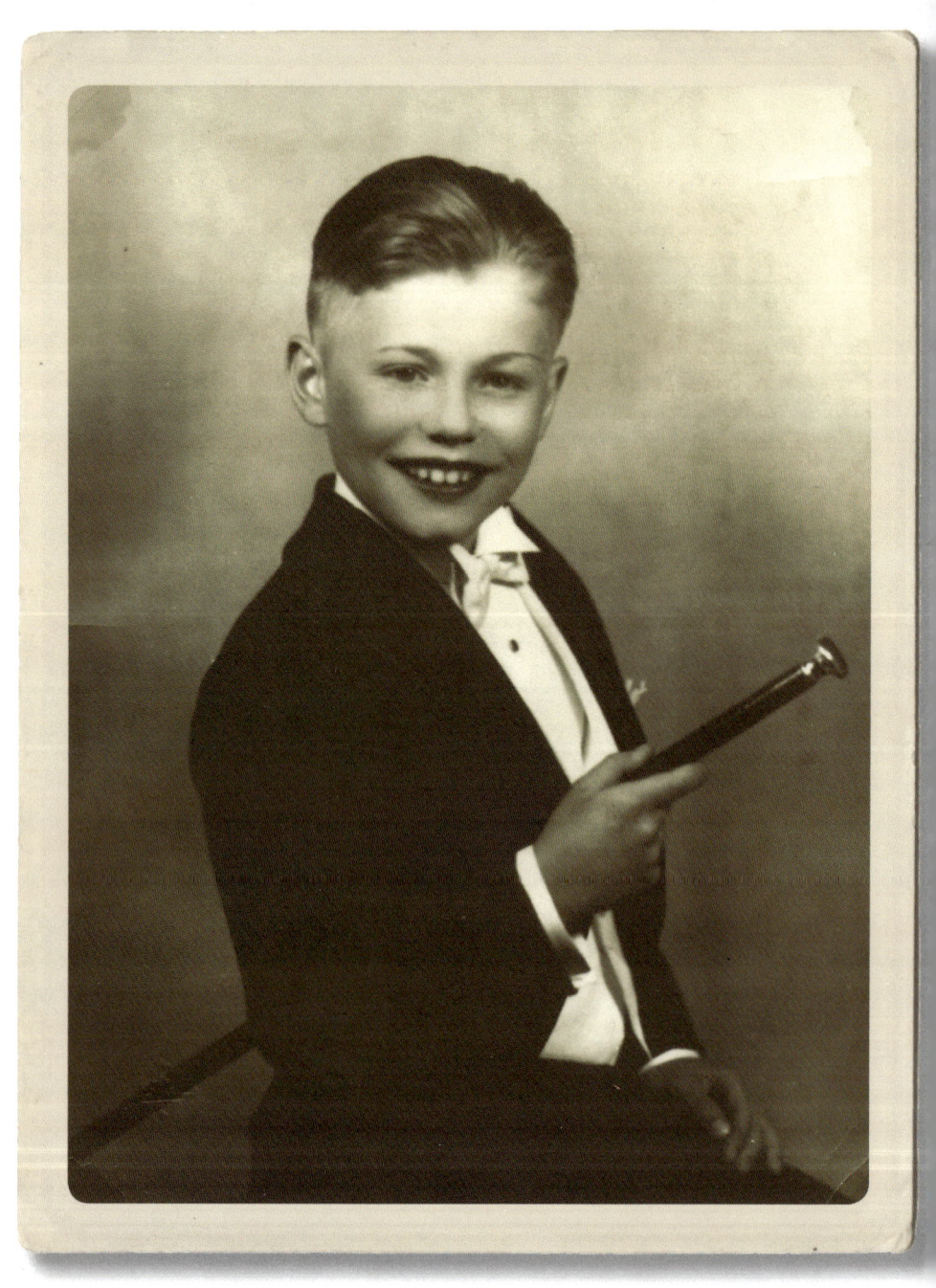

Young Bill, the entertainer, circa 1940

CHAPTER TWO

Bogie Lake

According to the family legend, Ed Muncey came from the hills of West Virginia at the tender age of twelve. "Came from" is a literal term derived from the fact that he ran away from home when he was severely disciplined by a school principal through the use of corporal punishment in the schools boiler room. Being of Irish descent, barefoot and dirt floor poor didn't endear him to his prospects of opportunity in a community that regularly advertised next to job listings "Irish need not apply."

Nevertheless, there were some residual benefits to growing up in an area of a long standing tradition at skilled wood working. West Virginia, Virginia, and North Carolina have a well-earned international reputation for quality hardwood furniture production. Apparently, Ed Muncey brought some skills with him to the forests of northern Michigan when he emigrated cross country. Legend also has it that he initiated and completed the sojourn by working as a fireman on the B and O railroad of Monopoly fame. A fireman is essentially a strong back that shovels coal into the locomotive for the princely sum of ten cents a day. In 1912, trains tied the United States together and anyone willing to work that hard could legitimately earn his way across country.

Whether he refined his wood working skills as a young adult upon arrival was never established but they were shared with his sons when the young family built themselves a summer cottage up on one of the many northern Michigan lakes called Bogie. Shop skills and discipline, wood working vocabulary and appreciation for attention to detail were ingrained into the young men and a cabin was the by product.

A popular magazine of the time was called Popular Mechanics. In it were shared articles and stories about the latest in high tech innovations such as automotive related components, practical inventions for the home and free plans for wood based structures such as bunk beds, kitchen cabinets and boats. The concept of "plywood" was the rage at the time of Bill's teenage years. A process that laminates or glues thin layers of wood to each other in a fashion that crosses the natural grain of the wood and creates a material or medium of relatively high strength at a fraction of the weight. The glue is flexible enough to allow for a new dimension of freedom in design that lent itself well to the curved bottoms and decks of boats with a lesser likelihood of leaking.

Plans for an eight foot hydroplane that would be powered by an outboard engine caught Bill's eye. Nights after school in the family garage provided the time to assemble the parts and pieces that he fashioned and manufactured by hand. Brass wood screws and anchor fast bronze nails were the latest and most respected fasteners for marine applications. Newspaper route money contributed to the weekly allowance that paid for them. As spring bloomed, the vessel came together and was joined at the transom by a ten horse outboard engine provided by Ed Muncey. The company pickup truck from Ed Muncey's Chevrolet enabled transport to Bogie Lake on one of the family weekends.

Father and his sons carried the creation to the water's edge at the community dock. With the transom extended off of the edge of the dock the outboard powerplant was attached securely and incorporated into the steering system. Although many of the smaller boats of the time were maneuvered via a tiller or handle attached to the engine itself, Bill was very proud of the steering wheel and cable system that made it possible to lean on his knees further forward and enhance acceleration when getting on a plane. The maiden voyage was remarkably uneventful and Bill was able to share driving it with his Dad and take his little brother for a ride with Raymond lying on the deck in front.

Summer brought the cessation of school and the perpetuation of America's passion for gasoline power. One of the more recent activities invented as a byproduct was water skiing. Standing on top of plywood slats attached to a person's feet and holding onto a rope or towline made it possible for someone to be literally pulled over the water if a boat with enough power was available. The more power a boat had and with enough stability, a boat could even pull more than one skier at a time. Although wartime gasoline rationing was impending, American families continued the tradition of weekend outings in the family car to the country. The state of Michigan provided plenty of destinations by way of hundreds of lakes and dwellings created and designed specifically for this motoring pastime called "motels." Although the Munceys were fortunate enough to own a vacation cottage on the lake, the people of Bogie Lake produced some community structures of attraction.

As an appendage to a local resort, a floating ski jump was built to embrace the colorful pastime and afford skiers the opportunity to actually sail through the air by being pulled over the jump. Stoutly constructed out of wood the jump could be floated to the middle of the lake and lined up for a boat to speed by pulling its adventurous enthusiast. The structure itself was novel enough to draw regional attention and the local promoters did not hesitate to apply its presence and possible use to encourage visiting vacationers to keep a watchful eye. Ski boats and even skis could be rented and the new born skiing industry provided a self perpetuating attraction that helped to fill motels and restaurants.

Gasoline power and propulsion also made it possible for younger people to enjoy dramatically more freedom and liberty. Bill's mother, Esther, acquired her driver's license at the green age of twelve. Although automobiles were usually physically regulated by the restriction to pavement or dirt roads, boats enjoyed a freedom of motion that fueled a fertile imagination. It would not be uncommon to see a group of younger boating enthusiasts tied together in a communal "raft" in the middle of a Michigan lake sharing conversations and beverages.

One thing that was interesting about Bogie Lake was the fact that another lake was right next to it, separated by a relatively thin natural bridge of land - just wide enough to allow for a two lane blacktop road. A driver crossing could easily observe waterborne activities on both lakes with a simple turn of the head.

At some point never established, Bill connected the words "plywood", "ski jump", and "two lakes" in one sentence. In review, the thought may have been a byproduct of a lively "rafting conversation." Nevertheless, the concept of using the ski jump to launch his outboard-powered race boat into the air and making it possible to jump from one lake to the other captured his imagination. The project contained all the elements attractive to a young man: careful planning, a demonstration of skill and daring, and enough notoriety, if properly executed, to impress girls.

There were several sequential steps involved to achieve success. The first was the use of the ski jump itself. The owners weren't initially impressed with the idea. Although placing the ski jump close enough to the edge of the lake was relatively easy, the idea of damage to the structure tempered their enthusiasm. Bill's energy, promotional zeal and assurance that he wouldn't actually attempt the feat until the end of the tourist season swayed their judgment. Besides, he was just a kid who probably wouldn't follow through anyway, but if he did, the anticipation of a repeat would carry over into the next tourist season - and could possibly help increase business. Win-win.

The next step was mathematical. Distances had to be measured and the jumping had to be practiced; not over the roadway but a length determined to be equal to the distance from the ski jump where it sat. The hull needed to be weighed and balanced so that it would maintain a level attitude in the air. Where he placed his own body would make a substantial difference. The octane rating of the fuel he ran would affect the horsepower output of his engine. The attention to detail was a satisfying challenge in itself and Bill bent to the task with quiet determination.

He decided early on that he would make two practice runs. One run would be for the practical experience of just making a boat slide up and over the ski jump and the other for the needed distance itself. Wax that he used on the bottom of his snow skis found its way to the running surfaces of the hydroplane. He enlisted the assistance of his friend, Tim Egan to bring one of the resort's rental boats out as a "chase" boat and stand by at a distance. Without fanfare or notice to the community, they made their way onto the lake early in the morning one weekday and conducted their initial launch.

It probably goes without saying that of course Ed and Ester had no idea that their eldest son was contemplating such a feat. Other than Tim, whom only half believed that Bill would go through with it, and the resort owners who completely believed Bill would not go through with it, no one had any idea of the imminent attempt. As luck would have it, there was virtually no one on the lake that morning to witness the event. In retrospect, that was just as well.

Since the first time was merely to experience and practice the concept of actually performing the act of jumping, Bill didn't commit all of the resources of his speedy craft to the effort. Instead he chose what he would have called a more conservative approach. This was literally the truth since when he actually contacted the

CHAPTER TWO

bottom of the ramp, he was at substantially less than full throttle. The resulting effort did accomplish a "jump", but he had attained barely enough speed to drag himself over the edge at the top of the ramp. The distance carried in the air was negligible, but technically effective enough to provide important information: information such as the fact that if he did not establish a method to keep his nose up on landing, he would enjoy a face full of water. Although a large smile creased that face immediately after the test, Bill was thoroughly soaked from head to knee. The boat was operated from a kneeling position, and Bill had been kneeling into the cascade of water that tumbled over the bow on impact. Smiling, right-side up and wet was considered a success.

After bringing the boat back to the dock so that he and Tim could check for things like cracks, dents and other damage, it was concluded there was still time for a more determined effort that morning. After passing their rudimentary safety inspection and quickly refueling, they headed back out to line up for the approach. Tim was admittedly impressed and a little amazed that Bill had gone through with it. Although they had known each other since early childhood and Tim had to concede that he had never seen Bill back down from a commitment, this type of challenge seemed a little extraordinary and out of the way. There weren't even any girls around.

This time Bill decided that he would sit a little further back so that the bow of the boat might have a greater tendency to stay up. The hand throttle was located on the right side midway down the cockpit allowing for the flexibility. He also increased that throttle in order to gain enough speed to propel him the required distance from the ramp. Once again he had remembered to unlock the transom latch so that the lower unit of the outboard powerplant could swing back when it came in contact with the ramp. Although they had not re-waxed the bottom of the boat for the second effort, the distance achieved on the attempt was more than enough to carry the boat and its driver the needed distance. It was a lot dryer too. He hadn't moved much further back, so Bill was pleased that he had managed to guess the appropriate amount.

This time, the period in the air seemed a lot longer also. There was a moment when he actually had time to glance across the lake at their summer cottage and recognize his little brother, Raymond, out in the yard raking leaves. There had been a brief moment of appreciation of the fact that this particular vantage point was unique and transient. It was a perspective that no one else would probably approach or appreciate unless they happened to be a water skier or some other fool like himself trying to jump a boat off of a ski jump. The sense of independence and individuality was one that would grow stronger with time. Seeing Raymond going about his daily autumn chores enhanced the perspective of the difference between them. Raymond would never be this impractical.

A loud plop resonated across the lake when the boat hit the water. In an effort that would become his trademark in later years, he conserved the engine by releasing the throttle and allowing the powerplant to idle the moment that the boat launched onto the ramp. Always conserve the equipment. He would later learn that there would be times in competition where one would be compelled to abuse the equipment, so the effort to conserve had to be a discipline always maintained.

Subsequent inspection by the boys established that the little craft was remarkably resilient and the pair proceeded to plan the actual effort. While they both began to realize the gravity of what they were trying to accomplish, they both proceeded with a legitimate sense of confidence.

The first task was to determine the best (thinnest) portion of the land bridge to jump. It not only needed to be of minimal width, but the ski jump itself had to be able to get close enough to take advantage of it. The depth at the shoreline varied so this proved to be a surveying adventure.

Although the boat seemed to carry itself off the ramp high enough, it made good sense to anticipate stopping any traffic traversing the road during the effort. Therefore, someone would actually have to stand on the road to act as a monitor. Tim could attend to this since they hadn't needed a chase boat in either test and getting one into the other lake would be tough anyway.

As Jump Day approached, Bill followed his self-composed check list in a diligent fashion. Re-waxing the bottom of the boat, checking and securing the electrical connections on the engine, and mixing the fuel were some of the items he addressed. Checking the seams on his life jacket and oiling his leather football helmet were personal issues to which he attended. He hadn't worn the helmet

CHAPTER TWO

before but as an afterthought, it didn't appear to be a bad idea. As a wingback, he had earned the nickname "Moose" on his school's football team. Enthusiastic participation had kept him in good physical shape. The seed of a commitment to safety planted itself and would stay with him the rest of his life.

"Why not be as safe as you can?" Bill thought, "It's not like there is something more important to do."

Fall in the state of Michigan may be the most colorful place in the world to be during that time of year. As the massive trees of the northern American forests prepare to release their leaves and slide into a winter slumber, the colors of the dominant canopy glow and pulse in the sidelong autumn light.

Although the sun came out unusually bright that morning, the trees rimming Bogie Lake appeared reluctant to wake up to bear witness to the event about occur. The boys had borrowed the delivery truck from Ed Muncey's Chevrolet to transport the boat and equipment down to the lake's edge. They would need it again when they transported the boat back from the adjacent lake, after all Bill couldn't jump back. Even the water in Bogie Lake itself quietly considered sleeping in as the sun's rays lifted sheets of morning mist off of its cool surface. The resulting fog rose to catch the colors of gold and silver enhancing the natural pallet provided by the attendant trees as the mist wafted into the tree line. The quiet scene was subdued and apparently detached in a mystical way that lent an extraordinary sense of purpose to their efforts, almost as witness and testament to the resolute young men.

Sounds of the pickup's doors closing seemed unusually loud, while the cough and initial sputter of its engine starting was more pronounced than usual. They did not wait for the warm air of the cab radiator to defog the inside of the windshield by convection through the dash board. A quick couple of swipes of gloved hands and they were on their way. Having already secured the ski jump in position the day before enabled them to concentrate on the actual task at hand. Curiously, Bill hadn't notified the media or even the resort owners of the actual time of the attempt. He presumed that once the feat was accomplished, their eyewitness accounts would be adequate to assure its authenticity. With eager determination, they backed the pickup down to the lake and off loaded the hull on to the community dock. Carefully setting it in the water, they secured the outboard engine and fired it up in neutral.

As the engine warmed up, Tim hurried back to the truck and proceeded to his position on the land bridge to ensure Bill's unobstructed passage into the other lake. Sitting on the edge of the dock with his two feet in the cockpit holding off the boat, Bill donned his life jacket and helmet. Observing Tim's progress, he turned and set down on his knees while grabbing the steering wheel with one hand and the hand throttle in his right. Satisfied that the engine was warm enough to allow all the parts to move together properly, he glanced out over the water. Letting the engine idle, he carefully reached around and levered the engine into the forward gear. Turning now to focus straight ahead, he gently squeezed the throttle and motored out onto the lake. Leaning his body weight ahead and over the steering wheel accomplished the relatively quick acceleration of the boat onto a planing attitude.

No other boats were on the lake that morning, no fisherman or skiers to have to consider when lining up his run at the jump. The outboard powerplant ran smoothly and evenly. A little more squeeze to the throttle brought the anticipated response and the little boat began to prance off the pontoons, or sponsons, attached to either side toward the front. These sponsons helped trap air under the boat that made it possible for the craft to literally fly over the water. This relatively new technology had barely been considered within the last fifty years. The improvement of performance over the traditional planing displacement hulls was dramatic and particularly appreciated as Bill leaned over and brought the boat around in an arc to line up with the ski jump. Picking up speed as he approached, Bill noticed the cool air lacing over his fingers on the steering wheel and tugging at the unfastened straps of his helmet.

"Should have tied those," he thought.

With the jump looming straight ahead, he depressed the throttle to the maximum setting in order to get the last measure of horsepower out of the engine. Stretching back to assure the desired nose-up position once the boat left the jump, Bill raced ahead and onto the ramp. The initial impact of the sponsons on the ramp sent a muffled echo out ahead as boat and driver slid upwards toward the sky in a terrific rush. Bill had cut the throttle at the last possible moment leaving the engine to idle as it hurtled off the edge of the jump

Chapter Two

into the air. Making a special effort to keep his shoulders square to the steering wheel, he hoped to maintain the desired balance of weight and wind resistance in order to enhance a level flight.

The nose was high enough to obscure vision straight ahead, but he could see off to his immediate right the roadway below with Tim standing on the white line in front of a patient driver in a green sedan. The actual sound of the wind as it sailed past him was evident in the absence of the ski jump acting as a sounding board for the engine. Bill dared to turn his head and look down at the shoreline as it seemed to stand still beneath him.

Actually it was standing still beneath him.

It was never determined with any degree of certainty what caused it, either too much wind resistance with the nose up a shade too high or perhaps he cut the throttles just a shade too soon, but in any case, the forward motion of the frail little craft had slowed down considerably. Although Bill was immediately aware of the problem, there wasn't a thing he could do about it. The nose continued to rise slightly while the transom and the engine tended to drop. Bill leaned ahead to bear his body weight forward but the effect was negligible. The overall effect was similar to a 4 x 8 sheet of plywood trying to push its way through the air. It also seemed that the driver and boat descended much more rapidly than they had climbed.

Looking back down at the pavement, through uncanny situational awareness, Bill promptly and accurately estimated that the lower unit or propeller end of his engine would most likely land somewhere near the white line on the road. Dropping with the grace of a bag of wet cement, the pair fell tail down. With both hands firmly wrapped around the steering wheel, he looked over to his right at Tim in front of the green sedan.

People that survive accidents often suggest that time can appear to slow down during a critical phase and a person's attention to detail slams into overdrive. Bill recalled later how Tim's arms were in the air over his head waving for some reason that was not then or ever really clear. Bill noticed that Tim's eyes and mouth were open in an expression matching that of the driver behind the wheel of the green sedan.

Anyone who has stepped on an aluminum can has heard the approximate sound of a ten horsepower outboard engine hitting asphalt from 25 feet in the air. Upon impact, the lower unit of the outboard engine folded up like a compressing accordion. The transom of the boat snapped off with the engine head. Bill's knees pushed the separated bottom of the boat on a cushion of air onto the road. The bow and steering wheel housing stayed airborne, if you could still call it that, a little longer before slamming flat onto the street leaving Bill kneeling with a lone detached steering wheel still in his hands. Splinters, cable, aluminum castings, pulleys, wires and transom plugs scattered in every direction. The hull and engine absorbed most of impact leaving the driver remarkably unscathed.

The silence that followed was only punctuated by the sound of the idling engine in the green sedan patiently waiting for what was going to happen next. The sedan driver brought his nose up to his steering wheel to peek over and down at the hapless boat driver now sitting on his ankles with his steering wheel in his lap. Tim ran over to help Bill stand up. The pair simply looked around at the debris that was once a boat. They proceeded to pick up the pieces and unceremoniously deposit them in the back of the Ed Muncey Chevrolet delivery truck. There wasn't really anything to say. An expletive or two certainly could have been appropriate but Bill realized that things unquestionably could have been worse.

As the two pulled the borrowed ski jump back into its position later in the day, Bill began to form an opinion that would resurface years later, "Sometimes records are seriously overrated".

Bill's parents, Ed and Esther Muncey

Bill and his son, Kenton, operating the same type of hydroplane that Bill jumped out of Bogie Lake many years earlier.

CHAPTER THREE

Pheasant Hunting

The first drop of blood appeared as a pear shaped fleck in the palm of his hand. The significance of it at first eluded Bill. He looked down at his hand and quietly shook his head as if that action could discount or dismiss the cause.

Then another drop appeared.

It had been a cold, crisp autumn morning in the chilled and foggy north woods of Michigan. The sunshine chased the mist into swirls that dissipated through the trees into the air. A bush-strewn meadow that they had walked into had taken on a mystical surreal quality. An occasional chirp from a bird claiming its territory underscored the solitude of the moment.

The two teenage boys cautiously stalked their prey into the clearing. Heat from the morning sun briefly gathered on their faces, only to be swept away by the cold air with each step. Small foggy plumes of breath funneled out of their mouths as they carefully chose each step. They sensed more than heard the bird's presence back by the tree line.

Michigan forests are famous for their autumn colors. Spectacular starbursts of orange and yellow leap out from the landscape on pallets of evergreen. The sound of dropping leaves becomes the commonplace white noise of the forest. Because of that, the small plodding steps of a twenty-pound pheasant are discernible to an attentive ear.

Both boys had been hunting together before, however, with less than modest success. Both were determined to demonstrate and develop their prowess as hunters. Until this year, the annual outing had been a ritual of sorts. Every fall, Bill and Tim would accompany Tim's father pheasant hunting in these woods. The boys would flush out the pheasant when the opportunity arose and Tim's father, Arne, would actually discharge the weapon. This year, the boys were by themselves for the first time.

Arne had been steadfast and earnest in teaching the boys safe hunting practices and firearms safety. Although all three had carried weapons, only the designated shooter would have a chambered round.

Pheasant Hunting

The two young hunters waded into the meadow waist high in brush and grass. Their red and white plaid jackets contradicted the immediate bland surroundings comprised of earth tones and fall hues. Even if someone were color blind, the patterns of the checkered jackets would stand out.

A patch of faintly green grass ahead twitched and shimmied. Both hunters noticed the movement and froze and stared. The patch was silent. A modest fog-scattering breeze camouflaged any other movement in the grass.

With his weapon held across his chest in the port arms position, Bill quietly stepped toward the turf a hundred feet ahead. At the same time, Tim carefully opened his shotgun and slid a cartridge as inaudibly as possible into the gun's barrel. Closing it, Tim brought his weapon up to point toward two o'clock of his position. Safeties were on both of their weapons. Bill moved closer while Tim held his ground. The stillness in the meadow had remained consistent since Bill began moving. Both of them knew the routine. The hunter in front flushes out the bird, the hunter behind tracks and shoots the bird. Pretty simple.

As Bill moved closer to the patch of grass, the sun slid behind the clouds. Shadows rippled across the clearing and sunlight seemed to strobe against the trees. The overall effect achieved a sea change. Birds chirped and a crackle of branches could be heard off to their right. And then the pheasant flew!

Bill saw it ten feet ahead of him. It caught his eye when it was five feet in the air, a slow graceful arc up to his left. For an instant, a sunbeam caught the bird in flight as if it were spotlighted on a stage. Bill briefly wondered why Tim hadn't fired yet. The problem was that he had.

It's amazing how quickly someone can become accustomed to the uncommon. Flashing images and dancing shadows blended easily with a gentle hand picking him up by the shoulders and hurling him head over heels into the bushes. It almost came to Bill as no particular surprise as he sailed through the air much like that pheasant.

Whether Tim was temporarily disoriented, or that he pulled the trigger too late or too early was never determined. By the time that the pattern of shot reached Bill, it was eighteen inches wide and spreading. With enough energy to rip a hood off a car, individual

Chapter Three

shot burrowed its way into his back, shoulders, neck and head. The impact of the charge catapulted Bill into a heap several feet away but still conscious.

Slowly he brought himself up to his hands and knees. Holding his right hand in front of his face, the wounds began to bleed onto it. It took a moment for Bill to comprehend what had happened. He had taken spills and tumbles racing boats and had always collected his senses quickly regaining control. But this was different. This was bad. On a primitive fundamental level, he knew that this was very bad. Nevertheless, some needs are constant. Gaining control is one of them, he reasoned. Bill knew even if he could not, he had to act as though he could. Control was progress and progress would be his ally. It could hardly get worse. Forcing foreboding aside, he innately knew that fear, panic and timidity were his enemies.

"Stop the bleeding, get to help." He had to keep it simple.

Tim didn't realize that he had dropped his shotgun while running to Bill. All Tim could say was a stream of "Ohmygodohmygodohmygod. " The look of horror and confusion on Tim's face gave Bill his first verification of how bad things were. Bill knew that the massive pain probably on the way was currently curtained by shock. This was good he knew, and yet that was bad too. Shock can kill you if you wait too long. Bill knew that there was no time to waste. His shirt stuck to his chest as he tried to stand up. Flaps and shreds from his plaid jacket hung down In front of him. Putting his hands on his knees, he pushed himself upright. Satisfied that he could stand and not weave much, he turned to face Tim.

It took all of Bill's deliberation to look into the terrified face and say, "Tim, we have to get to a hospital. "

With the utterance of that sentence, Tim's jaw stopped quivering. His eyes stopped darting and the inexplicable need to wave his hands about evaporated. In one motion, Tim bent over at the waist, wrapped his arm around Bill's middle and picked him up on his shoulder. Tim felt his friend was weightless as he raced over the thawing ground to Bill's Chevy.

The doctors were able to remove most of the buckshot. Some was too close to the spine for a doctor's knife, and was left. In telling the tale to his 12-year-old son many years later, Bill said it was the most painful ordeal of his life.

Upon hearing the story, his son contemplated on the nature of the relationship between Bill and his friend afterwards. "More than ample acreage for hard feelings and recrimination," his son thought. He asked how his Dad felt about his friend after the shooting, and the situation on whole. Bill's response lent insight to an attitude that still generates benefit today.

"I was just glad that I wasn't the one to pull the trigger."

CHAPTER FOUR

Big Break

Oily smoke and flames billowed out of one of the engines on the right wing of the bomber. As it promptly began losing altitude, the flames spread out over the wing. Members of the ten man crew could be seen from a distance to be leaping into the subzero, oxygen-starved air at 18,000 feet pulling at rip cords that would open their parachutes.

The enemy airplane that had caused the damage flew by for another run at the wounded aircraft slowing down to focus its aim. From a mile away, an American lieutenant looked down at the throttle control for his single seat airplane. Powered by a 1700 cubic inch V-12 Allison engine, it developed over 1,000 horsepower at a cruising rate of about 2200 revolutions per minute(RPM). The horsepower output was considerably more at the 2800 RPM he was currently pushing the engine to, and could go even higher if needed. Considering it was his job to chase enemy aircraft away from the bombers, the pilot felt compelled to close the distance and engage the enemy. Reaching over, he removed the stops that limited the levers allowing fuel into his powerplant. Pressing the levers near his right knee forward, the 23-year-old moved them into the position of War Emergency. This setting increased the horsepower output up to 50% and allowed the engine to cool itself more efficiently at the higher RPM. The airframe twisted slightly and shuddered with the greater application of power. Hurtling through the air at over 300 MPH, the young pilot from Akron, Ohio quickly closed the gap between the two adversaries.

The Allison engine thundered through the unmuffled exhaust as it consumed its 130/145 high octane gasoline. The high performance fuel, coupled with the supercharged engine, enabled the pilot to maintain the element of surprise. He flew through the stratosphere to find the bomber was being mercilessly pummeled by its predator. The enemy broke off the attack too late to avoid the approaching cannon. Round after round slammed into the enemy's single engine causing its own oily smoke and flames to furl out over the fuselage as its pilot prepared to reach for his own rip cord.

Immediately after World War II, thousands of these Allison

engines found their way into the common market as war surplus. Not only was it surplus, but also fairly obsolete for airplane use by virtue of the emergence of the jet engine which had recently been embraced by the aircraft community. The relatively sudden end to hostilities left an American production juggernaut that made an inexpensive source of very high horsepower and torque readily available to the public via military surplus.

On the other hand, it was an aircraft engine that required a sophisticated method to simply start and run at idle, much less develop the higher RPM needed to create the optimum horsepower. Applying the aircraft powerplants to a maritime environment that would respond promptly in a competitive situation was a challenge that taxed the most creative of fabricators. Nevertheless, it was apparent that these engines' successful application would permanently alter and enhance boat racing.

It was possible, however, for a race driver to scrap or damage the engine during the starting procedure before he even got underway. Many a driver experienced great frustration when going through the steps which had to be undertaken in absolute sequential order and at a prescribed rate in time. Leaving out a step or performing one too late, or too soon, would leave the engine unresponsive or 'washed down' and unable to start. That scenario would be more desirable than to over rev the engine causing what was called a "lean condition. " The dreaded back fire could break the engine into pieces with great force. The whole procedure was more than a little intimidating even to the most experienced operators.

The evolution of watercraft had reached a crest 50 years earlier when a Frenchman had attached gasoline power to a hull design that became known as a hydroplane. 'Hydro' being Greek for water and 'plane' indicated moving over it. The quick burning petroleum enhanced response and the overall lighter weight of the powerplant and its required fuel combined to establish a maritime operating platform of great potential. With the hull traveling over the water instead of pushing through it with a traditional planing displacement design, it encountered less drag and a greater rate of acceleration. Relatively smaller versions had demonstrated this potential in tangible ways prior to World War II, but the global conflict accelerated the production technology of materials that enabled much heavier craft to get lighter. Plywood, aluminum, and

Chapter Four

magnesium were some of the benefactors of development.

The oldest son of Esther and Ed Muncey, Bill graduated early from high school in the Detroit suburb of Royal Oak, Michigan. A genuine aptitude for playing and writing music had earned him a summer term at a prestigious music academy and the resultant credits allowed early scholastic release. This amazed Ed Muncey who saw little value in musical pursuits and felt that any further effort in that direction would be detrimental to his child. He appreciated the dedication and discipline needed to play well. He encouraged Bill up to a point but was also convinced that other interests would provide greater long term benefits.

The success of Ed Muncey's Chevrolet dealership had been slow but steady through the war years. The end of hostilities had welcomed back every G.I. to the idea of prosperity and the benefits entitled to the victors. Often these anticipated benefits materialized in the form of a new affordable automobile. Moreover, many service members came to Ed Muncey's Chevrolet. The resulting relationships laid the groundwork for a customer base that would grow and prosper over the years. Ed had a gift for making friends and genuinely identified with a young couple addressing financial challenges. To Ed it did not seem that long ago since the young Muncey couple had rented an apartment above a bowling alley and Bill's first crib had been the apartment's bathtub.

Prosperity had ushered Ed's family into a new and more comfortable home in Royal Oak. Ed built a game room in the basement and invited his friends over for the Friday night poker game. On occasion, this weekly fixture hosted the attendance of some of the more involved friends and associates in the community which included the mayor and chief of police. People in the know who could make things happen in the burgeoning economy of post war Detroit would congregate and converse about their comings and goings. It was during one of these Friday nights that Ed happened on the idea of helping his eldest get a ride in one of the latest model race boats. As is often the case, turning points in a person's career often hinge on someone knowing a friend who knows a friend.

Conversation had come up about a boat that was successfully using one of the very powerful Allison engines and testing it out on the Detroit River. This hydroplane could be heard testing as far away as McNichols Avenue. Ed happened to know the brothers who owned it, as they had often stopped by the dealership to admire the latest automobiles General Motors had to offer.

Ed had supported his son in his efforts to race boats partly as a means to maintain his interest in the latest technologies and partly as a method to direct his attention away from music. It was in Ed and Esther's opinion that an appreciation of music and a good singing voice were important for church and high school dances, but the temptation of pursuing music as a career was more likely to lead to a life of financial uncertainty and an association with nefarious characters. If pressed, Ed would have admitted that he was honestly disturbed to see that at the tender age of eight years old, Bill would rather spend five or six hours a day voluntarily playing on Esther's piano than be outside getting in trouble with the other kids in the neighborhood. Bill's interests had evolved beyond the piano to include proficiency with the clarinet, the trombone and his generation's version of the electric guitar called the saxophone.

It was almost a curse that Bill had true talent, if not genius, for playing and writing music and had earned the local respect as a musician. He had his own band and had even gone so far as to adopt the stage name of Stan Arno. While performing on stage, Bill would wear a pair of clear horn-rimmed glasses that enhanced his intellectual image like the popular band leaders Benny Goodman and Glenn Miller.

"It may require dedication and intelligence but it isn't likely to earn a steady paycheck," Ed thought. Better that Ed encourage Bill's pursuit of activities that would absorb his youthful passions and passing interests. His support of boat racing had addressed that need and it seemed to provide the kind of commitment that might continue to hold his attention.

Ed had been pleased to see Bill dedicate time to observing the boat races held across from the Detroit Yacht Club on the Detroit River. Ed recalled that when Bill was sixteen years old, he would speak of his heroes on the water like Chuck Thompson and "Wild Bill" Cantrell with a certain reverence not associated with band leaders. This was a chance for Ed to participate in and contribute to his son's interests without crowding. After all, Ed couldn't play a musical note and wasn't able to share the musical aspect of his sons life.

A conversation with a friend led to a conversation with another friend that brought Ed to Al Fallon, one of the owners of the Miss Great Lakes boat. Having driven it in competition himself, Al was personally acquainted with the complexities of grafting the technology of an aircraft powerplant into the wooden dimensions and constraints of a watercraft. It was never established whether Ed Muncey actually paid Fallon to provide the test ride for Bill or whether Bill was simply encouraged to show up at the right time, but a date was determined and Ed was able to convey the opportunity to his eldest son. Ed had been openly supportive of his son's involvement with power boat racing. In exchange, Bill would help at the Chevrolet dealership. Bill would later joke about how when it came to doing the parts inventory over in the service department he would list to himself, "This part for the dealership, this part for the race boat."

Ed offered no objection provided Bill replaced all parts used and maintained an adequate inventory. Whether Ed realized it at the time or not, an appreciation of music can compel healthy respect for mathematics and this proficiency encouraged and enabled Bill to be a participant in the family business. Music also insisted on an accurate appreciation for timing which would prove pivotal in future pursuits.

Upon learning of the opportunity to operate a full size hydroplane, Bill was hardly able to contain himself. He promptly introduced himself to the owner over the phone and made himself available to help prepare the boat over at Al's shop. Without pause, Bill got personally acquainted with Al and proceeded to become familiar with the engine and the controls.

Compared to the inline six cylinder 235 cubic inch automotive engine that propelled his own race boat, the Allison V 12 of 1710 cubic inches was daunting. Massive by comparison and weighing up to a ton when finally configured for a marine application, the propulsion system weighed ten times what Bill was used to. It also developed five times the horsepower. An eager learner, Bill pummeled Fallon with questions about anticipated situations. Patiently, Fallon explained the starting procedure and had Bill start the engine while it sat on the trailer in his shop. This wasn't a simple task. Although Bill had taken flying lessons at Wayne County airport, the V-12 was substantially different from the more common radial style powerplants in air planes. To add a dimension of difficulty, the standard aircraft controls were modified to accommodate the varying situations common to boat racing and implemented an air control that was attached to a right hand foot pedal. Although this took on the appearance of the traditional gas pedal in an automobile, it had more in common with the hand control on a farm tractor. The difference was important and Fallon had apprehensions as to whether the young novice could accommodate the distinction in the beginning.

Instead of the simple on/off switch and starter button that Bill had on the dash of his Chevrolet powered sixteen foot hydroplane, the dash board of the Miss Great Lakes was a panel of switches and gauges Bill had never seen before. There was a master switch, a switch for the electric fuel pump that enhanced the performance of the mechanical pump built into the engine, a two sided switch that ungrounded the magneto, a switch that sent power to the starter motor and yet another switch that opened a small valve allowing fuel to bleed into a small fuel injection system aimed directly toward the combustion chambers in order to simply start the engine. Another switch enhanced the spark to twenty four spark plugs. Some switches were turned on and stayed on; some weren't used after the powerplant started running. Then there were the fuel/air mixture control levers that required adjustment as the powerplant was started and again after it got under way. The sequence of steps was critical and could cause substantial damage to the engine if not properly applied. Bill quickly realized that it took both hands to start the boat. "When do I grab the steering wheel?" Bill asked himself.

Fallon chuckled as he patiently explained the systems and showed the enthusiastic young man the procedures needed to operate the boat. He recalled the first time he took the Miss Great Lakes out onto the water and remembered that it was initially intimidating on its maiden voyage. Add that the totally submerged propeller had a tendency to push the bow high into the air as the boat achieved the proper planing attitude, it made for a disorienting experience. Being unable to see straight ahead in the beginning could present a problem. That was something that couldn't be replicated in the boat shop and could be a challenge when attempting to leave the Detroit Yacht Club where the boat was scheduled to be launched. Fallon was going to have to give this some thought.

Chapter Four

Although Bill was quick to share his enthusiasm with his father, he wasn't too anxious to share the possibility of the experience with his immediate friends. Bill would later state "I turned pro at eighteen." With an implied confidence, the transition from capable grass roots competitor was a magnified leap. Amplified by the fact that this was going to happen in front of his hometown as the son of a locally well-known personality and he had more than his share of distractions. He wasn't in any hurry to encourage the presence of the media and was comfortable in the knowledge that this was simply an unpromoted test. Nevertheless, sometimes a friend tells a friend who tells a friend.

The great day arrived with a drizzle in the morning that dramatically contributed to the humidity that only a Midwest city like Detroit can generate. Sultry and clammy, the pace of preparation at the water's edge was deliberate but casual. Like any good crew chief, Fallon liked check lists. Working his way down it created a level of confidence with each check mark. Bill walked beside him and tried to learn as much as he could. There were a lot of new features and technology involved with this type of boat and Bill absorbed everything that he could. He knew that his questions may seem trivial and draw attention to the fact that he lacked experience but the only way to overcome that was with a steady application of curiosity and optimism. Esther had often told him, "You can do anything that you set your mind to." Time had born that truth out on many occasions. Learning music at her knee at an early age when she taught piano in their home was probably the most pronounced example of that advice. Bill was not unduly intimidated by the huge musical toy that he was allowed to play with in their living room at the age of eight and he had faith that this larger maritime toy was also something he could master.

Fallon showed patience and an engaging sense of humor that inevitably encouraged the young driver. Although Fallon was quick to impress upon any driver the need to consistently conserve the equipment, he also understood that there was a fine line between conserving and achieving maximum performance. He knew from personal experience that sometimes the line gets blurred. The test drive wasn't intended to be anything more than just that. Ed Muncey had assured Fallon that should Bill break something, Ed would make good on it. The possibility that the test could be a stepping stone to a permanent ride for Bill was remote because Fallon already had a capable and dedicated driver.

There weren't any witnesses on shore to appreciate the attention to detail that the crew had paid to preparing the boat. The morning sun was rising into a cloudless sky and the river seemed tranquil and deceptively tame. The Detroit River had the well-earned reputation of being the most treacherous in the world. The race course surveyed by the American Power Boat Association was laid out to have the first corner of the pear shaped oval down by the Belle Isle Bridge. The concrete supports for the bridge had created swells and depressions that weren't often observable to the naked eye but at high speed could throw a boat around in unpredictable and dangerous ways. Learning how to read the water and handle the constantly changing surface conditions was an educational curve that was acquired in separated seconds and minutes of driving over time.

There was one witness out on the race course, however. Down by the bridge, Ed had brought out the family pleasure boat to view the event. He hadn't told Bill that he would be there. He often observed his sons activities from afar. He felt that if he told Bill that he would be there, it may make him nervous and self-conscious but he wouldn't go out of his way to conceal it. He let his son know that he was interested and would attend an event if he could. All members of the Muncey family were raised with the attitude that your commitment to work came first, observing popular pastimes came far down the list. Nevertheless, Ed had made a special effort to be there.

This was a big deal.

Bill was intensely focused on the tasks at hand. The sounds of car horns honking in traffic over on Jefferson Avenue across the river didn't offer the slightest distraction. The boat had been launched and paddled by hand over alongside to the yacht clubs guest dock. Fueling was being completed by the crew. Bill was putting on his life jacket and helmet as he and Al reviewed once again the starting procedures of the behemoth powerplant. Bill had fired the uncoupled engine on the trailer to warm it up and get the oil well circulated. All had gone well during preparations, but Fallon had his apprehensions. With the propeller in the water, encountering a load, the timing and sequence of action is different. No advice in the world can replicate the situational awareness needed to start and control the craft. There were cases where the driver never did get the engine started and the boat had to be brought back to the dock after each unsuccessful attempt.

The cockpit of the Miss Great Lakes didn't have a seat belt. The idea was controversial and the prevailing wisdom was that if the boat got into trouble the driver needed to get out easily. Boats can sink fast and there shouldn't be anything to slow the escape down. Bill was in the habit of carrying a rag or two in the belt of his life jacket. He did this for two reasons, the first being the occasional need to wipe oil or water off of his goggles, the other was to use the rag as a plug should a leak develop in the hull or a drain plug be lost.

The other side of the equation was the possibility that a bucking and bouncing hull could actually eject the driver. The steering wheel took on more significance than simply aiming the boat. It had to act as a huge handle to help keep the driver in the boat. Stainless steel sealed in rubber was the ultimate configuration for such a device. Often up to twenty inches in diameter, this rotating circle of safety was designed to flex and bend as the driver was bounced around the cockpit trying to hold himself in and maintain a steady course while strategically placed padding and upholstery provided more than cosmetic functions.

Upper body strength was another consideration. It took a substantial amount to physically hold oneself in line with the throttle or adjust the body's position as it bent and twisted with the attitude of the boat. In the tradition of popular body builders of the time, Bill worked out with a boxer's punching bag every day. That coupled with high school football and hockey had kept him in peak physical condition.

Although flight suits were available and shop coveralls were common, Bill wore a pair of blue jeans and a white T-shirt under his life jacket. Black tennis shoes provided traction and cotton balls stuffed into his ears protected his eardrums from the unmuffled exhaust directly to the side and front of him. Wiggling down into the tight fitting seat, he and Al went over the starting procedure and the anticipated route. There was a chase boat now out on the water in front of the yacht club being operated by Al's brother. Should the need arise, it could easily tow the Miss Great Lakes back to the dock.

Fallon's apprehensions of the load of the river throwing off the novice's timing proved to be well founded. After using the tow line three times to bring the Miss Great Lakes back to the dock , the collective opinion was that Bill was "washing down the cylinders" which is hydroplane-ese for getting too much gasoline to the combustion chamber by applying the full fuel throttle lever too soon. He could get the engine to fire but the acquired knack of knowing just the right time and rate of application to apply '"full rich" (aircraft-speak for all available fuel flow) eluded him and Bill would "put out the fire", meaning there was so much gasoline present that it saturated the sparkplugs. The batteries were wearing down and if something was not done soon, all this test would verify was that the Miss Great Lakes did not leak much.

The only immediate solution to the problem that day was for Al Fallon to start it himself. The sequence and timing was an acquired sense developed from practice. As Bill prepared to try again, Al stepped from the dock onto the deck of the boat next to the cockpit. Dropping down on his knees next to Bill's right side, Al said, "Why don't I work the fuel control lever while you operate the fuel injection and the starter?"

At first Bill thought that this was a great idea, until he realized that Al would still be kneeling on the deck when the boat got underway. A puzzled look came over Bill's face and he asked, "But, Al, where are you going to sit when we get going?" Al quickly looked down on the deck and said, "Don't worry about that. I'll just swim to shore."

Now it was Bill's turn to look down. Somewhat embarrassed Bill asked, "You mean you'll just help me get it started and then jump overboard?"

Al nodded. Bill knew that there weren't very many more turns left in the starter before the batteries were depleted. Even the starter was sounding tired. Apparently, this was the only way Bill was going to drive a boat on the river that day. After contemplating the scenario for what seemed like a long time, Bill looked up at Al and said "Thanks, Al."

Fallon nodded and looked up from his crouch to make eye contact with his brother at the helm of the chase boat thirty feet off the dock. With a wave of his hand and a fraternal nod, Fallon signaled him to idle off into the current. Bill caught Al's gaze as

Chapter Four

he looked back at the young driver and nodded. Bill reached over for the starter button and spring-loaded primer switch. Depressing the foot pedal about a quarter of an inch at the tip, Bill pressed the starter button while flicking the primer switch. Almost immediately, the collector style exhaust pipes belched black fuel laden smoke back at the pair. Fallon promptly shoved the lever to full rich and Bill inexplicably knew to depress the throttle a good two inches further. The transom dipped, the bow lifted and the Miss Great Lakes lurched into the main current of the Detroit River. Bill suddenly realized that he was totally but temporarily blind looking straight ahead, as Al had warned him would happen. He leaned to the left of the windshield and looked off toward the chase boat to try and get a sense of direction. By stepping a little further into the throttle, the transom appeared to come back up and let the bow drop back down. Looking over to the right again he realized that Al Fallon was gone. Taking his finger off of the starter button and releasing the primer switch, he converted the control of the engine to the foot throttle and idle rich lever.

The sensations assailing the young novice came from a myriad of sources. A cyclic vibration shimmied its way up the propeller shaft between his legs and was gone as the hull continued to pick up speed. The black smoke that had bellowed out of the Inconel exhaust pipes had cleared up and appeared to be cleaner while 24 spark plugs efficiently burned the fuel being sent to the 12 cylinders. Four light-weight sodium-filled valves per cylinder rotated the charge into exhaust and then overboard. The sound of thousands of spinning, meshing and rocking parts was lost in the throaty roar of a leviathan of power that commonly conquered the sky. Modest rolling waves working their way down the river were quashed out of the way as boat and driver shouldered their way onto the waterway.

The spray of water that had peeled up from the bow as Bill was getting the hydroplane into a planing attitude had disappeared. He noticed less vibration from the impact of the water and more of the sense of being suspended over the surface. At about 2200 RPM, the boat seemed to completely break free of the surface and leap from swell to swell. The rate of acceleration increased and the buffeting of the wind became a force to be reckoned with in spite of the windshield. Bill had to exert effort to exhale against the wind, and then let the force of motion fill his lungs with each inhale. The roar of the engine was deafening as the powerplant reached 3000 RPM.

Time on the water with a high performance craft is measured in minutes and seconds of experience. Bill had acquired hours at the helm of nimble vessels such as stock outboard powered runabouts and 16 foot automotive-powered hydroplanes. A keen sense of attitude and balance had been honed from hundreds of thousands of waves, ripples, and rolling swells. Operating this much larger boat was a completely new set of references unfamiliar and demanding. He determined that because the hull felt sluggish and slow to respond he must be traveling a slow rate of speed. "Now that I have it up and going," he thought, "I need to show that I can make it go fast."

As the need to turn the boat loomed ahead, Bill scanned his gauges before establishing a radius. Oil pressure was at 80 pounds and steady; fuel pressure to the supercharger was 20 pounds and the boost or manifold pressure from the supercharger to the combustion chambers was at 65 inches of mercury. All systems were healthy. What amazed him was his speed. He was going almost 100 miles per hour! What was sluggish in this boat would have been out of control in any other boat he had ever driven. Gently turning the wheel, the boat promptly responded to the helm and laid out a lazy arc that brought Bill through the first corner and straight down the shoreline in front of the Whittier Hotel.

Keeping well away from the docks and warehouses on the city shore, Bill waved at a familiar cabin cruiser as he headed into the larger Belle Isle Bridge corner. Realizing that his Dad had come to see him run was a big deal. Ed wore his dark blue captain's hat back on his balding head and with a big smile waved back. His spectacles reflected the elongated liquid roostertail that shot skyward from the propeller of the race boat entering into the corner. Bill comfortably wheeled over the same swells over which he had seen legends like Danny Foster and Bill Cantrell drive. Rocking gently from side to side, the hull appeared to casually negotiate the apex of the corner as she easily thumped and bumped her way over the current, back around to line up alongside the yacht club docks. Gar Wood had put the Miss America hydroplane through her paces on this same river. Bill realized he had just entered into a very select and brutal fraternity of individuals who shared a unique and

Chapter Four

almost indescribable set of experiences. At that time, there were not more than a 100 people in the world who had the slightest idea of what he was experiencing. The edge of competence demanded from members of this community was sharp and unforgiving.

Straightening out, the Miss Great Lakes planted her transom and the wavering RPM from the fluctuating load of the corner evolved into a steady drone that resonated throughout the hull. Like a wooden amplifier, the boat's plywood hull broadcast the sounds of its engine as if it were music aired over an aquatic stage to listeners miles away. In that day, it was the sound of progress. Heads turned and ears cocked to discern its source. The pulse of the great Motor City quickened a bit. A workman sitting down to open his lunch pail paused to reflect and consider that in his community at that moment and on that day someone was trying something new and special. A secretary sitting at her desk unwrapping the wax paper from around her homemade sandwich looked up to notice that the glass in the nearby window frame vibrated slightly and she smiled. Change was in the air and that was exciting. These were good sounds and good signs.

The end of his first lap in an Unlimited-type hydroplane contained all the elements of excitement and the demands of concentration Bill had expected. The gauges continued to reflect a healthy state of performance. He kept the engine RPM at approximately 3200 as he flew past the yacht club. Looking over at Al Fallon as he went by, Bill noticed that there were interested bystanders walking down to the dock. Although his body language didn't indicate any concern, Al had a towel draped over his shoulders due to his recent swim. The rising temperature of the air that early afternoon flowed over the bow of the boat around the powerplant and delivered a funnel of heat that caused Bill to uncomfortably perspire under his life jacket. His left foot dangled unemployed beneath his seat in the cockpit. There weren't any brakes in a race boat.

Curiously, there weren't any other boats out on the river at that time. This was a welcome surprise as Bill completed two more laps before heading back to the dock. Being blessed with exceptionally good 20/10 eyesight enabled Bill to look over from quite a distance and observe Al with both arms waving in the air, the universal signal amongst all levels of boat racers to bring it back to the dock. Although Bill may have been challenged to get the boat started and away from the dock, he demonstrated an unusual aptitude to know just when to pull the fuel control lever back to shut off the gas and flick the magneto switch to the grounded position. Correctly anticipating the tug of the river's current, he was able to drift the bow of the boat up to the dock without the assistance of the chase boat. It may have appeared to be a small thing but Bill felt a measure of redemption for the humbling beginning of his ride.

Al was all smiles as he extended his hand to help Bill off of the deck of the boat onto the dock. The gap between Bill's two front teeth which would become his trademark someday was plainly visible as Bill's wide smile was equally evident. With a tremendous sense of satisfaction, they both looked down at the marvelous powerplant nestled in the boat visibly emanating blurred images of heat wafting off the enormous valve covers. A quiet sense of accomplishment and indebtedness surfaced in the younger man's mind. Someone had taken a chance with him by giving him this opportunity and he was quick to state his appreciation. Al tried to minimize the issue but Bill was profuse with his thanks.

"Anytime you need someone to go swimming for you", Bill said, "just let me know."

The overall mood of the moment shifted slightly as everyone's attention diverted to an apparently agitated man coming onto the dock. Waving his arms and shouting, Fallon recognized the man as the actual driver of his race boat. Although he couldn't make out what he was saying at first, Fallon was unpleasantly surprised to realize his driver had apparently been drinking. Shouldering his way through the small crowd of onlookers, the driver sidestepped Al and confronted Bill.

"Who do you think you are trying to steal my ride?" the man demanded.

Bill had seen him approaching out of the corner of his eye. Instinctively, he felt the individual was someone familiar; at least someone he had seen before. Although not personally acquainted, Bill recognized him as the driver of record of the Miss Great Lakes. He was one of the personalities that he had often cheered and rooted for from the shore as a fan. Bill had always regarded drivers like him with a tremendous degree of respect if not reverence. To Bill's young and naïve mind, this fellow must be attempting to congratulate him on a successful run, perhaps even share experi-

CHAPTER FOUR

ences driver to driver. It had been Bill's experience throughout his participation in boat racing, that it was a sport of gentlemen and sportsmen. After all, the marine environment was naturally hostile. Everyone wanted the best for everyone else, particularly with regards to safety and fair competition. Bill stepped around Al to extend his hand by way of introduction.

With profound satisfaction, Ed Muncey looked on from the deck of his boat. Upon completion of the successful run, the mood on the dock had been visibly celebratory. Unaware of the specific difficulties that had to be overcome to get the boat out onto the water, Ed had seen his eldest son hold his own and operate one of the fastest boats in the world out on the Detroit River. He felt a keen sense of pride for having contributed to one of the most exciting days of his son's life. He was quick to realize that Bill was justifiably too preoccupied in discussion with the Crew Chief to look up and notice Ed's proximity. On the other hand, as an experienced adult who had learned to fend for himself out in the unprotected world at a young age, he was also quick to recognize the body language of one of the 'celebrants' on the dock as anything but congratulatory.

Bill's quick reflexes fended off the first blow that had been aimed at his head with his left forearm.

"Reflex first, response second," Bill thought. He hadn't actually heard anything that this fellow had said but he suddenly realized the intent. Another right hook launched in his direction with lightning speed. Time seemed to slow down as Bill raised his left arm again to deflect the punch. A breeze from the river delivered the scent of whisky to Bill's nose that immediately confirmed that this situation wasn't going to be resolved with calm deliberation. Off balance both psychologically and physically, the blow was easily deflected and Bill answered with one of his own. Although Bill was no stranger to fisticuffs, it clearly was not his forte. Aiming at the enraged drivers jaw, Bill's swing went wide of the mark and caught the man in the windpipe knocking him back a step. His adversary reached up for his own throat and began coughing and gagging. Frantically attempting to suck air, he dropped to his knees.

"Call an ambulance!" Bill heard someone say in the background. After regaining his balance, he stared down at the hapless driver now lying on his side, winded and wheezing. Helplessly Bill looked over at Al and then back down at the dock. Unclenching his fists, he stepped back away from the scene while some men kneeled on the dock to provide aid. The silence that followed was punctuated only by the frantic drumming of feet on the wooden planks as someone ran to find a telephone and summon help.

Although it was never his intent to do so, Bill went on to replace that driver in the cockpit of the Miss Great Lakes. It was not supposed to be his "big break"; it just worked out that way.

The P-39 Air Cobra utilized the same Allison engine that was later converted for hydroplane racing.

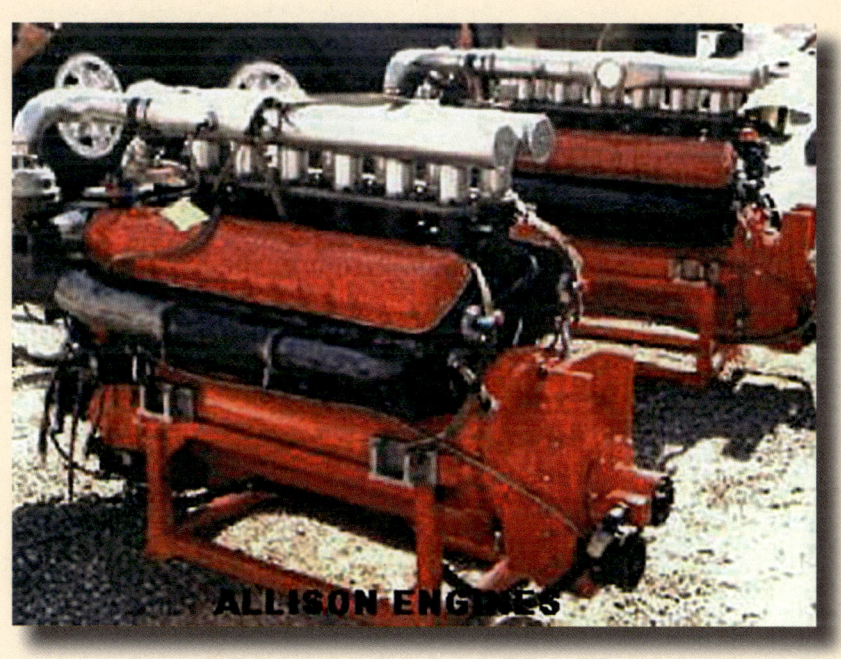

The Allison engine eventually developed up to 3000 horsepower.

Gar Wood was an inspiration to many boat racing enthusiasts

As a teenager, Bill Muncey would watch drivers like "Wild Bill" Cantrell pictured here and Chuck Thompson race on the Detroit River.

The Ed Muncey Chevrolet dealership in Detroit, Michigan.

CHAPTER FIVE

Raven Hair

Thick, luxurious, raven hair. Although he never realized how susceptible he was to a woman's hair, that was the first thing he noticed about Kitsy Graham sitting on the other side of the Creative Writing class Bill was taking at Rollins College in Central Florida.

The next thing he noticed was that she was outspoken. This bothered him a little, at first. He wasn't sure that he liked her candor. It was, after all, a creative writing class. How complicated could it be? However, after a few hours in the same classroom, he began to realize that she took writing seriously. One of his frat brothers, Donnie Wilson, mentioned that Kit was a journalism major and her questions to the professor hinted she was one of those women who saw no reason that there could be a career for a woman outside of or in place of being a wife and raising a family. He wasn't sure he liked any of that either.

Oh, Kit had heard about Bill Muncey. She was convinced that he was just about everything that her parents could think of that would go on the negative side of the ledger for proper suitors. First, he was a musician who played the saxophone. That, in and of itself, relegated him to irresponsible status. Although she had to admit that she had heard him play and that in fact he was very good, musicians were notorious for imprudent behavior and participation in nefarious activities on the saltier side of the tracks.

Yet, she did like the saxophone.

Then there was the motorcycle. Although he had a brand new Chevrolet, he seemed to prefer using his 1947 Indian motorcycle to get around. It seemed a contradiction of sorts. Apparently, his family was relatively well to do. They could not only afford to send him to a good college, but provided excellent transportation - with four wheels.

"Why would he prefer riding around on a motorcycle?" she asked herself.

Although her brother Mac had one himself and seemed to derive great pleasure from not only operating it but also understanding its mechanics, it was not the safest way to travel and not particularly accommodating when it came to dates.

As if to put icing on the cake, he was the President of his fraternity. That didn't seem to be anything more than a license to organize parties, distribute and consume alcohol and, oh yeah, play loud music. The end result of those activities was never particularly responsible or presentable either.

Yet he wasn't especially hard to look at.

Kit had been raised by a well-established family of Scottish ancestry that had spent over 150 years in America. A direct descendant to Malcolm Graham, the Duke of Montrose, her family had immigrated to America and prosperously participated in the growing nation's industrial development. During the American Civil War, they had contributed to and prospered from their representation for and distribution of the products of the Remington Rand Company which included the famous rifle.

Her father was an engineer by education. A graduate of Massachusetts Institute of Technology (M.I.T.) with eleven patents to his name, he had provided well for his family and had actually been able to be one of Roosevelt's " Dollar a Year" men during World War II. As an administrator working with the British Air Ministry which implemented America's Lend Lease program, he had been recognized and appreciated by Great Britain with the award as a Knight of the British Empire (K.B.E.). Malcolm and Eleanor Graham had sent their children to the best schools with the best of intentions. She had been close friends with the daughters of the best of New England society, such as Jacqueline Bouvier who went on to become Jackie Kennedy, and socialized with children of foreign dignitaries such as the Shah of Iran. It would be safe to assume that her parents wouldn't be particularly pleased to hear that their eldest child was not dating the son of a Senator or business magnate, but a music-playing, motorcycle- riding marketing major.

Yet he asked insightful questions in class.

She asked around and found that the other girls at her sorority verified his reputation for owning a car that was capable of 90 MPH. And he drove it that fast. He was even known to fly airplanes and race boats. Although he had graduated from General Motors School of Business Administration with a major in marketing, he showed no sign of settling down in the near future. To complete the image of piratical adventure and devious behavior, he sometimes wore an eye patch to class. Rumor had it that the need

Chapter Five

was legitimate from a hockey accident and that light caused him discomfort sometimes but it did suit the rakish image.

Yet he certainly wasn't boring.

She knew that studying wasn't the primary purpose for his suggestion to share an ice cream cone and go over their notes for an upcoming test. In spite of that, she was surprised herself when she promptly responded with a "Sure, why not?" It was impetuous and somewhat out of character for her.

"What's the worst that can happen?" she asked herself.

The most disarming aspect to this man's approach was his self deprecating sense of humor. He had the ability to laugh at himself and once you realized that he wasn't that keen on taking himself too seriously, he would slip in a serious point or address a substantial matter. Before you knew it, you were having a constructive conversation that went beyond the immediately pressing matters of initial discussion. She guessed that Bill genuinely liked people. He possessed a certain level of unobtrusive confidence that was lacking in other people she knew. It wasn't born of the arrogance of good fortune but she guessed that it had been acquired by independent experience.

Their first date had been an adventure of sorts. She had made the mistake of mentioning that her brother also owned a motorcycle and that she had enjoyed riding on it. That prompted an invitation to ride his. Although her sentiment had been sincerely stated, she was hardly in the position now to say that riding on his would not be fun. Any misgivings would have to be set aside. In later years, she would recall this marked the first time that she discerned that even simple things with Bill could take on a bigger than life dimension.

The ride was determined to be a reward of sorts for their successful efforts to prepare for a test. From the very beginning of their relationship, Bill demonstrated a knack for creating a fun conspiracy about the simplest of plans. Kit was put off, amused, and impressed all at the same time when they typed up their respective essays on her typewriter. She had to admit that Bill was the fastest hunt-and-peck typist she had ever seen. It was obvious that no one had ever taught him how to type. Both index fingers virtually flew over the keys as he hammered out his paper. The flurry of inefficiency still seemed to produce a decent word count.

"Amazing," she thought.

Later she realized that his "Why not try it?" attitude was an integral part of Bill's psychological makeup. She had been raised around an equestrian life style. Horsemanship was almost an art form in her family. Hours upon hours as an adolescent were spent embracing the discipline, vocabulary and care. Her family invested in stable fees and riding lessons. Mucking out stalls to help pay for those lessons had ingrained a respect and admiration for good horsemanship. Her cousin was an Olympic trainer for the U.S. team. Form, balance and grace on a horse were all personal signatures of style.

Bill, on the other hand, had learned how to be a capable polo player by simply "Getting on the horse and going," he said.

"Amazing." she thought.

After securely tying her scarf over her head effectively protecting her long, thick hair from the imminent wind, they embarked on a motorcycle ride that was designed to take them to what Bill had said was, "The best ice cream in central Florida." The motorcycle was loud, powerful and boisterous. She smiled to herself as they accelerated out onto the highway.

"Not especially unlike its owner," she thought.

If some obscure historian had to pick some time and place that could exemplify the American South, central Florida in spring would be a good choice. Quiet, unimposing, and essentially comfortable, it demonstrated a way of life that was productive yet relaxed. Within 50 years, the central Florida area would accumulate over 8 million people within 100 miles of Orlando, but in the late 1940's of post-war America, it was a semi-rural setting inadvertently designed for young lovers to get acquainted.

Dynamically optimistic, Kit found Bill's enthusiasm generally alluring. Although her high I.Q. told her that many of the points he made were 25% optimism and 75% fact, the basic discrepancies were generally harmless. It was difficult not to find his enthusiasm curiously magnetic. She promptly created an endearing nickname for him that they both laughed about. Borrowing part of a popular moniker of the day referring to a manipulator as a "con artist", she came to call him "Con". He definitely practiced the art of modifying an uncomfortable situation into something more pleasant than it was.

Chapter Five

The kickstand of the motorcycle frequently would spring out while they were underway causing Bill to pull over and try different methods of securing it. By their third date, these frequent stops became opportunities for Bill to steal a kiss. Later in life Kit often wondered if the malfunction wasn't deliberate. It certainly was convenient and the delay was never considered a problem. It was like they weren't in a hurry to get anywhere because they were always already there.

Her major in journalism and a minor in history gave her an inquisitive perspective on world affairs and contemporary matters. Not unlike a lot of American women of the time, the feeling of empowerment honestly earned from their roles on the home front in World War II had caused a change. Kit was capable and motivated to create and embrace a new posture for women in American society. She had been a nurse as a teenager volunteering at hospitals stateside during the conflict. She had attended dances at West Point and appreciated and admired the war time commitment the young men felt. The Battle of the Bulge represented the personal loss of a boyfriend for her. Her generation was being pushed onto a world stage and she didn't feel particularly resistant to the idea. It did come to pass that future historians such as Tom Brokaw would refer to hers as "The Greatest Generation."

For some reason, Bill made her feel that all things were possible. He didn't come from a family that was steeped in tradition. As she got to know him over the following summer, the new found prosperity that his family had encountered was not unlike the general attitude prevalent on the streets of America. Maybe she was imposing her perspective on an unsuspecting victim, but Bill seemed to represent the optimism she wanted to feel.

Then there was the accident.

He was by himself flying a single engine airplane that he had rented. It had run out of gas and Bill had been forced to crash land. By way of explanation, Bill had simply laughed it off and said that he had had to "set her down early." Instead of dwelling on it and elaborating on heroic details, he would change the subject and move on to subjects that are more light-hearted. She felt that it wasn't that he did not realize the seriousness of the matter; it was because he had learned a valuable lesson and moved on.

This man was interesting. A contradiction of sorts, different from anyone she had met up until that time. She realized that he had an attraction that she couldn't quite put her finger on. Her sorority sisters would inquire what the big deal was about this new suitor and she was unusually short on words. Finally she would shrug her shoulders and smile by way of an answer. She did not really come up with a good answer until her eldest of the three sons she had with Bill asked her during her golden years. "Mom," he inquired, "I've seen pictures of Dad when you first met him and I've also seen pictures of other boyfriends. Dad wasn't especially good looking. What attracted you to him in the first place?"

She pondered the question for the last time, smiled and asked back, "Did you ever hear him play saxophone?"

Mary "Kitsy" Graham. Photo courtesy of the Departement of College Archives and Special Collections, Olin Library, Rollins College, Winter Park, Florida.

Bill's yearbook photo at Rollins College. Photo courtesy of the Department of College Archives and Special Collections, Olin Library, Rollins College, Winter Park, Florida

A young Bill Muncey with his saxophone.

CHAPTER SIX

Oranges

The engine coughed. A brief but abrupt audible space in the languid drone that Bill was enjoying as he flew over the lush green landscape of central Florida. The small radial powerplant had performed flawlessly on takeoff 15 minutes ago, pulling the tandem seat aircraft to altitude with ease. Leveling off at a thousand feet, he had set a course to buzz over his campus at Rollins College. Bill had not been soloing long so he wanted to make this trip simple and the mission direct: a common and recognizable landmark, make a 180-degree turn and then back to the airfield. Besides, rentals were by the hour.

Bill had learned that when driving hydroplanes it was sensible to place cotton swabs in his ears when sitting behind an engine and even with that, the resonance of the powerplant was still invasive. However in an airplane it wasn't particularly unpleasant. Sometimes it was actually soothing. He had a new girlfriend. Her name was Kitsy Graham and flying might be the kind of thing she would like to share. The hum and the balanced harmonics could almost put you to sleep if the experience itself wasn't exhilarating. Bill's Uncle Gallemore had been a pilot; flown with Chenault in the American Volunteer Group in China during World War II. His mother, Esther, had told Bill of the thrill she recalled when his uncle had taken her for a flight under a bridge. He was killed in action during the war so flying created a sense of connection with his uncle for Bill.

Central Florida could provide some of the best flying in the world and today was no exception. "Visibility Unlimited" was written in chalk on the board hanging on the wall in the rental office back at the field. The semi-tropical landscape contrasting with the deep blue of the sea revealed an environment new and foreign to a kid from the inner city of Detroit.

It was partly for this reason that Ed and Esther Muncey had sent their eldest away to Rollins College. Something new and different, maybe even exotic, but still near enough to family if assistance was needed. Ed's brother Ray lived nearby. Neither Ed nor Ray had attended college. In fact Ed had not made it beyond the sixth grade in school. When he was "college age" Ed was scraping out a living standing on street corners hustling cars to earn enough money to feed his new wife and baby. No one had even vaguely considered the idea that Esther needed an education that included college. Although her parents could have easily afforded it, she would marry and devote her life to being a fitting wife and mother. Both Ed and Esther were very pleased with the idea of being able to send their child to college, and were living vicariously through him. Bill was able to do things that were beyond their grasps at the same age. Bill's grades were good enough to warrant an extended education and if he was going to become more involved in the family automobile business, he would need a sound and well rounded education. His son's aptitude for numbers displayed at a tender age further caused Ed to parentally shake his head with pride. He was pleased to believe that his son could go far.

On the national scale, America's passionate affair with the internal combustion engine had reaped exponential benefits. Its development had not only enabled a dramatic expansion of transportation capabilities for commercial application, it also provided a dimension of freedom and liberty never imagined by younger citizens fewer than two generations before. Even the airplane had progressed in leaps and bounds since World War 1 to become accessible to the average American. The aspect of renting made that access even easier. Ed didn't mind that Bill would invest a portion of his budget toward learning to fly. Although he personally abhorred the idea of flying himself, Ed knew that a lot of the younger generation were enthused with the idea. He very much wanted his children to fit in and be happy.

As a young man, Ed knew what it was like to not fit in. Muncey was an Irish name and he had come from a time and place in America when that distinction was a compulsion for social ostracism. Just being of Irish descent was enough to publically disqualify an applicant from some forms of employment. When his own children asked what kind of name Muncey was, he would simply say, "It's an American name."

On the other hand, Esther Gallemore of English descent did not have any idea what that type of discrimination was like and Ed was determined that his wife and children would remain ignorant of the phenomenon. America was experiencing an exciting time of relative social unity and prosperity after World War II and Ed considered himself lucky to be able to provide as well as he did.

The aircraft's engine coughed again. A sea change of attitude began to settle over Bill. One cough in an airplane was worth attention and valid consideration of possible causes. A second cough demanded an immediate evaluation of potentially extreme circumstances accompanied by an appropriate sense of dread. The drone of the powerplant continued but Bill's perception had to be the consideration of "for how long?"

Dozens of scenarios and causes flooded across his mind. "Was it fuel, ignition or a lack of oil causing the engine to seize?" Bill asked himself.

He checked the oil pressure as well as he could from the cockpit by glancing at the gauge on the dash and it looked fine. The ignition was a lot harder because all the wiring was securely tucked under the engine cowling in front of him. The fuel on the other hand was easy. Bill had addressed it traditionally as he did his walk around the aircraft prior to take off. Directly in front of the cockpit on top of the fuel tank was a small hole that a steel rod poked up through. It was attached to an air-filled ball that floated on top of the fuel in the tank. The height of the rod projecting out of the top of the tank indicated fuel level. Pretty simple.

The drone of the engine suddenly stopped. Replaced by the sound of air slip streaming past the wingtips, the transition catapulted Bill into an urgent sequence of decisions. He knew that regardless of the cause, he and his airplane were going to make an unscheduled landing in the immediate future. Although the rental glided well and was a good flyer, they were definitely going down fast. Glancing over to his right he saw streets and a canal traversing his glide path. However to the left he was relieved to see a cultivated field of grass that stretched well beyond his length of descent. Tipping his wing down to the left he began to scrub off altitude to descend and reach for the cushion of chlorophyll in the relatively soft field of grass.

The initial apprehension that accompanied the realization that he was going to be forced to land was replaced by the drive to minimize the difficulties and mitigate the damages that might be coming his way. Looking about he noticed that there were not any buildings nearby that might provide a telephone that could bring help; on the other hand they were not there to run into either. The nearest road was a mile away which would have been great to land on and could provide the option to hitchhike back to town. A thousand options and possible alternatives cascaded through Bill's mind as the little airplane promptly lost altitude and quickly spanned the distance to the field. Bill started his procedure to prepare for a crash landing.

Although it sounded melodramatic, he knew that any good pilot had to keep his nerves under control in any circumstances and as calmly as possible anticipate a situation where everything that can go wrong does. Bill reached over and shut off the fuel. Even though he strongly suspected faulty ignition, he still grounded the magneto and turned off the primary source of electricity in the event that an errant spark find a ruptured fuel tank. As ridiculous as it seemed at the time he briefly recalled a Tom Swift episode that he had read as a child where the hero stayed calm and cool under pressure. The contrast of perception between the young reader he was then and the young student he was now wasn't lost on Bill. "Staying calm and cool," he thought, "was easy to read but a challenge to do."

Although he knew that the airplane had its wheels fixed in the down position, he looked to verify out of force of habit. "Always look," his instructor had told him. While looking at one of the wheels he noticed it was slowly turning from the resistance to the wind. Past the wheel in his line of sight, the green blur of the grass progressed below. He could make out tiny little orange flecks embedded in the grass.

Suddenly Bill realized it was not a field of grass at all, but actually an orange grove. In a flurry of thoughts, he considered his options but grimly determined that there wasn't room to glide anywhere else, nor was there time to do anything but pay attention and attempt to fly the little aircraft through the trees to the ground. Part of him understood how silly this intention was, but on the other hand, part of him also observed that if he was not doing whatever he could to minimize the risk, the alternative was a complacency that invited the worst possible result.

"Work the situation," he thought. "Besides, what else am I going to do?"

A fatalistic determination that probably represented itself on his face with compressed lips, clenched teeth and a firm jaw settled

Chapter Six

into the 5"8" frame strapped to the seat. He unconsciously tightened the seatbelt as the fuselage dropped in between the first pair of trees. A branch seemed to reach up and grab the tip of a blade of the propeller snapping it off. The tug of that impact briefly pulled the nose of the plane and Bill instinctively adjusted and compensated the aircraft's attitude. The sound of still more branches impacting the skin of the fuselage made its presence known with "whacks" and "whumps" that resonated thickly up through the airframe. The horizon was filling up hurriedly with greens and oranges while the yellow of his plane contrasted sharply against the scenery. As out of place as it may have seemed, it occurred to Bill that the contrast of color might help searchers find him easier.

The sounds of striking branches became a staccato of signals indicating the wings were now falling onto the top of the orange grove. It was remarkably similar to how it would sound dragging a broom across the head of a drum.

Then the wings were gone.

The impact hurled Bill's torso across the strap at his lap. His head came within an inch of the dashboard while the joystick mercifully tipped forward and avoided impaling Bill. The body of the airplane dropped to the ground like a rock and bounced on its wheels back up into the tree limbs before it settled into a slow but steady roll to a stop.

Bill was surprised that he was not dizzy or disoriented by the violence of the landing. It struck him that he could now include himself among that elite circle of pilots who personally appreciated the irony of the statement, "Any landing you walk away from is a good landing."

The quiet was invasive. Although secluded and embraced by the swathing canopy of green and orange, Bill could look down the rows of citrus trees and see a road crossing his line of sight a half mile away. He could not see any traffic driving by and he knew that unless someone happened to be looking up when he descended, no one would probably know that he had crashed. There was no reason for anyone to be looking for him. He climbed up and out of the cockpit dropping to the ground beside the fuselage. A quick tour around the aircraft determined two important facts: the wings had separated from the airplane cleanly and the wheels were straight and intact.

A nagging curiosity then overcame him. He knew that he may never clearly understand why the plane had lost power but he was compelled to try and find the reason. Folding up the side panel that covered one side of the engine, Bill peered inside. He had an understanding of mechanics and did not see anything obvious or out of place. The wires from the ignition system were all, apparently, where they should be. He then slid the fuel line back from the carburetor where it entered from the fuel tank. He aimed the open end of the fuel line away from the engine as he separated it from carburetor so that no fuel would spill. Nothing came out. He looked back up at the little rod sticking up through the top of the fuel tank. It still showed a full tank. He pressed down on it. With a little pressure, it dropped down and signified its landing at the bottom of the dry fuel tank with an echoing and hollow thud.

After a long moment, it dawned on Bill the significance of the fact and what it represented. The ground crew at least twice prior to take off had checked the aircraft. He also knew that ultimately the responsibility was his. He was the pilot and in the end, he would be the individual who paid the price for neglect or carelessness. He briefly thought about the freckle-faced kid with whom he had spoken back at the airfield, the energetic and lanky red headed boy with the big grin who was paying for his flying time by caring for the airplanes. There was not a dishonest or lazy bone in his body, but obviously, something had distracted him from completing his checklist on this aircraft. Their introduction had been brief, still Bill knew the youngster was going to feel bad about his part in this misadventure.

Bill had excelled in team sports. Football, hockey and baseball had all been cooperative concepts that while providing a tangible return on success, didn't anticipate a catastrophe or failure. His interfacing with the airfield attendant was a new kind of team effort. He began to appreciate the respect and attention to detail required to excel in motorsports more fervently. One thoughtless oversight …

Walking out to the road, Bill spotted a man leading a mule and cart. Both men were surprised to see each other. Bill was surprised because he had never actually seen a mule pulling a cart. Maybe at the picture show, but never in person. The farmer was surprised because here was a disheveled young man standing in the middle of his orange grove.

After the pair had exchanged a brief acknowledgement, Bill explained his situation. He felt a deep sense of responsibility for the circumstances he was in and wanted to do whatever he could to help minimize the damage to this man's orange grove.

"Do you have a truck that could pull my airplane out to the road? " Bill asked.

"I don't think our truck could get down the row to it," the farmer said. "The rows are too close together. We usually walk or use carts if we need to get down there," he explained.

At that point, both of them looked at the mule.

"How much do those aero planes weigh?" the farmer asked.

Block, tackle, rope, a mule, and twenty dollars finally got the fuselage out to the road. Prior to the effort, Bill had gone to the farmhouse and called the airfield to let them know why he was late and that they might want to bring a trailer to the farm. It took four people to get the wings out of the trees.

ORANGES

CHAPTER SEVEN

The Army Years

"Greetings. Your friends and neighbors have selected you to represent them in the armed forces of the United States. "

Bill could remember the opening paragraph of his draft notification verbatim 30 years after the fact. Fresh out of college with a new wife, a steady job, a roof over their heads and a child on the way, he definitely had his hands full. Nevertheless, 10,000 miles away two countries were at war. A clear cut undeniable example of unprovoked aggression had occurred and America as a nation had been drawn into its resolution. Tens of thousands of young men from across the country were being drafted into the conflict. World War II was still very fresh in the minds of the American public and the bitter taste of isolationism that inadvertently prolonged it was still lingering. There was not a family in the United States that did not have participation at some level with the planet-wide conflagration that had irretrievably altered America's role in the world. With America's victory in WWII came a somber resolve that this would never happen again. A declining President had championed the forming of the United Nations after the war as the primary step toward averting a repeat. Between World War I and its sequel, the infant League of Nations had failed to act in the face of similar aggression and the cost had been devastating.

After a prompt and spirited debate about North Korea's unprovoked aggression against its neighbor to the south, the United Nations had reached a determination and a call to action uttered across the globe. The United States had been of the first to answer. Younger brothers were taking up the torch handed over by their older siblings returning home with stories of service from Germany and Japan. Bill's Uncle Gallemore had been lost in the skies over China as a "Flying Tiger" fighting the Japanese. During Bill's high school years, he could not walk a block in town or his own neighborhood without being reminded by a star in a house window, or a sign in a store front soliciting war bonds, that there were responsibilities beyond one's friends and family.

While she had been journalism major in college, Kit Muncey's minor had been in history. She had a keen sense of history that was not lost on contemporary news. She read Bill's induction notice with the apprehension of a new wife and mother. Their family had barely been started and now the chief breadwinner was being called away. For her parents the Second World War had been an immediate and constant presence in their household. Kit's father, Malcolm Graham, had been an active member of the US Air Ministry. They lived in Washington D.C. and he participated in the implementation of the Lend Lease program between the U.S. and Great Britain. As an example, her father was the one who had decided where Rolls Royce would alternately build its aircraft engines as Germany attempted to bomb England into submission. Malcolm had been rewarded with the recognition as a Knight of the British Empire (KBE) as a statement of appreciation from a grateful nation. Nevertheless, war had always been somewhat remote. Now it was here, in-your-face, and immediate.

A sense of community and responsibility was inherent in the Muncey household. Ed Muncey had been too young for the draft of World War I just as Bill's age had excluded him from World War II. Ed, however, prospered with the return of the veterans. America's passion for automobiles had grown over the decades and Ed Muncey's Chevrolet dealership was in the right place at the right time.

Bill might have been referred to as "the rich kid" in high school, but that affluence did not preclude him from the responsibilities of any other young man. Additionally, the hockey injury that had temporarily cost him sight in one eye cleared up and he was now blessed with somewhat noteworthy 20-10 vision. His hunting forays into the forests of Northern Michigan had taught him to be a good shot with a rifle or shotgun. He was definitely sound military material.

On the other hand, his family's prosperity did bring a substantial level of security. His sense of family encouraged him to believe that regardless of what happened while he completed his military service, his family would be looked after. Kit got along well with her in-laws and should she need support, emotional or otherwise, Bill knew his family would continue to provide it. Nevertheless, after Bill finished, Kit chose to stay with her own family in Connecticut for the birth of their first child. During the course of the Korean War, as it came to be called, over 20,000 troops were mustered

Chapter Seven

from the Midwest. During this tumultuous time Bill made a friendship that would continue the rest of his life.

Lee Schoenith was the same age as Bill, from an equally well-to-do family in Detroit. The Schoenith family owned and operated a company called Gale Enterprises which machined and manufactured tools and components for industrial applications. Bill and Lee shared an interest in high performance machines. Lee had heard of Bill indirectly as the son of E.L. Muncey. Anyone who had access to a radio in the Detroit area in those days had heard of Ed Muncey's Chevrolet. As they became better acquainted during the Army's basic training, Lee would tease his new friend, "If Chevrolets were such good cars, how come the police always used Fords? Obviously, criminals use Chevys! "

Bill would confirm part of this taunt when he would smuggle Lee off base in the trunk of his Chevy while on leave.

The benefits of high school sports paid dividends in basic training. In those days of leather helmets and sharpened cleats, football was a brutal sport. Bill played wingback on the offensive line of Royal Oak High School's football team where he learned the valuable lesson of "the sprint." A tremendous spurt of energy applied at a brief but rapid pace could often overpower an opponent or obstacle. Not being a large or stout young man, Bill relied on agility and ability to sprint accurately in sports whether it was football or hockey. In the face of adversity, this bent often made the winning difference. It also taught endurance. Bill learned that often the day was not victorious because of agility or clever strategies, but sometimes it just came down to who was still standing at the end of the day.

On one occasion, as Bill was tackled with the football, he fell forward into the slippery mud with his right hand outstretched in front of him and the ball tucked under his left arm. An opponent ran directly on top of his extended hand and Bill watched as the cleats nailed his hand into the mud-covered turf. His father was in the stand and Bill did not want to bench. He quickly concealed his wounds with a poultice dressing of sticky Michigan mud and he finished the game. This level of commitment and determination created the kind of tangible results that would apply well to military situations.

The demands of basic training included confining the recruits to the base. Leave was sparingly allocated and usually had to be earned. As an incentive, the drill sergeants had offered a two-day weekend pass to the recruit that could complete the obstacle course first without infraction. The need for a recruit to take his training seriously and earnestly apply himself became more apparent as tales of successful attacks of human waves against the American lines were filtering back to the public from the Korean peninsula. Nevertheless, the sergeants decided as a live fire drill, the passes could provide some extra motivation.

Bill missed his wife. Being young, in love and wanting to be anywhere other than an Army base compelled him to complete the course in a competitive fashion. The acrid smell of cordite wafting across the course from the fifty-caliber machine gun that was chunking out rounds over his head added a surreal dimension to the challenge of this particular sprint. With rounds whizzing and tearing through the air inches above his helmet, Bill heeded the advice from his instructors to keep his "head and butt down."

A spattering of rain mixed with a rippling breeze that tumbled leaves across and over the obstacle course splotched his muddy uniform. The cackle of the drill sergeants mingled with the sub sonic thumping of the concussion charges that were being detonated to replicate an actual assault. It all seemed distant and remote from the task at hand. His objective was simple, single minded and focused.

"Get to the end of the course. Keep your head down. Get to the end of the course. Keep your head down." It became a chant.

At the same time, he wiggled and twisted under the strands of barbed wire, under and through the pools of mud and muck with indifference. Later in life, he wished that it might have been a determination to do his patriotic duty, a sense of being a better soldier or perhaps a desire to be especially competitive with his fellow recruits that compelled him to excel. But in the end he had to admit that he just wanted to be with his wife.

When all was said and done, he completed the course in the fastest time.

"Okay, soldier," his Drill Sergeant said," Let me see you do that again!" So he did and earned the other weekend pass.

Years later, students of the sport of hydroplane racing would acknowledge that the kind of aggression demonstrated by accelerat-

Chapter Seven

ing out of the corner was well suited to the "sprint mentality" Bill possessed. Instead of a "steady as she goes" attitude, circle racing rewards pulses of aggression. He couldn't know it at the time, but Bill had an aptitude that would lend itself well to his impending profession.

For a young American couple, it was a time that seemed larger than life. Rumors of extensive communist conspiracies marched over the front page of the Detroit Free Press. Exotic places earned terrifying names like Pork Chop Hill by rendering some of its defenders into unidentifiable fragments. Seemingly sedated destinations like Chosen Reservoir took on ominous meanings with the reversal of the fortunes of war. The conflict had initially gone well in the eyes of the American public. The military prowess of the Allies from World War II had seemed to overwhelm the relatively tiny nations that were involved. One of the most illustrious and decorated American heroes, General Douglas MacArthur, had led the troops back up the Korean peninsula and apparently contained the situation.

Then another superpower had gotten involved from the opposing side. Apparently feeling that its border was threatened, the Red Chinese flooded over the Yalu River and pushed the United Nations forces down the peninsula and almost into the Sea of Japan. The U.N. death toll sky rocketed. Although the American media tended to minimize the setbacks, stories of tremendous hardship and loss filtered back to the public. Rumors of World War III were on people's lips with an atomic perspective that was frightening to consider.

As Lee and Bill contemplated their future deployment, Lee would shrug off any ominous possibility and suggest that with the political influence of his family, he felt secure that he would not be sent to the front lines. Although it was reassuring for a pair of naive young men to consider this as a realistic perspective, Bill knew that even if such an option existed from his side of the equation, it would not be something his father would pursue.

As it worked out, Bill's musical acumen saved him from the caldron and crucible of war. With the grim humor that only two good friends can have, Bill would tease Lee about it in later years.

"Merely because I could play a saxophone, I was shipped off to a military band in Germany while Lee, with all his political connections, got himself sent to Korea and got wounded," he would say. "Of the 20,000 troops drafted from my part of the country, only 500 were sent somewhere other than Korea."

Although very pregnant at the time of his deployment, Kit was delighted. Bill would be in Europe when the baby was born, but living with her parents during the interim and knowing that Bill was relatively safe in Germany provided great comfort to her.

The passage across the Atlantic in a troopship with thousands of other soldiers was an experience that remained with Bill for the rest of his life. Packed like sardines in the fetid confines of sweaty steel bulkheads and swinging back and forth in their allocated hammocks in the throes of a storm, the relatively short crossing was exacerbated by a new found tendency toward seasickness.

The United States Army found it prudent to indoctrinate every arriving soldier that came through the military facility created at the former concentration camp called Dachau. It would be difficult to find a more appropriate explanation for why a force of arms may be necessary with the least amount of words than to have an American soldier tour the infamous encampment. Bill later said to his children, "You could still smell the ovens." The fact that over five million people were systematically murdered through this and similar facilities wasn't lost on the young Detroiter. Spirited collegiate debate and polite dinner conversations back in the States took on an appropriate invasive and distinct dimension when personally witnessing the means of the heinous crimes. It was a sobering experience that ultimately impressed upon Bill a social consciousness that remained with him for the rest of his life.

To add another perspective to his adult life, shortly after Bill's arrival in Europe, his son was born in Greenwich, Connecticut near his in-laws. Although William Edward Muncey, Jr. was born with a slight case of asthmatic bronchitis, Bill was informed by telegram that his wife and child were healthy and five weeks later mother and son made the same Atlantic crossing by airplane to join him. The nearest town to his base in Germany was called Straubing and although it had been eight years since the cessation of hostilities, continental Europe was still suffering through the strains of reconstruction and rationing from the world war. As an example, Kit would schedule the ironing of diapers to the wee hours of the morning when their section of the electrical grid was turned on.

Chapter Seven

Nevertheless, any hardship real or imagined was easy for the young couple to take in stride. They knew that they were very lucky to be there.

Promoted to the rank of corporal, the Army was prompt to capitalize on Bill's experience as a band leader. His participation as a rank and file musician with popular swing bands led by celebrities such as Gene Krupa and Harry James wasn't lost on his superiors either. Morale was important to the occupying forces in Europe and the familiar melodies of Glenn Miller and Benny Goodman offered a reassuring reminder of home. The local dance halls and airfields found that John Phillip Sousa balanced with the beat of Sing, Sing, Sing, or Little Brown Jug.

During his adolescence, he had led his own band at local dances with the pseudonym Stan Arno. Wearing a pair of plain black horn rimmed glasses, he had sported the image that was popular of the day. Stan Arno and his Orchestra had provided Bill live performance experience in front of a crowd that gave him a confidence on which the Army could capitalize. Arranging music while teaching other soldiers on how to perform helped develop his leadership skills. Although some had convinced their recruiters that they knew how to play an instrument, many lacked basic music reading capabilities needed to perform in a band. One soldier implored Bill to teach him "the trick" to reading music.

"No trick," Bill said. "Just read one note at a time."

With the European community trying to rebound and share in the relative prosperity of the 1950's, the dollars from the American serviceman helped stimulate the economy. Kit and Bill spent their time off duty touring the European country side. Investing in the purchase of a 1936 two seat BMW enabled them to travel down to Italy over the weekend or visit the Bavarian Alps on a tight budget.

In spite of the fact that the Army strongly encouraged him to stay, Bill chose to set aside his option to re-enlist. Although he and his wife had made the most of their time in the service and he was quick to realize that they had been more fortunate than most, he was eager to pick up the thread of the career he and his family had carved out for him back home. There was a prosperous Chevrolet dealership back in Detroit that beckoned his participation.

When the time came, the young Munceys returned to America along with their nimble BMW.

THE ARMY YEARS

Bill Muncey meeting his new son, Wil, while stationed in Germany.

Lee Schoenith at the Mount Baker race pits on Lake Washington in Seattle.

CHAPTER EIGHT

Every Way But Straight

"She wanted to go every way but straight," was the way Bill described the Miss Great Lakes hydroplane when he drove her on the Detroit River. Setting the race boat through her paces in an attempt to qualify for the regatta on the Lake Saint Clair end of the river, he had wrestled her around the five mile oval laid out in front of the Detroit Yacht Club. Although of a later design, the Miss Great Lakes was a hydroplane that still sported a totally submerged propeller. The evolution of high performance propeller design had embraced the concept where only the tip of each blade pierced the water's surface. Due to this disparity, she often resembled a boat that was arguing with the water rather than gracefully flying over it.

On the other hand, Bill was grateful for the opportunity to participate in this hometown event in the first place. Although he had done an adequate job during a previous test drive of the vessel, he was not the official designated driver and his option of participating was nil until an unfortunate string of bad luck visited the Miss Great Lakes camp. The original engine had failed and the representative owner, Al Fallon was unable to replace it. His test drive had thoroughly whetted Bill's appetite for greater participation at any level and he had volunteered as available crew if Al needed help. Bill was willing to do just about anything just to stay involved. Push a broom, tend a bow line, or swab out the oil in the bilge that was commonly present in race boats were chores that he would jump at for the opportunity just to be there. He knew the odds he would ever actually be a driver were minimal but it didn't matter. He would be part of the show and that was enough.

Bill remembered it was not that long ago that he was standing on the shore of the Detroit River down in front of the Whittier Hotel as a spectator cheering on his heroes Chuck Thompson, Gar Wood, and "Wild" Bill Cantrell. There was something about the roar of the unmuffled exhaust of the monstrous engines and the sheer volume and presence of the weighty but polished craft that appealed to him. Hailing from a community that prided itself on the nick name the "motor city" Bill took a special delight in witnessing the progress of marine motorsports in his own back yard.

Starting in boats powered by outboard engines in competition within the ranks of the American Power Boat Association, Bill had learned at the age of 12 that jockeying a hydroplane around a race course was more akin to dance moves than wrestling holds. The relatively small 12-foot plywood hulls were nimble and required a substantial amount of focus and concentration especially at top speed, but this felt more like grappling the steering wheel and pointing the craft in a general direction where she might agree to go.

The disappointment of the team was prevalent and almost irreversible when it was determined that the marvelous V-12 Allison aircraft engine that propelled the hydroplane over the waves was badly damaged. Owner Fallon lacked the resources at the time to replace it and it was apparent that the team would have to sit out the race. Harnessing an enormous 1700 cubic inches of internal combustion, the Allison engines were becoming more available, but not readily nearby. Moreover, they definitely were not cheap.

Mostly because of his inexperience and naiveté, Bill began to form a plan. Hatching an expression that he would go on to share often in life, he asked himself, "Why buy when you can borrow?"

He had no idea where to start but he quietly approached Al Fallon alone after the disparaging news had been shared with the crew. Big breaks often actually happen incrementally in small doses and with apparently ineffectual steps. Often it takes 20 years of quiet but steadfast determination to become "an overnight success." This was not one of those times. Bill knew that what he was about to propose was a big deal. Logic said it was most likely unattainable, but he also had learned from his father that as a salesman, "You have to ask for the order."

His father, Ed Muncey, had risen to a substantial level of success by ignoring the restraints of his humble beginnings and wholeheartedly committing himself to the task at hand. Bill had definitely learned that there was no shame in being ambitious.

Al Fallon had taken a liking to Bill. The kid always showed up to help out on the team. He didn't know much, but he was always eager to learn and there was not a job he wouldn't do. In spite of the financial success of Bill's famous father, the young man did not seem to take on airs and definitely got along well with the rest of the crew. On the other hand, Al had to respect the fact that Bill was not one to back down from a challenge either. The test drive that Bill had taken in the Miss Great Lakes had ended up with an unwarranted and unanticipated altercation on the dock between Bill and the driver of record that involved fisticuffs and Bill had stood his ground in spite of the surprise. E.L. Muncey's son had earned a lot of respect that day.

Nevertheless, Bill's voice was low and small when he first spoke to Al of the idea. Wringing a dry shop rag in his hands out in front of him, Bill looked up at Al and asked, "If I can find us an engine and help get it in the boat, can I drive her in the race?"

Bill's suggestion wasn't entirely unwarranted from a capability point of view. Al was aware that Bill had done a lot of driving in the "limited inboard" ranks and was no stranger to the racing procedures, course flags, and terminology. He knew that Bill had driven other people's boats before and he had established a competent reputation. He always brought the equipment back in good shape. It was rumored that on occasion Bill would drive up to sixteen heats in a weekend.

At that point, Al had two considerations: the kid probably could not come up with the equipment in the first place and if he did, it was not as if his boat was going to make it into the race some other way. "Where would you get an engine?" Al asked.

"Oh, I don't know. They're just around. I'll start asking," Bill offered. Simple to say, not so simple to do.

Finally, Al considered the original driver for the boat. It wasn't as if he was going to get this boat back on the water. If Bill could actually pull it off, why not?

"Sure, Kid. If you can find an engine and help get it in the boat, you can have the ride. I don't have any money, otherwise I'd be doing it myself, so you really have to do this on your own," Al said.

Al went on to ask him if he was sure that he really wanted to do this and Bill replied, "Just open the door."

"I need to get busy." Bill said, "Can I use your telephone?"

"He's already asking to borrow my telephone." Al thought. He had to laugh to himself. With a quiet shrug Al Fallon said, "Sure, kid. Knock yourself out."

After many calls and conversations, favors called in and favors promised, Bill's inquiries led him to the gatehouse of the one man within 100 miles who had the equipment and could make it available in time. Several factors had to line up: the right equipment, in time, near enough and under the right terms. As he got out of the car to speak with the guard at the gate, he pondered the last factor. Exhausting his savings account, he might have enough money to place a respectable down payment, maybe a $100.

Although he worked hard on weekends at E.L. Muncey's Chevrolet dealership, it was a family maxim that he would never get paid more than anyone else performing the same duties would. His Dad had said, "You're going to have to work twice as hard as anyone else just because you're my son. And because I'm your old man, you'll get paid half as much." Ed had laughed and thrown his arm around his eldest son's shoulder to pull him closer. Looking down from his six foot height Ed had chuckled and said, "Nothing worthwhile comes easy, son."

Although the money part hadn't actually worked out that poorly, the attitude was pervasive. None of the Muncey boys was pampered. Even Bill's little brother Raymond had been cast adrift from an allowance at 16 and was given a job washing cars at the dealership.

"Is Mr. Wood at home?" Bill asked the security guard at the gate.

"Who is inquiring?" the guard responded.

"I'm Bill Muncey, E.L.Muncey's son," Bill said. "I'm here to talk to him about some business."

Bill hoped that his family name might lend some weight to his inquiry. His father was reasonably well-known in the Detroit community from all the advertising that the dealership did. The little plug certainly couldn't hurt.

"Do you have an appointment?" the guard asked still not giving up the information Bill requested.

"No, but I've been told that he is the man that I need to talk to, " Bill said realizing as the words came out of his mouth, they sounded pretty ineffectual.

"You need to call and make an appointment, kid. Gar Wood is a busy man. Then you'll need to be put on my access list so that I can call up to the house before I can let you in," the guard said. Clean shaven and in a crisp, pressed dark blue uniform, the security guard's demeanor was polite, direct and unassailable. Persuasion at this point was futile.

Chapter Eight

"Thanks," Bill said, "I'll be back."

The guard nodded.

Bill had no idea how he would make that happen in time. He did not even know if Mr. Wood was in the country, much less at home. If he was at home, there wasn't any guarantee that he would even see him. After all, Gar Wood was an exceptionally successful business man that just happened to also be a boat racer. He would hardly have time to talk with a virtual stranger about a single engine for a race boat. And then there was the money thing.

Discouraged and disappointed, Bill turned his car around in the driveway and drove down the long driveway to the thoroughfare. Turning right he glanced back toward the walled Wood estate and noticed a side street that ran across the far side of the property. Turning again onto the back road, he pulled his car up off the road and out of sight behind some trees and got out to consider his options. There weren't many because there wasn't much time.

It was about ten o'clock on a soft, sultry Saturday morning. August was a humid month for the Motor City. The trees along the Wood estates wall were full, tall, and green. The grass between the wall and the road was well manicured. Twisting vines of dark green ivy had laid claim to the wall itself decades ago. Brick red peeked out from behind a corduroy carpet of evergreen cascading down the wall's side. A slow cool breeze from the Detroit River caused the thick leaves on the trees overhead to rustle and at the same time remind Bill why he was standing there.

The fact that he was 22 years old and much too old to be forgiven for such childish behavior was not lost on Bill as he clambered up and over the wall behind the Wood estate. The fact that trespassing was a crime didn't elude him either.

"E.L. Muncey's son arrested!" briefly crossed his mind as he marched toward the back door of the main house and the servants' entrance near the kitchen. Soundly knocking, he really had no idea what he would say to whoever answered the door.

Fully expecting a maid, cook, or butler to respond to his knock, Bill's jaw dropped slightly when a bathrobed and slippered Gar Wood swung the door open. With his silver hair a little disheveled and a folded newspaper in his hand, Wood cocked his head sideways and said, "Hello. Can I help you?"

A smaller voice from Gar Wood, Jr. sitting at the kitchen table called out, "Who is it, Dad?"

Of course, Bill recognized the man immediately. He had never actually met him, but Bill had seen Gar Wood at the controls of the race boat, Miss America, on the news reels at the movie theater. On occasion, Gar Wood had shown up at local boat races as a celebrated spectator. In addition, of course, Bill had watched him race on the Detroit River. Although Bill experienced a certain degree of awe and respect, he also knew that Gar Wood put his bathrobe on one arm at a time like anyone else.

"My name is Bill Muncey and I am working with Al Fallon trying to get his boat ready for the Harmsworth and the Silver Cup." Pausing, he was unsure how to go on.

Trespassing and intruding upon the legend who was still in his bathrobe obviously trying to enjoy a quiet morning in the privacy of his own home with his son; well, that might have been a bridge too far.

"I wish Mr. Fallon all the luck in the world but what has that to do with me?" Wood asked.

"We need an engine." Bill blurted out, "and we've heard that you are the mostly likely source within the time available. I'm sorry about coming up to the back door like this but your security guard is very good at his job and we're just about out of time."

Wood recognized Bill as one of the local youngsters racing at the Region 6 regattas of the American Power Boat Association. Often driving other people's boats, this young man had made consistent and good starts using unfamiliar equipment. For a moment, Wood was intrigued. For some reason he assumed that this young man would be driving.

"I might have an engine that would suit your purposes," Wood said. "I think that it might be a later model than the one Fallon has been running but it should get the job done. Why don't you call my office Monday and we will see what we can do?"

"Why that would be swell, Mr. Wood," Bill said. "And I'm really sorry about disturbing your morning."

Without another word, Gar Wood simply nodded and closed the door. And with that quiet nod from Gar, Bill Muncey's vast career as a driver of Unlimited Hydroplanes was genuinely launched.

The thrash by the Miss Great Lakes team that followed was characteristic of the kind of effort common in motorsports. No

Chapter Eight

one had seriously expected anyone to come up with a replacement engine in the first place. The powerplant was of a later model in the second place and while it developed more horsepower than the original, it had minor adjustments and unique components of fabrication required for installation.

The Harmsworth Trophy was an international award created by an English publisher to excite marine motorsports. Any country could participate but any intended competitor had to pass a brutal qualification process. Only teams that met those demands would be allowed to represent their country in pursuit of the elusive prize. On the other hand, the Detroit Silver Cup was scheduled to follow just a few days after the Harmsworth qualifications.

Gar Wood was true to his word and although he himself didn't actually speak again with Bill, Bill's phone call to Wood's office was accepted and the engine was delivered to the address Bill gave. The team feverishly swapped the powerplants and prepared the boat for racing.

By 1950, the concept of the surface piercing propeller had established itself as a technological edge needed for a true hydroplane race boat to be competitive. The traditional submerged propeller could still compete well on the race course, but the handwriting was on the wall. This fact didn't deter the enthusiasm of the Miss Great Lakes team. The optimism and determination of the young driver to be was contagious.

Although he was slow to admit it, Bill also possessed a respectable mechanical aptitude that the Miss Great Lakes team found valuable in its preparations. The fabrication process for the needed parts and the mating of the aircraft components to a marine application was painstakingly detailed and had to be done right the first time. There wouldn't be time for a second effort. Bill would say later in life that the installation of systems into race boats was one of his favorite parts of racing.

Starting an Allison engine in a race boat on the trailer is a somewhat complicated and sometimes dangerous process. The gearbox must be disconnected from the propeller shaft and water has to be pumped to the engine if it is going to be run for any appreciable amount of time. The relatively sophisticated fueling system had the potential for leaks and careful scrutiny by the crew was a big part of the testing process prior to committing the boat to the isolation of the race course. The high octane fuel was especially volatile and presented a problem that would be difficult to deal with away from the shore.

The fact that the load presented against the propeller was missing when tested on the trailer made the sensitivity of the driver to varying conditions irreplaceable. Since his initial test drive in the Miss Great Lakes, Bill had practiced starting her at every opportunity. His first ride in her had been particularly inglorious in that Al Fallon had to start the engine for Bill, then jump overboard, and swim back to shore in order for Bill to continue driving from the cockpit.

The magic moment of starting the new engine arrived and necessitated crew members to stand at either ends of the engine on the wooden deck of the boat armed with CO_2 fire bottles. Aiming the hosed nozzles at the most likely source of fuel leaks, each crew member nodded their readiness to Bill prior to his initiating the starting sequence. After returning their nods, Bill's gaze dropped to the bilge. An acute sense of hearing was a prerequisite to starting this behemoth of an engine. The cyclic rotation of the pistons needed to be coordinated precisely with the pulse of the primary fuel injection system. The graduation of successful ignition had to be seamlessly altered from the primary system to the main one without interruption. If attempted too quickly, the sparkplugs could be washed down and the fire would go out. Once stopped, the engine was difficult to refire. If attempted too slowly, a lean condition could be created that would cause a backfire in the supercharger or "altitude compensator" and the subsequent explosion could break the engine, injure a crew member, or worse.

As he had learned from playing the piano as a small boy practice makes perfect, and this time Bill fired the engine up without incident. The increased power of the new engine compared to the old one was immediately evident. The responsibility to keep it running now was all his. Fully aware of the nature of that charge, Bill put the Miss Great Lakes through her paces for the Harmsworth on the bumpy Detroit River on September 2. The pressure to perform on an international stage in front of his home town was pronounced. Fans and media from all over the world had congregated to see competition hopefuls attempt qualifying laps for the prestigious Harmsworth. The Silver Cup was scheduled for two days later.

Chapter Eight

The additional power of the newer engine created so much hydraulic lift at the propeller that it kept climbing out of the water. This called for constant adjustment at the steering wheel to compensate for the varying attitude of the hull and rudder. Half of the time the Miss Great Lakes behaved like a traditional displacement boat as she settled down in the corners but by the end of the straightaways, she more resembled a full-on airplane. Fortunately for the new driver there wasn't anyone else on the race course and Bill was afforded the opportunity to get better acquainted with the new configuration without the risk to other boats. By the end of his qualifying lap attempts Bill had developed a very respectable qualifying speed of 92 MPH average lap speed over the three-mile course. Some onlookers were amazed that the tired race boat had it in her.

One spectator in particular recognized that it wasn't so much the boat but the aptitude of this driver who coaxed more performance out of the craft than she was accustomed to giving up. A man who would have a tremendous influence on the future of boat racing, Ted Jones, was an accomplished aircraft engineer for the Boeing Airplane Company from Seattle, Washington. His family would go on to be profoundly influential in the design and development of hydroplanes for at least three generations. That day he was impressed with the apparent prowess of the young driver from Detroit. The idea of a hydroplane race boat that actually flew completely out of the water was not enthusiastically embraced by the established rank and file of the marine motorsport community. It was a concept that demanded quick reflexes and an open mind. Ted determined that he would have to keep an eye on this young man.

The crew of the Miss Great Lakes was excited and relieved that their steed had performed so well. A lot of preparation and effort extended and attention to detail had been maintained in spite of crew fatigue. Fallon was not as elated as the rest.

"Going faster was all well and good," he thought, "but more speed and greater power comes at a price." Fallon carefully inspected the hull for any signs of stress and its own fatigue.

Although the qualifying speed was respectable, the Miss Great Lakes was not selected to represent the United States for the Harmsworth Trophy Race. This decision, however, in no way affected her ability to participate in the Silver Cup.

The Detroit Yacht Club sprawled and loomed at the same time. The clubhouse pressed up against the shoreline of the Detroit River with acres of docks reaching like tentacles out into the current. With beige walls and a dull brick red roof, the center section of the main structure climbed three stories into the Detroit sky. Tall leafy trees surrounded the grounds. In those days of boat racing, every team that competed at the Silver Cup level was representing their home town yacht club. In some cases, it was a requirement to list on the race entry form which yacht club a team represented. Communities with a maritime heritage like Buffalo, Detroit, and London strove for sportsmanlike prominence amongst each other, often creating and hosting their own cups and regattas. The Silver Cup was Detroit's own. Its big brother trophy race, the Gold Cup, and its attendant regatta could travel to the club that represented the winning team, but the Silver Cup remained in Detroit regardless of the outcome.

To participate in the Silver Cup was immense to Bill. As a crew member, it would have been a big deal, much less as a driver. Qualifying for the Harmsworth was one thing, while competing in the Silver Cup was another. He knew that the competition was formidable and his primary concern was to keep the equipment alive and healthy for the duration of the event. Often, the winner in this type of contest was determined by who was still running at the end of the day rather than who went the fastest. He realized that getting this ride was essentially a fluke and the opportunity may never present itself again. Maybe Mr. Fallon had harbored doubts about whether Bill could get an engine and then second thoughts about putting a relatively untested rookie behind the wheel of his boat. Nevertheless, here he was and he had made the most of what he had. The qualifying attempt for the Harmsworth had been respectable and even if he never drove one of these bigger boats again Bill could be proud of that.

This Silver Cup had drawn his parents and little brother to the stands. His aunt Madge and Uncle Bill were also there. The sun had gotten an early start that day. A cloudless sky helped create a warm morning and the sun shone unrestricted as its beams twinkled off the tips of gentle waves on the river. The crew solemnly held the boat in place at the dock, while Bill sat quietly in the cockpit waiting for the five minute gun which would sound the opening of the

Chapter Eight

race course allowing for the contestants to move on to the watery track. The boat gently rocked where she was moored, and Bill stared resolutely at the dashboard and its many gauges waiting for the official countdown to the five minute gun. The air was still and the hum of the crowd seemed a million miles away.

The report of the small cannon was almost startling. Since the gearbox was bolted directly to the propeller shaft and there was not a clutch or conventional transmission, as soon as Bill achieved ignition the Miss Great Lakes climbed up out of the water. The sheer force of the hull pulling away from the dock created a flood and tumble of cascading river water hurled across the dock. Experienced crew members were well out of the way by that time while the newly initiated laughed off the soaking. In the heat of the day, they would dry off soon enough.

Bringing her promptly up on a level plane, the Miss Great Lakes made her way parallel to the shoreline heading down toward the Belle Isle Bridge. The heat of the engine funneled under the dashboard back over Bills legs, up his torso and out of the cockpit. The temperature inside the boat began to rise as the engine warmed up. On a hot day like today, the cockpit temperature might reach a staggering 120 degrees.

With his eyes returning often to the gages on the dashboard, Bill maintained a constant vigil on the engine. The pressure of the oil and fuel were his main concern; 80 pounds of oil pressure and 20 pounds for the fuel. When in doubt, shut it off.

As he turned the bow left into the corner, a handful of water bounced up from below his legs and splashed across his face and goggles. It felt good and welcoming as it cooled off Bill's cheeks.

No, it was not good.

Pulling a shop rag out from behind the belt of his life jacket, he wiped the water away from his goggles.

He asked himself, "Where the heck did the water come from, and why was it up in my face?" Looking down below his feet, he saw a torrent of water gushing up through a fist sized hole that had formed in front of where the propeller shaft went through the bottom of the boat. The housing that held the seals and bearings for the propeller shaft was called a shaft log. Apparently, the additional strain of the increased horsepower had caused the log to bend and twist against the forward end where it met the bottom of the hull and tore away some material. As the water poured in through the bottom of the boat, the spinning propeller shaft caught it and flung it up into the air past Bill's face and the problem was growing.

Once the water had found a point of entry, it was able to pull and tug at the edges of the opening. The force of the boat moving over the water at this speed was considerable with the added advantage of leverage. The sheer volume of spray increased and started to obscure Bill's vision. He had already adjusted his mindset from a mode of competitive exploitation to damage control and a "cut your losses" approach. With the sole intention of saving the boat, he began to understand that not only was the volume coming in fast enough that he probably wouldn't make it back to the dock, the point of shutting it off and waiting for an aid boat was going to be moot.

Now, he couldn't see. It was not unlike trying to steer in a shower. Leaning out over the right side of the cockpit, he caught a brief glimpse of the area inside the race course called the infield. There were patrol boats stationed there and that represented the quickest possible source of a tow line and aid. As he turned the Miss Great Lakes in that direction, his shower grew bigger.

The possibility of being completely blinded began to occur to him. Although his speed was rapidly diminishing, the mass of material he represented would be formidable should he impact another vessel. He was out of time and out of options. He had to shut the boat down.

Grounding out the magneto with a turn of a switch was the first step. By rote, Bill went through the shut down sequence. Any serious driver will practice this exercise dozens and dozens of times until it becomes a single act of reflex. The faster and more efficiently a driver can do it, the less damage will be caused and the less repair work the crew will have to do. A few seconds can save thousands of dollars and hundreds of man hours. Bill had spent hours simply sitting in that cockpit practicing. All the practice now paid off in that a quick shut down minimized the damage that the river was doing to the bottom of the boat. The water level had reached his ankle on the foot pedal as the boat quickly came to a stop.

As the hull settled down off of a plane, the volume of water that had collected against the insides of the transom in the back of the

Chapter Eight

boat flowed forward around his calves. The spray had stopped and Bill could look down and see that the hole wasn't appreciably larger than when he had first seen it. Pulling the rag back out of his belt he leaned down and tried to use it to plug the opening. The water pressure pushed his rag back into the boat. Looking up he saw a patrol boat idling in his direction.

"There is no way that they can know what kind of trouble I'm in," Bill ruefully thought to himself. He waved his arms over his head and tried to encourage the skipper of the patrol boat to speed up.

Calculating the time before the patrol boat would get there, factoring in the time it will take to secure a tow line to the bow and allowing for the added volume of water to flow into the boat Bill quickly concluded there simply wasn't enough time at the rate of flow.

"Work the problem, " he thought. " Do something to slow the flow." The idea of simply leaving the boat never crossed his mind. "What are my options?"

In a compulsive flash of insight, he realized that his life jacket could be pressed against the hole to staunch the flow. Wresting it off he rapidly swung it down below him and followed it under the steering wheel to push it into location against the hole. Wedging it tightly between his chest and the torrent coming into the boat appeared to have the desired effect.

By this point, water was coming in over the sides of the engine compartment and cockpit.

He could hear someone calling to him from out on the patrol boat. The sound of water splashing against the engine also reached his ears. The Miss Great Lakes was sinking faster.

It was time to get out.

He could not move. In his enthusiastic effort to wedge the life jacket against the hole in the bottom of the boat, he had also inadvertently wedged his back up against the steering wheel. The tangle of his legs against the underside of the seat compounded matters. The water level quickly rose up over his head as the bow of the race boat nosed under the river's surface. A torrential cascade of the cold Detroit River enveloped the cockpit muffling the shouts of the rescuers. The ensuing silence was replaced by a frantic underwater buzz of propellers.

Some primordial sense of urgency set in. The growing darkness surrounding him as the boat quickly sank deeper accelerated the alarm and the pace of adrenalin. Bordering on panic, he wrestled with the jacket and twisted against the bottom of the steering wheel while trying to find a foothold against which he could press. Turning and contorting, his left knee grazed the engine stringer and he pushed himself out from under the steering wheel's curved edge which had been lodged between his shoulder blades.

Spinning up and out, Bill scrambled and flailed his way upward kicking against the deck. Gasping loudly as he broke the surface, he was looking directly into the astonished face of the patrol boat skipper.

"That boat and I were on our way to the bottom of the Detroit River," he later recalled.

Years later, Bill would acknowledge that he had pushed the Miss Great Lakes too hard in his efforts to qualify her for the Harmsworth. One way or another he should have been more conservative or more responsible in the operation of the boat. He was the driver. She was in his care and he had not brought her back to the dock.

Gar Wood sent him the bill for the engine.

Bill as a young Unlimited Hydroplane driver

Dan Arena, Lee Schoenith, and Bill Cantrell

The Miss Great Lakes race boat provided Bill his first Unlimited ride in the early '50's.

CHAPTER NINE

A Dumb Idea

"To date, this is probably the dumbest idea I have ever had," Bill thought. Initially, like a lot of stupid moves, it had seemed like a great adventure, transplanting his young family 3,000 miles from home to a new city, a new job and a new life. He was deliberately separating himself from the comforts and support of the familial home and financial security on which he privately feared he had become dependent.

"Could I make it on my own?" he had asked himself.

At this particular instant, he was asking himself an entirely different kind of question. "What on earth was I thinking?"

The offer in Seattle, Washington had been somewhat of a surprise. In the beginning, it was supposed to be an opportunity to merely test drive some equipment. Ted Jones and the Associated Grocers group had formed a racing team and built a new hydroplane. Christened the Miss Thriftway, it had incorporated many of the present-day hydroplane design features plus some substantial refinements that Ted had personally developed for high performance boats over the last five years. Jones had been impressed with the driving aptitude he thought he had observed in Bill on the Detroit River when Bill had driven the Miss Great Lakes. Wanting a fresh point of view, Ted invited Bill to come "out west" for a visit and test-drive the new boat.

Bill was technically under an exclusive contract to Horace Dodge of the Dodge automobile manufacturing family to drive race boats for him. Horace relented to Bill's request and agreed to loan Muncey to the new team for input. It would certainly be convenient to try and blame Horace's generosity on the fix in which Bill now found himself. Unfortunately, this was a serious situation and blaming someone else for the circumstances was not going to stop the the falling snowflakes that were getting larger.

Seattle was regarded by most of Bill's acquaintances as existing on the edge of the world somewhere out near the Arctic Circle where the grey weather is usually rain relieved by an upgrade to periods of snow. Eskimos resided in igloos on every street corner.

His high school buddies had regarded Bill Muncey as perhaps

one of the richest kids in school. Why would he want to exile himself to some frozen, remote, and isolated corner of the country? Back in high school, he demonstrated his independence and financial creativity by pocketing the lunch money his parents gave him and waiting tables during lunch period at the café across the street from the high school to pay for his own meals. This Seattle move was an exponential leap in exercising that independence.

Bill's family was less than enthusiastic about the idea that boat racing could be anything more than an exciting hobby, much less a career that could generate a real paycheck to support a family. However, the offer to permanently drive the Miss Thriftway included a modest salary and when Bill relayed the proposal to his parents he couldn't help but feel a certain degree of validation. Bill's wife, Kit, was skeptical initially, but relented when Bill's father threw his support behind the young couple and offered to finance their first new house out in the Pacific Northwest.

Somehow, Ed Muncey had identified with his son's adventure. Even Ed's brother, Bill, tried to talk his namesake out of transplanting to Seattle and throwing his hat in with boat racing. Bill's uncle extolled the virtues of the responsible husband and father and fervently tried to discourage his nephew from making the commitment but in the end, Ed and Esther Muncey supported their son and his bride in their decision to move.

The plan was for Bill to take his four year old son, William Jr., and drive West in the family station wagon. Kit and two year old Dorian would fly out two weeks later.

This father and son quality time was a great idea on paper. It was even a great idea on a map. The mid-1950's America saw a dramatic expansion in transportation capabilities by way of the highway. After a brutal lesson learned from his adversaries in World War II, President Eisenhower had leant his considerable political credit toward updating and enhancing the mass transit systems cross country so that shipping of commodities could be better facilitated. What this did for the average citizen was made it possible to drive one's personal automobile from one side of the country to the other via inter-state highways. The transit expansion had been time consuming and expensive and the highway system's support infrastructure was much better in some states than others. Telephone availability was often spotty or nonexistent and there were vast stretches of paved interstate that traversed mile after mile of uninhabited open range.

On the map that Kit and Bill had studied, the highway ran straight across the state of South Dakota with no towns or large metropolitan areas to speak of. At the time this had seemed like a good thing - better cruising speed, especially at night. Bill liked to drive at night. It was healthier for the equipment and safer, he reasoned.

On the other hand, it could also be a not-so-good idea, especially when it was snowing. It had never occurred to either of them that the weather would play a substantial role in the trip. Bill had snow chains and he had driven in the snow plenty of times in Detroit. How bad could it be?

What they had not factored in were service stations that closed in the evening. After the first one, Bill had simply pulled back onto the highway anticipating another opportunity just down the road. After the second one, it had started to snow. Big flakes, lazy, floating tumblers that somehow reminded him of sheets of plywood. They were innocuous flakes, innocent, and unthreatening. As he traveled on into the night, the isolation amidst the broad expanse of the American plain was serene.

"Not a light in sight," Bill thought.

The station wagon was equipped with a V-8 265 c.i. engine that was not only powerful but reliably spun a six volt generator that in turn spun a heater fan that kept Bill and little William warm and comfortable in the well-sealed interior. The vacuum created by the big V-8 powered the windshield wipers and maintained a feeling of security against the elements outside.

"Not even a headlight," Bill observed.

In a vague and unsettling way, he began to realize that he had not seen another car in either direction for quite some time. The fact seemed curious.

"Not even the occasional trucker," Bill pondered to himself. Looking down at the fuel gage, he started to do the math of miles per gallon versus distance needed to travel. William was sleeping on the bench seat next to him oblivious to any sense of anxiety or concern. Looking over, Bill considered that William had been a pretty good boy so far on the trip. Only one time had he misbehaved and that was when he had let himself out of the car as Bill

A Dumb Idea

visited with a friend while leaving Michigan. Ultimately, Bill chastised himself for leaving his son alone in the first place. He was, after all, only four years old.

Watching his son sleep, securely wrapped up in his Disneyland Davy Crockett blanket brought home by contrast the fact that they truly were in the middle of nowhere. The sheets of snowy plywood had turned into small flurries of chips from a table saw. The wind had picked up, causing the flurries to whirl and twist in the conical beams of the head lights. The engine deceptively droned on at a comfortable cruising speed while the radio tinnily picked up stations two states away. A soft carpet of white frosting was beginning to collect on the black top and Bill noticed a distinct absence of tire tracks in either direction.

It occurred to Bill at this time how vulnerable they really were. Aside from his own perennial optimism, he had no real reason to think that they would find a gas station soon. In fact, he had no reason to think that there would even be a warm or dry place to pull off the road. The amount of gas in the tank was dangerously low. They needed fuel to not only move, but also to simply make heat. If the conditions that were developing outside were any indication, the need for heat would soon out-rank the need for travel.

The sun had recently set and they had hours to endure before the daylight could make a substantial temperature difference. If worse came to worse, he could flag someone down for help.

"But when would that happen?" he asked himself. At this point, he had not seen a soul for over an hour. In this part of the country, they closed sections of the highway down to traffic so that travelers would not get stranded or skid off the road and be buried in the snow.

"Had he missed a sign or signal?" he wondered.

Snow flurries conspired into a floating blanket that shrouded the front of the turquoise and white station wagon. Diminishing vision forced Bill to dramatically reduce his speed. He considered that going slower might conserve gas. On the other hand, maybe not. He seemed to recall that the engine was most efficient operating at a slightly faster pace than he was currently traveling.

The muffler sounded louder. It took him a moment to understand that the increasing density of the snow he was traveling through acted like a tunnel deflecting the sound of his exhaust back against

Chapter Nine

the body of the car.

Bill turned on the cabin light to look over William blissfully asleep on the seat. He and Kit had even talked about the "fellas" stopping in at their friend Bill Stead's ranch in Nevada on the way to Seattle. There were plans and then there were plans. The needle of the gas gauge had stopped wiggling against the letter E.

His tires made a crushed and padded sound as the wheels rolled over the thickening virgin snow. In the back of the station wagon there was their cherished phonograph player encased in a buffet type piece of bleached wood furniture. In addition to a radio, it could also hold a substantial amount of LP high fidelity vinyl records. Next to, it was the family dining room buffet with the dining room table disassembled, wrapped, and padded on top of both pieces. The dining room chairs made up the puzzle. Only after a complex merging, had the chairs been able to make this trip. Intermingled with the whole load were Bill and Kit's clothes safely folded and layered into two suitcases. They were relatively large suitcases. It occurred to Bill that the size of the suitcases might be a good thing.

There still was not a light in sight. This did not really indicate much since visibility was poor. The snow began to take on the appearance of a mid-western blizzard. Bill originally felt that he had two simple choices: One was to keep driving in the hope that a gas station or some form of heated shelter would appear. This involved a substantial consumption of fuel. The other choice was to stop on the side of the road and run the engine only to provide heat. The second option would allow them a longer time to wait for help to arrive from either direction. Hopefully, in either case, he could get out of the car in time to signal his need to another driver. Neither choice was a particularly attractive alternative.

A third choice was beginning to present itself. It seemed ridiculous at first but became more viable as time went on. In either of the first two choices, when he ran out of gas, the heat would go. It is simple physics. At that point, he would have to decide whether to wait and try to contain heat within the car or get out and try to walk to safety. Stories of people freezing to death in their cars during blizzards popped into Bill's head. Getting out and trying to walk somewhere did not seem like a stroke of genius either.

"How do I care for my son?" Bill asked himself.

A Dumb Idea

He certainly could not expect a four year old boy to walk anywhere in this weather. He did not have the clothes for it anyway. His little fingers and toes would freeze! Then the image in the rear view mirror caught his eye. The suitcases were actually quite large. If he removed most of the contents of one, he could probably get William to fit inside, well insulated with articles of clothing. If he cut a couple of holes in the side panels of the suitcase, William could see and breathe as Bill carried him by the suitcase handle. It just might work.

On the other hand, it just might be another dumb idea! How long did he think that he could walk in a blizzard until he succumbed to the cold himself? Then what would happen to his son? He would be locked inside a suitcase with snow piling up on top. Nevertheless, it was an option.

At one time, Ed Muncey Chevrolet had been the largest Chevrolet dealership in the world. Although Ed had reduced his personal participation of late, it was still a lucrative and ongoing concern. Bill was raised and educated with the intention of participating in the family business. Ironically, it was during that educational process that Bill had developed the idea of doing something else. As a Marketing Major at the General Motors Institute of Business Administration, Bill had been impressed with the power of mass communication such as radio and more recently, television. During his adolescence, he had witnessed firsthand the ability of radio to express and communicate ideas to vast audiences across continents. Edward R. Murrow broadcasting from London during the Blitz had left a profound impression on an entire nation. Music played in a ballroom in San Francisco could be danced to in New York. Testimony before a committee in Washington D.C. could be seen in real time by viewers in Washington State. The growing motorsports audiences and Bill's aptitude for successful participation as a competitor had underlined the possibility of a career totally independent of any advantages gained from a fortunate birthright.

His father had made a similar sojourn as a young man from West Virginia. Although Ed's effort had been more out of necessity, transplanting himself into a new way of life was not entirely foreign. In an underlying sense, Bill felt that his father was maintaining a certain degree of respect for this bold move. Now, if he could just get there.

Chapter Nine

Ironically, Bill thought to himself, "If I hadn't let my temper get the better of me, I would have avoided this whole mess in the first place."

The first time Bill met Ted Jones had been under rather dubious circumstances. Bill had been straddling the engine compartment across the front of his personal race boat. It was stored on its trailer parked in the back lot of the Muncey car dealership in Detroit off of McKinley Avenue. A six cylinder Chevrolet engine was suspended by a hoist over the boat and Bill was trying to remove the harmonic balancer that was attached to its crankshaft. It was turning into an exercise in patience. A wheel puller was not easily available and Bill was crudely using a wedge of wood fashioned from a 2x4 to tap between the balancer and the block to force it off the crank. The whole process was not going well.

He hated borrowing tools from the dealership's mechanics. They needed them to earn a living and he was the owner's son. The whole idea just rubbed him the wrong way. So here he was, trying to replace an engine without the right tools for the job. Instead of pressing the circular balancer off, he was just creating a great way to dent the timing chain cover.

"Swell," he had thought to himself, "and now here comes some well-intended fan to ask questions about race boats and shoot the breeze about how fast they go. Just great!"

"You really ought to get the right tool for the job," as the stranger opened the conversation.

"It just keeps getting better," Bill thought sarcastically. "Maybe he doesn't realize that perhaps I wanted to dent the timing chain cover."

The temptation to make a smart aleck remark to this tall, dark haired boating enthusiast was almost overwhelming. On the other hand, there was something about this fellow standing there in his sport coat without a hat and with a Western style string tie that seemed vaguely familiar. Maybe he was a new salesman calling on the dealership or a representative from the Chevrolet factory. It didn't really matter, he thought as his frustration abated. He was showing some interest in Bill's project and that deserved a polite response.

"I don't like borrowing the mechanics' tools," Bill offered. "I managed to get a good deal on this engine and I'm eager to see how it fits."

A Dumb Idea

Standing up in the engine well, Bill stepped onto the deck and down to the ground wiping his hands off on his pant legs as he dropped, and offering one to the man.

"My name's Bill, what's yours?" he asked.

The familiarity began to grow as Bill got up closer and the stranger firmly grasped his hand in return and said, "My name is Ted."

Then it hit him like a brick. This guy was Ted Jones. Ted Jones had driven unlimited hydroplanes. Ted Jones had designed the fastest hydroplane in the world. Ted Jones was standing in the back parking lot of Ed Muncey's Chevrolet out of the blue and talking to a rookie driver about the proper procedure for removing a harmonic balancer from a 235 c.i. 6-cylinder gas engine. Ted Jones just shook his hand.

"Wait a minute," Bill thought, "Ted Jones did not just happen to be in the neighborhood. In fact, there is not even a race scheduled in the area for weeks."

Bill's pulse quickened.

Bill maintained his polite posture in a convincing fashion and scrambled internally to try and discern the reason for this living legend's visit.

"Do you follow the Limited class racing much?" Bill asked.

"I'm from out west and we have a lot of racing where I come from," Ted offered. "I try to watch when I can. I was out here on business recently and saw you run out on the river."

Although Bill was pleased with the opportunity of driving the Miss Great Lakes at the time, he still had mixed feelings about the whole episode at the Silver Cup, "She really liked to fly, but I might have pushed her too hard. I don't know if you saw, but I sunk her during the race," Bill said as he briefly looked down at the tire on his trailer.

"Yeah, I stayed around for the whole event," Ted understated. "You seemed to get as much as she had. It's too bad she didn't stay together."

With a modest amount of relief in his voice Bill asked, "So what brings you back to Detroit, Ted?"

To scholars of marine motorsports, the ensuing conversations created a ripple effect that influenced the design and refinement of high performance maritime craft for decades. Ted Jones was look-

Chapter Nine

ing for a driver that embraced the concept of a boat that flew over the water instead of through it and had the aptitude to use that capability in an aggressive and decisive fashion. The young Bill Muncey had displayed that aptitude. Bluntly, it was a young idea from a young engineer that required a young man to demonstrate it. To many well-respected naval engineers and designers it was a tremendous departure from the accepted and traditional discipline in both physics and hydrodynamics. A youthful, impolite outburst from Bill toward this interested but distracting stranger may have created an entirely different result that would not evolve into a desolate road in South Dakota.

The pad of snow on the road was getting thicker. If Bill had to stop in a hurry, it was likely that he would need to compensate his steering for a slide. It might even be to the point that an abrupt drop in speed could cause the traction to be lost under his rear driving wheels and cause the car to spin. He knew from experience driving in the snow that tire chains would be in order soon. There wasn't anywhere in sight for him to pull over and put them on. 'There isn't even a shoulder to speak of.

"Not that that would matter," Bill ruefully mused. "There aren't any cars to avoid anyway."

He had honestly reached the point where he would not be surprised if the car's engine just stopped. Inadvertently it seemed one decision a foregone conclusion. He would any minute now run out of gas and then wait for help until the heat was gone from the car. He would have to hope for a break in the weather...or perhaps break out the suitcase.

He wondered briefly if his father had ever felt so separated and adrift. When Bill had been born, Ed and Esther lived in an apartment above a bowling alley. Bill's first crib had been a bathtub - after he had graduated from a lower dresser drawer. Certainly, Ed Muncey had felt periods of indecision or doubt. Nevertheless, to Bill's knowledge, he had never put his family in danger.

"What was I thinking!" he chastised himself again.

At first, he thought it was something stuck to the headlight causing the light to deflect in a new way. A snowflake or two glittered differently. It took a moment at first for him to adjust to the idea that he was looking at a light in the distance. Like a blinking eye, it wavered and obscured its distance. Eventually Bill realized that it

A Dumb Idea

was not a car or truck but was attached to a fixed object. It wasn't a flame but an incandescent light. The light meant electricity. Electricity meant civilization. This meant that if worse came to worse he could walk there. The relief was profound. He hadn't noticed but he had been holding his breath in concentration and now exhaled dramatically.

As the car sputtered up next to the pumps at the gas station near a motel, Bill considered the close call and alternative endings. This frozen oasis could easily have been another twenty miles down the road. He could have just as easily lost his infamous temper with the tall dark stranger in the back lot and told him to mind his own business.

Half of the close calls in life might be avoided with thorough preparation but the other half would be left up to something else.

Left to Right; Ray Muncey, unknown, Ted Jones and Bill Muncey

Mira Slovak and Bill Muncey

The Presidents Cup. Left to right Kit Muncey, Bill Muncey, Willard Rhodes, and President Eisenhower

CHAPTER TEN

Nobody called him "Billy"

Bill Muncey's desk was humbly comprised of a pair of two-drawer, sheet metal file cabinets that were spaced far enough apart to allow for a wheeled swivel office chair to roll between them and a household door set on top of them to act as a writing surface. He was sitting at that desk in the early afternoon, when the phone rang.

At this time in American history, most homes had a telephone. Most likely, just one and they all had a rotary spin type dial. If a home was particularly posh, it might have more than one hard-wired telephone in strategic places around the premises. Bill was proud of the fact that there were three located in his house, one in the kitchen for his wife, Kit, and one next to their bed in addition to the one at the desk. It had not been that long ago that a long distance telephone call was a special situation requiring a trained operator's assistance to complete the call.

Bill picked up the call on the third ring and answered, "Good afternoon, can I help you?"

His eldest son, sitting in the den nearby, could hear the ensuing conversation. After a substantially long silence where Bill did not speak but only listened, Bill sat up straight in his chair lifting his elbow off the desk and speaking in a measured but deliberate tone into the phone. His son never forgot what he heard his father say next.

In a tone that he had never heard his father use before, Bill said, "If that is what you want, Mira can have every drop of blood in my body."

Subsequently, Bill's tone went up an octave and the focus was more intense. Although the child could only hear one side of the conversation, he knew something very significant was happening.

"I have no idea where to find Mira's brother." Bill went on, "Maybe somewhere in the Midwest. "

Although the kitchen was upstairs from the den, Bill's voice carried and Kit picked up on the unusual nature of the call. Walking to the top of the stairs where she could look down to Bill at his desk, she listened patiently with a mixing bowl in one hand and a wooden spoon in the other. Although she had not heard the first sentence, she knew by the tone of Bill's voice that there was a sense of urgency and alarm.

"I will make some phone calls, "Bill said, "and get back to you. Please keep me informed of any developments."

He took a deep breath and said, "Thank you for the call."

With a timeless gaze that only two people very close to each other can understand Bill looked up to Kit and said in a staccato of sentences, " Mira's been in an airplane accident. He's in very bad shape. It doesn't look good. He needs a lot of blood. I offered, but apparently he has a very rare blood type."

This was followed by a frightened look between them accompanied by a sense of helplessness.

Kit was the first to collect her thoughts and make a suggestion. Putting together the pieces of the conversation she had heard, she asked, " Do you think that your father out in Detroit might know some law enforcement people in the Midwest that could help find Mira's brother? "

The suggestion was hopeful and optimistic. Bill's father was well acquainted with community leaders. E.L. Muncey would know whom to call.

Bill's thoughts briefly flickered back to his adolescent years when he would volunteer to clean up the basement game room in the Muncey house after his father's Friday night poker games. Often E.L. would have the mayor or the chief of police over to play five card stud or "baseball". Bill's enthusiasm for housekeeping at the time had been enhanced by the possibility of finding the lost big bill or loose change left behind. These same friends of his father might be able to help Bill's friend.

To Kit Mira Slovak was not only a close family friend and the godfather of one of her children; he had once risked his own life to save her husband's. Truly a knight had fallen and although Bill had had his competitive differences with Mira over the years, Kit knew that there was not a power on earth that would dissuade Bill from rendering every possible effort to help. She recognized an expression of grim determination on Bill's face as he reached for the phone.

The regatta in Madison, Indiana was reputed to be one of the oldest in North America. With a population of about

Chapter Ten

10,000 people, the annual Independence Day event had evolved into a week-long celebration attracting six digit crowds. A sleepy town on the north shore of the Ohio River, Madison had once been a bustling port serving the farms and industries of the Midwest. Overtaken by the competitive rates and expedience of rail and truck transportation, Madison had devolved into the picturesque community attractive to tourists seeking a glimpse into the maritime nature of America's history. The community had developed the hydroplane regatta into a very marketable asset that attracted teams from thousands of miles away and cash-spending spectators and tourists from the surrounding states.

In 1957, the Miss Thriftway team was usually considered a contender at any regatta on the circuit. An article in the popular LIFE magazine referred to the boat in the context of "most racers consider the greatest hydroplane racing today."

Nevertheless, at the preceding President's Cup in Washington, D.C., the team ended the weekend with a less than stellar final heat due to damage to the left side or port sponson. Barely making way under her own power Miss Thriftway placed fifth and had to expedite repairs in order to make the regatta in Madison. A valiant effort by crewman Joe Lewis rendered her operable once again and she entered the hot pit area on the sandy shore of the Ohio amid a dry dusty cloud of optimism and high spirits.

In the first heat of the Indiana's Governors Cup, the Thriftway found itself opposing a formidable contender in the Miss Wahoo driven by Mira Slovak. Mira had demonstrated a remarkable aptitude for piloting a hydroplane considering his relatively recent immersion into the sport. Already an accomplished airplane pilot, he had successfully grafted his aerodynamic reflexes into the constantly shifting hydrodynamic arena to the dismay and consternation of his opponents. Additionally, he had achieved something more difficult to acquire; he had earned the respect if not downright admiration of the brutal fraternity of his fellow drivers.

In the aircraft community, his fellow pilots might call him a "good stick and rudder man". Deftly applying the discipline needed to be a professional pilot and allowing enough flexibility to compensate for a constantly changing maritime environment, Mira had also shown the courage and determination that underscores the difference between a rookie driver and "a good chauffeur" as

Bill would say.

Mira showed that kind of courage and determination to a national audience four years prior when as a Czechoslovakian airline pilot, he flew his aircraft to freedom over the Iron Curtain. Leaving the rest of his family regrettably behind, he embraced the concept of independence and liberty head on rather than remain in the relative security blanket of communism. Classically tall, dark and handsome with impeccable manners, America quickly reciprocated that embrace.

Bill had to contend with that capable combination on the race course in Madison that day.

A race on a river with an Unlimited type hydroplane is dramatically different from a race on a more placid body such as a lake. The swells created by the flow of the river move about with the changes in the river's volume and are affected by the ambient temperature on the water's surface. A one inch drop or rise of the river's top layer over a 100-foot span may be unnoticeable to the naked eye but is as dramatic in a hydroplane traveling in excess of 150 MPH as a car hitting a speed bump at 60 MPH. Add to that wakes and holes created by competitors' sponsons, transoms and propellers and there is a constantly changing race track with which to read and contend. Then factor the need to compensate for the river's own speed and a driver has another unique variable. Many a rookie driver has failed to consider this and bounced hard against the dock when coming in from the course. As an example, enter a corner at 159 MPH and you lose the race; enter at 160, you might win the race, but enter at 161 and you crash.

Most large rivers flow at a rate between five and nine MPH. A driver needs to account for a variable in his entrance speed of over ten MPH when racing on a river. In a worst case scenario, a miscalculation could force him to drift into another driver's lane with no time to react. Two well- matched opponents will find themselves orchestrating a high speed, hydrodynamic ballet in order to stay in contention.

Bill gained a slight position advantage over Mira in the first heat. Characteristically, Mira's pursuit was relentless and very aggressive. In the closely battled contest, Bill prevailed; however, it required him to set a 15-mile course lap average record of 112.312 MPH in order to stay ahead of his rival. That record would stand

Chapter Ten

for six years.

The luck of the draw found the two matched up for another heat the following day. The excitement and anticipation emanating from both shores of the Ohio were palpable as the two drivers guided their boats onto the race course amongst the other competitors after the five minute gun was fired. Onlookers witnessed the pair jockeying their steeds for the most advantageous position when the "one minute to the start" shot was fired and the full field of competitors came together into their respective lanes.

Bill leaned heavily into his boat's slightly superior speed as he made a legal start to the race and bounded into the first corner in the lead. The blue water that greeted him there enabled the Miss Thriftway's sponsons to claim a clean purchase of the surface and set a more stable radius. Mira, on the other hand, had to negotiate around Bill's position and contend with the white water created by Bill's wake, roostertail and propeller. These factors forced Mira to drive harder and deal with more horsepower-eating variables in order to press his pursuit.

Press his pursuit he did! Cantering up the Kentucky side straightaway, Bill was able to maintain his position, keenly aware that any deviation from the quickest path around the race course would be an error Mira would immediately exploit. Rapidly accelerating to speeds over 160 MPH, Bill knew that a mistake of that nature could promptly negate any speed advantage. With engine tachometers climbing to 75% beyond military combat redline and laying out watery roostertails hundreds of feet behind them, the pair proceeded to demonstrate an unpredictable repeat of the race the day before.

Slamming into the second corner, Bill managed to maintain his lead. Bouncing and bounding violently through the upriver current, he slightly increased his position advantage and galloped past the exit pin on the Indiana side of the oval race course. Both drivers were sitting in open cockpits and without any restraining device such as seatbelts or straps. Requiring substantial upper body strength just to hang onto the steering wheel, both drivers had to twist and turn in their respective seats to remain in their boats and not get thrown overboard. Rocking from side to side, it took focused and concentrated physical effort to keep the foot on the throttle, steer the boat and stay in the cockpit.

Mira pressed his pursuit.

No one was able to firmly establish from where the errant swell or wave came. Some thought that it was just a simple surface deviation of the Ohio River. Others thought that it was a patrol boat's wake. Regardless of the source, Miss Thriftway encountered an extraordinary roller on the Ohio River midway up the front chute. At the considerable speed that she was traveling, it served to act like a launching ramp and hurled boat and driver into the air.

In an interview on the subject Bill later said, "When you hit a bump and get thrown out of attitude, you know you've got to take the time to bring the boat back. When you can do that and not decrease your boat speed, then you've done something. It involves absolute control of the throttle with your foot and a real coordination between the throttle and the manifold pressure. It's all very slow, very coordinated. It can almost be a ... no, not a sensuous experience, but certainly an artistic one."

To gasping onlookers it seemed to take an eternity for the now airborne Miss Thriftway to come back down. The angle of the roller crossing the bow would dictate which sponson would absorb the brunt of impact. Cognizant of Mira's imminent presence and still very much in the game, Bill made the appropriate throttle adjustments in concert with the supercharger's manifold pressure. Modestly tugging on the steering wheel to allow for the change of course in the air due to the rollers angle of impact, Bill braced himself for the plunge of re-entry. The mahogany decked hull with the persimmon stripes sailed through the air with her bow slowly descending. Sunlight twinkled off her deck as the sponsons seesawed. The left sponson dipped.

The lumber industry uses high pressure jets of water to strip the bark from trees in route to the saw mill's blades. At 150 MPH, water has the density of 455 pounds per square inch. This also describes the consistency of asphalt.

A photographer for the Louisville Courier-Journal was standing in the judge's stand training his lens on the Miss Thriftway as she held off the Miss Wahoo's challenge. Jim Harlan's photos were later used in a magazine article that went on to say about the Miss Thriftway "...soaring ten feet, it burst like a clay target. "

Whether Joe Lewis' hurried repairs were at fault or whether any repair could have withstood that level of assault is certainly

CHAPTER TEN

debatable. If the repairs were what actually failed will never be determined because every shred of evidence was scattered across the Ohio River.

Tearing past the aluminum skin on the bottom of the left sponson, a sheet of water ripped into the bulkhead immediately behind the breach. Since the bulkhead was attached directly to the engine rail or spine of the boat, the combined impact of the water and the leverage of the bulkhead frame succeeded in ripping the sponson open and off of the boat. A column of the Ohio the size of a bathtub barreled through the side of the Miss Thriftway just under the dashboard and steering wheel and plowed into Bill lifting him and his seat into the growing aquatic cloud of bits and pieces of plywood, aluminum shards, wires, fittings, and hoses that were once a race boat.

That cloud ultimately grew to over 100 feet tall as the ribs, panels and sheets of plywood and aluminum twisted and tumbled apart. Spectators gasped as the cloud developed shades of black, silver and gray that represented disintegrating components of a race boat. Bill was indistinguishable in the mass of water, sawdust, and metal. Tumbling head over heels in the black mist that surrounded him, the water tore and clawed at his clothes and life jacket. It succeeded in ripping off his wedding ring and watch. It shredded portions of his drivers' suit pulling the suit out from under his life jacket. Miraculously no bones were broken, but the pummeling of his torso ruptured his spleen. Eyes open but unable to adjust depth to focus, a surreal sense of drifting and floating came over him. The shock and speed of the experience distanced him from the impending pain.

Somersaulting and ricocheting off of flotsam and jetsam, Bill cartwheeled to a stop amid the watery field of wreckage. Now mercifully unconscious and temporarily vacated from the pain, his personally designed jacket kept him floating face up amid the wreckage debris.

From his distance behind, Mira was unable to see the errant roller that slithered across the race course. His eyes were focused primarily on the Miss Thriftway and looking for missteps of which he could take advantage. Just coming off of the corner himself, he did not notice anything unusual in the attitude of his opponent's boat midway up the front chute. But for no apparent reason, the

Thriftway's bow appeared to Mira to lift and the transom dropped slightly. It was a subtle difference but to trained eyes, it represented a change in the boat's attitude that could have substantial consequences. Mira knew that it wasn't the lifting of the bow itself that was significant. It was the compression of the transom into the water that foretold the danger. With nowhere for the propeller to go but down, the added thrust from a totally submerged pair of blades would wrest control of the boats delicate balance out of the drivers' hands. Depending upon the severity of the lift and the load on the propeller, the driver might not have time to recover.

Mira's jaw dropped as he watched the Miss Thriftway launch into the air. The thrust from the propeller was so substantial that it threw the back end of the boat up and out of the water and forced the bow back down into the Ohio like the down side of a seesaw when one child hops off. The left side of the hull hit the water first, the resultant impact created a mountain of spray and debris as the Miss Thriftway disintegrated right in front of Mira's eyes. It seemed that a blink of one eye was all the time it took to render a sleek and formidable race boat into a tumbling bundle of white water, splinters of plywood and twisted panels of aluminum.

Promptly lifting his foot off of the throttle, Mira caused the Miss Wahoo to decelerate. At a surprisingly quick rate, her speed matched that of the river amid a suspended field of debris, oil, and gasoline that had once been the Miss Thriftway. By a stroke of pure good fortune, his gaze quickly found and focused on Bill's floating body. In one motion, Mira grabbed the combing of his cockpit and pulled himself out of his seat and onto the deck of his boat. For a brief moment, he allowed his eye to survey the surrounding waters and grimly realized that the accident had happened so quickly that the search and rescue teams had not had time to react. The spectators, patrol boats and officials seemed to be sitting in stunned silence as the reality of what had just happened began to sink in. It was unlikely that crowds had ever been as silent.

Bill's body seemed limp and lifeless as it gently rocked back and forth in the eddies of the Ohio current. Without a moment's hesitation, Mira committed an act that would be recalled for decades within the racing community. He leapt from the relative safety of his deck into the water. The world class reflexes that enabled him to race hydroplanes and fly airplanes combined with selfless, moral courage to render aid to his fallen friend.

There was one problem.

Mira couldn't swim.

Without consideration for the dangers presented to himself by the copious amounts of high octane fuel and oil spreading its combustible mix around him and the cumbersome reality of his swimming limitations he flailed and dog paddled his way over to Bill's side.

Reaching Bill's inert body and spitting vile tasting water out of his mouth Mira spoke to his unconscious friend.

"I've got you Billy," Mira said aloud. Coughing and twisting in the current he struggled to keep Bill's head floating face up.

" Billy" was actually a term of endearment because he had learned early on that Bill decidedly didn't like anyone calling him that. For some reason that Mira never quite understood, Bill would smile whenever Mira called him that. Their shore side banter would often reach silly dimensions, Mira would call him "Billy" or "Munsley" in front of the cameras, and they would trade good-natured insults and taunts to the delight of fans and the media.

Nobody but Mira Slovak could get away with calling him "Billy."

Waving his arm as high over the water as possible, Mira tugged on the round collar of Bill's life jacket and signaled to the search and rescue team as it approached. As soon as the boat pulled up alongside the two men and rescuers actually laid hands on Bill, Mira clambered up over the gunnels and into the patrol boat. The medical examination began as the rescue boat was underway. Staying by Bill's side, Mira kept up a steady, reassuring voice to the unconscious driver.

In the years before helicopters made a substantial contribution to search and rescue efforts, the shore side ambulance was the primary mode of transportation to the hospital. Unfortunately, access from water's edge to the door of the ambulance could be completely blocked by the presence of the crowds and media rushing to the point where the rescue boat was landing. Crew and family could be isolated by a wall of well wishing but impenetrable spectators.

To avoid this problem, the race director routinely informed the drivers at the daily drivers meeting that in the event of an accident an announcement intended for them would come over the public address speakers that would say, "Drivers – take a walk."

This message would discretely notify them that there was a driver in a stretcher coming to shore and that all drivers should immediately walk over to a predetermined location at water's edge. Once there they would form a line, shoulder –to- shoulder up to the door of the waiting ambulance. They were instructed to actually hold hands in order to create a human fence discouraging fans and spectators from getting in the way of the stretcher bearers.

"Drivers - take a walk," came the announcement over the public address system.

As the patrol boat radioed Bill's condition to the paramedics, anxious crew chiefs, drivers, owners, and officials began the migration to the Indiana bank without saying a word. Competitive differences evaporated in the muggy air of the Ohio River Valley.

Some made up the line from the dock to the back door of the ambulance while others went passed the security guards onto the dock to assist in the actual transfer of Bill in his stretcher. Hand over hand and over head, Bill's stretcher was carried through the crowd to the shore. Mira stayed near his friend's side all the way to the ambulance. Bill's wife, Kit, and the Thriftway crew chief, Jack Ramsey, were able to garner the first real information about Bill's condition and prepared to follow the ambulance to the hospital.

Once the stretcher was secured to the ambulance floor, the door closed with a hollow thump and the back wheels spun gently in the sandy loam as the ambulance waddled back and forth up the beach to the road. Sirens wailing and red lights flashing, a police escort enveloped the station wagon-type emergency vehicle in order to expedite the trip to the hospital. Bill had not regained consciousness and his fate was uncertain. The fact that he was still breathing was the primary harbinger of hope. A pall of silence remained along the banks as the sirens wailed into the distance.

Twisted, torn, and ravaged by the Ohio, what remained of the Miss Thriftway was dragged through the current to shore. Wading and sometimes swimming to an advantageous position, crew members attempted to attach cables extending from a crane over head. Once his driver was safely away, Jack Ramsey turned his attention to directing his crew toward handling the remnants of what had thirty minutes prior been one of the fastest boats in the world.

The somnolent Indiana burg had willingly shed its peace and

Chapter Ten

tranquility to embrace the thunder and roar of the hydroplanes. Now the sultry air of summer was pierced by the high pitched whine of a chorus of sirens as the caravan wound its way to the Kings Daughters hospital nearby. Virtually within walking distance of the shore side pit area, it had the appropriate facilities for a small riverside town. Lacking an operating table or even a gurney, it did not have the equipment to deal with high level trauma or violent injuries.

Bill began to regain consciousness on the hospital floor lying in the stretcher in which the search and rescue team had originally placed him at the crash site. Most of his driver's suit had been torn off during the accident and his life jacket had been removed en route. A blanket draped over him was now pulled back to allow a doctor's survey. The immediate diagnosis confirmed that inexplicably there were not any broken bones; however, there was certainly damage to internal organs. The tumble and tangle of the centrifugal forces Bill had just encountered had torn his stomach loose and damaged his kidneys and spleen. He had also seriously bitten his tongue and the swelling of his abdomen indicated that there was internal bleeding.

The shroud of fog that had surrounded him initially began to dissipate as he discerned sounds and voices. White noise took on understandable structure and Bill could recognize individuals that were talking nearby. The linoleum one square foot tiles on the floor alternated between a faded yellow and a chocolate brown. Bill studied this and found it oddly interesting. Clutches of different conversations were humming independently around the hall where he lay and echoed above him. One of the first voices he heard was that of his teammate, Joe Lewis, asking a doctor, "Is he going to live?"

The physician responded, "We don't know for sure yet."

Bill could hear Mira's thick accent and was curiously comforted. Nurses asked friends and family to wait in a small area that served as a waiting room. Kit and Mira, among others, began the tireless vigil of sitting, praying, and waiting for updates.

Ted Jones paced back and forth across the small room. Kit Muncey uttered without malice but pragmatic resignation, "Most boat designing is done in the waiting rooms of hospitals."

Bill's extremities were showing signs of the trauma by swelling.

His arms, legs and neck had enlarged dramatically and the medical staff determined that what Bill needed was beyond their capabilities. Although there were excellent facilities nearby, it was determined that Bill should be immediately flown to Seattle for the best medical care. The route chosen would take him via Chicago where he would be shuttled from a charter onto a commercial flight. Time was of the essence since internal bleeding was confirmed.

Although doctors administered pain killers, Bill's swollen tongue made it difficult for him to be understood. He was able to convey that he wanted his friends and family nearby and that this extended to Mira. Strangers surrounded him and it was mildly disturbing to notice one occasionally frown and slowly shake his or her head. When told that he was going to be transported to an airport nearby and flown to Chicago, Bill insisted that the pilot be Mira. A drugged or dying man is allowed his eccentricities and the attending medical staff went along with the charade. Mira accompanied Bill to the airport and boarded the plane by his side. The aircraft was a light twin Piper Apache designed to carry four people. The two seats on the passenger side were removed to allow for Bill's stretcher to be secured to the floor.

As pain killers took effect, Bill was better able to make himself understood. He was a pilot himself and appreciated the common thread of efficiency and discipline required to earn the license. Nevertheless, he insisted that the original pilot of the aircraft take a back seat and let Mira, the only individual entrusted with the task, fly him to the nearest major airport. Mira gently tried to talk his friend out of this opinion but Bill was adamant. Anyone who knew Bill could recognize the futility of trying to dissuade him from a position once he committed himself. By the resolute set of Bill's jaw, Mira could read his friend's face and realize that some compromise must be determined. A brief conversation with the other pilot reached an accommodation and the three found themselves huddled into the aircraft and taxiing out on to the sparse runway of the rural riverside airport.

O'Hare International Airport near Chicago, Illinois was the destination and Mira played a personal role in arranging for Bill's transfer to the subsequent flight to Seattle. Mira's employer, Bill Boeing, operated a large corporation that manufactured passenger airplanes. In fact, the aircraft that Bill would be transferred to was

Chapter Ten

a Boeing plane. While still in Madison, Mira called his boss and asked that he help with the arrangements. Subsequently when the trio arrived in Chicago, airport personnel were able to direct the single engine aircraft adjacent to a regularly scheduled flight and facilitate the transfer onboard. Bill continued to insist that Mira accompany him and the flight crew arranged a portion of the first class cabin to allow Slovak to sit next to the stretcher.

The combination of bruises and swelling from the internal bleeding made applying seat belts an episode of agony for Bill so the pilot of the aircraft made an exception and allowed Mira to belt himself in and simply hold the stretcher in place. Nevertheless, turbulence encountered during the flight jolted and rocked Bill on the stretcher compelling him to cry out in pain. Mira could offer his friend little more than a soothing voice and well intended words of encouragement.

As the airplane approached Boeing Field in Seattle, a crowd of fans and boat racing enthusiasts gathered.

Now, nearly ten years later, another crowd gathered near an airfield. This time it was Mira's return; the occasion Mira's remarkable completion of a solo flight from Europe to an airfield in California in a glider type aircraft propelled by a Volkswagen engine and named the Spirit of Santa Paula. Another aircraft rose up to meet and escort him down for the landing. The flight had taken him half way around the world and had been well promoted within the aircraft community. The substantial attendance of spectators was visible from the air on his approach.

Mira pulled up to the right and alongside to his escort, gradually scrubbing off their altitude, and lining up to the airfield. As they approached, his escort tipped his wings and rose up and to the left. Mira decided to follow his escort and come around for another approach giving the crowds below a modest demonstration of his remarkable aircraft. Had it been a later model aircraft the stall alarms would have given him notice. They did not because this craft didn't have any.

For what seemed like an eternity, Mira and his glider hung in the air, nose up and suspended by what momentum he had acquired. Instantly realizing his situation, he knew that he had precious little room between himself and the ground to recover control of his aircraft. For a moment he was simply occupying a small box hundreds of feet in the air that was beginning to fall like a rock. Urgently ignoring the sickening feeling in the pit of his stomach, with great control and careful deliberation he began the time consuming process of regaining a flying attitude and gathering lift under his wings.

The concrete of the Santa Paula streets below seemed to rush up to meet him. Rooftops, chimneys and television antennas appeared with crystal clarity. Adrenaline helped him absorb and process the tremendous amount of information separating the valuable such as distance and altitude from citizens walking their dogs or enthusiasts pointing toward the sky. Bringing the nose back around and aiming toward the airfield he could almost reach out and pull himself onto the tarmac of the runway. Mentally willing himself into straight and level flight with his reflexes and training gleaned from thousands of hours in the air, Mira stabilized the aircrafts attitude.

Too little, too late.

The Spirit of Santa Paula plunged into a large irrigation ditch just short of the runway. Hurtling its pilot out of his seat and through the frame against the concrete sides of the causeway, Mira's bones broke and his internal organs hemorrhaged. He found himself lying on his back amongst the debris, covered in dust and profusely spilling blood.

By one of those uncanny turns of fate, a citizen happened to be driving her car down the road next to the ditch and had looked up just in time to see the crash. She was completely unaware of anything special at the airport that day. Nevertheless, she happened to look up and more astoundingly, she happened to be a nurse.

What she did over the next five minutes kept the pilot alive. Coming upon Mira's dust-covered semi- conscious body, she immediately observed blood coming out of his ears, nose and mouth and employed her training to render aid. It was a substantial amount of time before anyone else was able to find them and assist. By the time Mira was transported to a hospital, two facts had been determined, he had lost a tremendous amount of blood, and he had a rare blood type.

"....Mira can have every drop of blood in my body. " Bill had said. The debt he felt he owed could never be repaid in full. Frantically sifting through options, Bill summoned up that Mira's brother, Jaroslav, lived somewhere in the Midwest.

The circular stains from cups of coffee overlapped on his desk

Chapter Ten

pad as he called around the country through the night waking relatives and friends trying to locate Jaro. It was quietly tense in the Muncey house as the morning hours approached. In the end, it was a combination of help from Bill's brother, Raymond, his father, Ed and networking with the Indiana State Police that resulted in finding Mira's brother. Literally pulling him over on the side of the highway, State Troopers informed Jaro of his brother's plight. The police escorted him to the nearest hospital with sirens blaring and the indispensable transfusion was secured for transport.

Mira went on to make a full recovery from his injuries.

Although still convinced that the debt he owed could never be completely paid, Bill Muncey had felt the need to at least try to make a small down payment.

After all, nobody but Mira could call him Billy.

Nobody Called Him Billy

Bill, sporting his famous gap-toothed smile.

The Miss Thriftway hydroplane returns to the dock from the race course.

Accident Sequence Shots

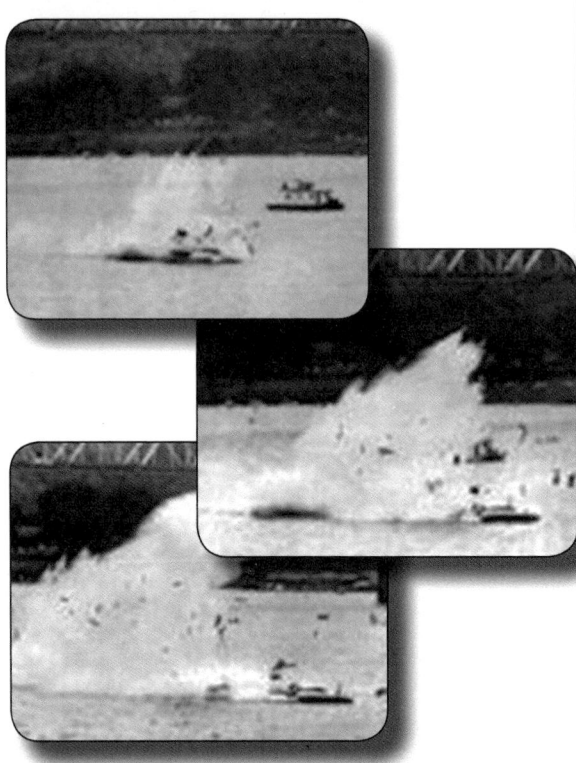

Competition takes second place to life saving maneuvers as rival teams help transport Bill Muncey from the dock after a serious accident.

Bill driving the Miss Thriftway hydroplane as it disintegrates on the Ohio River.

With reflexes developed in the cockpit of an airplane, Mira Slovak flew the Miss Wahoo race boat over the toughest race courses in the country. This Photo from Lake Chelan, WA courtesy of Ron Harsin.

Mira Slovak spanned the globe to set a worlds record in his Volkswagen powered airplane.

Wil, Jr. seated in the father & son quarter-midget race car.

Bill leans against the bow of the Thrifty Chevrolier while Thriftway crewman Joe Lewis inspects the transom.

CHAPTER ELEVEN

He had to Wrestle

Bill had to wrestle with it. Kit hadn't exactly leapt at the idea, and upon reflection, he had to reexamine the wisdom himself but in the end he was convinced it was a good idea. First, there was the father and son thing. William was five years old. There weren't a lot of things that he had to share with his son. His job kept him away from home a lot. Whatever they did together had to be reasonably compact, memorable and special; especially special.

Then there was the discipline thing. This particular endeavor ruthlessly demanded an attention to detail and a respect for instructions. William would have to learn how to use equipment in a very responsible way in front of a lot of people. This had to happen in order to participate effectively and for his own safety. Learning how to do this at the tender age of five could be of great benefit for future activities.

Speaking of crowds, Bill reasoned that if William could participate without being intimidated or influenced by the fact that these activities drew crowds, which would also be a future asset. The sport that Bill was considering was drawing in audiences and participants from across the country. The Northwest chapter was substantial.

The start-up expense in terms of dollars was significant. There was special equipment and apparels to be acquired. It would require the use of the family car. It could get complicated, but in the end, Bill successfully wrestled with the fact that introducing his impressionable eldest son to the sport of car racing was a good idea.

The race cars were called Quarter Midgets. They were very small, less than four feet in length. They were also under powered. A small gasoline engine similar to a lawn mower powerplant propelled them around a condensed oval asphalt race track. The driver was strapped in with a seat belt and a shoulder strap. He wore a helmet, goggles and gloves. The car had a substantial roll bar. It had a hand brake.

Bill did his research and attended several events. He brought Kit to one of the local races and even she had to admit that it appeared safe. The idea of a fast ball hurtling across a baseball diamond scared her more. Little boys got bruised and broke their arms. Relatively speaking, compared to tree houses and backyard football, this rigidly supervised activity could actually be safer.

Bill often said publically and privately, "It's a competitive world out there. "

As a parent, anything he could do to prepare his children for that competitive world was a step to be considered. He spoke with other fathers and realized this could also develop a dialogue with his son that would be impossible to replicate at any other level.

The Muncey family decided to pursue car racing.

Bill was not a total stranger to car racing himself but his participation had been limited. He was able to find a car and trailer in the newspaper's classifieds. Once the decision had been reached, Bill committed himself to the endeavor with his characteristic enthusiasm and optimism. The helmet had to be of the highest quality. The goggles were identical to Bill's, only they were the smallest version available. Aircraft standards in quality and literally developed for combat, the goggles could deflect dirt and debris thrown up from the track very effectively.

The gloves proved to be the greatest challenge to acquire. William was small, and finding a pair of leather gloves that would provide protection but still allow dexterity was harder than Bill thought. Kit was the one who suggested they use a pair of women's riding gloves.

Washington is the "Evergreen State" and Christmas in the Pacific Northwest inevitably exudes the scents of fir, pine, or spruce. Households throughout are thick with the traditional Yuletide fragrance by Christmas morning. Colored lights sparkle and glow on the family Christmas tree over an array of dazzlingly wrapped packages. It was almost a life statement that the race car had to be parked among them under the tree in a manner that feigned normalcy. This was impossible, of course, but Bill was amused to try. Eventually, it was nestled as close as possible to the lowest boughs front and center to the view of first perception when the two boys came into the Muncey family living room.

Primarily gloss white in color, it had the red number 62 painted on the tail cowling, and Bill had arranged to have the local celebrity cartooning weatherman, Bob Hale, paint the image of a kittenish tiger bounding across the front cowl. The roll bar towered above

Chapter Eleven

the seat and gleamed in chrome plate. The hand brake was also chrome with a white knob on its end.

Bill could not remember a recent Christmas when he was as excited as he heard his two boys coming down the stairs from their room Christmas morning. The only apprehension he had was how his youngest son, Dorian would react. Being only three years old, he probably would not fully understand the car's capabilities. For that matter, neither would William.

It would be interesting.

The two boys came into the room side by side. Instinctively, Dorian looked away from the car to the other gifts somehow knowing that the car was not of concern to him. William, on the other hand, stopped walking and stared. Looking over at Bill, the facial expressions exchanged told volumes as the message was conveyed between parent and son that this particular gift had a lot to do with him. William's eyes got wide and his mouth opened. He still did not move. He looked over at his mother and she smiled. Looking back at the car, he took a step forward and pointed to the tiger on the front of the race car.

Kit pointed at a gift and nodded to Dorian who promptly proceeded to unwrap it. William took another step and placed his hand on the chromed roll bar looking down into the cockpit.

"This is for me?" he asked.

Kit and Bill nodded in unison. Although there were other presents exchanged that Christmas morning, the race car pretty much dominated the conversations.

On a particular subsequent Saturday morning, several fathers and their designated drivers appeared at a local track along with their race cars. Coming from around the Pacific Northwest, they were attending the one and only safety class provided by the regional Quarter Midget Club. During the course of the day, the teams learned about flags, driving in formation, regulation safety apparel, racing rules and codes of conduct. It was the first opportunity for Bill and William to spend time together outside the immediate family unit. It was a good thing.

Every parent was expected to spend time as a flagman on the race course and offer his or her services in helping to conduct the race. There were basic signals indicating what to do in certain circumstances such as a vehicle stopped on the track, or which flag to display to drivers at different points in the race. In the event of an accident, each flagman knew what his particular duties would be and what flags to display.

Bill had not really spent any personal time with someone substantially younger than he since he had left home. Brother Raymond was six years younger and as the older brother, Bill had been responsible for his care and concerns countless times. He could not help but notice some of the familiar perspectives and responses in this current situation. On more than one occasion, he inadvertently called his son Raymond.

The safety course was instructive and William seemed to grasp the essentials. He was very trusting and Bill was able to offer advice and suggestions without having to overcome barriers of doubt, reservation, or questions.

William's hand-to-eye coordination seemed adequate to the task and he genuinely enjoyed operating the vehicle. He was not afraid of the equipment or the situation in which he was being put. When it came time to drive the car onto its trailer, William was confident and reasonably accurate.

Shortly after that session, the two took the car to the local baseball field parking lot and set up a mock course so that they could practice putting the car through its paces. Bill taught his son how to overcome the tendency to slow down for the corners and set up the radius for his car. It was an important time for the pair and they prepared for the upcoming season with anticipation.

Kit was pleased to see her two "men" working together and becoming a dynamic team. Conversations about racing strategies were common at the dinner table the family shared most evenings. Bill tried to be reserved but Kit knew he was anxious. This was a big deal.

William would be starting the first grade in the fall. The circuit started in the early spring. Although there were tracks around the region, most of the racing occurred at a track located relatively close to home at the north end of Seattle in a shopping mall parking lot. There were bleachers and a judge's stand. A wooden fence surrounded the track. Grass covered the infield. If the weather was kind, spectator attendance was respectable.

At the first races, the pair had decided to present a conservative approach on the track. Bill was concerned about the open wheel

Chapter Eleven

aspect to the cars and cautioned his son to be cautious when attempting to overtake another driver. It was important to convey to his son that he was not racing against another boy but against another car. On the other hand, the kids did talk amongst each other and Bill described proper behavior when it came time to display good sportsmanship. On the other hand, Bill did not hesitate to embolden aggressive behavior when it came time to defend a position on the course or discourage and frustrate another car trying to overtake.

"Always look over both shoulders," Bill would say. They learned later that not all the other boys did that.

The cars were started by being pushed by a parent. All the cars would be grouped together and they started in rows, side by side. It was common for up to 12 cars to run in the same race or heat. Row after row would be pushed and started until all the cars had lined up in their respective and previously designated positions. The parents would individually push their child's car and then promptly assume their assigned positions as flagmen on the inside perimeter of the track. A yellow flag would be displayed until all the cars were started and the group of competitors was moving along at a comparative speed in a loose but organized pack. Once that level of operation had been universally achieved, a master flagman would wave a green flag as they passed the judge's stand or tower signifying the official start of the race, and the drivers would be allowed to accelerate at their discretion.

The order of start was determined by draw or finish in that the winners of a previous heat would be relegated to the back of the pack at the subsequent race. The first car on the front row nearest the corner was introduced to the spectators as being "on the bubble". Each individual driver was introduced to the crowd at least once during the course of the weekend's activities.

Bill was pleased with William's progress and it was about this time that both Kit and Bill decided to call their son "Wil". Kit was determined that her eldest son would have an identity as separate and independent from his namesake as possible. Although a junior, he would earn his own place and perspective. She liked the idea of dropping the second 'l' when it came time to spell her son's name. Bill's main concern was that his son did not acquire the moniker "Billy". For some reason that he never did quite understand, he personally disliked the nickname and did not want to visit the same imposition on William.

It was on one particular weekend late in the first season that everything seemed to come together. Wil had won the initial heat which placed him at the back of the pack at the subsequent heat. There were an unusual number of competitors attending the races that weekend. With twelve cars on the track at once, Wil's position at the back was a challenge to overcome. Engine performance was regulated and commonly inspected so that one car did not have an undue advantage by virtue of mere horsepower. Although Wil had shown a basic aptitude for driving, it was going to be very difficult for him to work his way up through the pack to a prominent position in the laps allowed.

Bill's surprise expanded as the pack moved through the first corner after the green flag dropped. At each corner of the oval track, Wil ducked inside the car he was trying to overtake. His position improved by two places with each lap. This fact was not lost on the announcer who seemed to be getting more excited at the passing of each car. The crowd cheered as the drama unfolded. Everyone wondered if there was enough time. For some reason, all the other drivers tended to stay in the middle of the track enabling Wil to duck underneath and literally drive a lesser distance. Finally, he came upon the leading car. It was painted a baby blue and displayed the number 52 on its tail. The boy driving was named Bud Green and had a well earned reputation of being a capable and aggressive driver. Bud was well aware of Wil's presence and capably held off the challenge. Keeping the lane next to the corner closed off, the time for assault passed and Wil earned a second place finish. Respectable and impressive. Bill could not have been prouder.

After praising him for the good job that Wil had done Bill asked, "Why didn't you try to take him from the outside?"

Wil responded with, " I don't think that I'm fast enough".

The final heat came around and father and son were anxious to get back on the track. The announcer had primed the crowd and the impending rematch between "62" and "52" was being well promoted. The green flag dropped and the pair proceeded to dice and dip around the corners. Bill looked on expectantly, clenching his flag tightly. Virtually unaware of any other cars on the track,

Chapter Eleven

he absently watched like any other spectator. Back and forth, the two drivers jockeyed for an advantage. Back and forth, they traded positions. Exposed wheels spinning inches from each other, each driver leaned over the side of their cockpits and into the corners as they circled the track. Five years old and they were driving like seasoned veterans. Grim determination was on their young faces. The collective roar of all twelve cars seemed unusually deafening.

Then it happened.

Bill's gut tightened as he asked himself, "What have I done?"

Bill's brother Raymond was about five years old back in 1939 when Bill talked him into doing it. Bill had acquired some plywood from a crate down at the family car dealership. Plywood was sophisticated in those days. Relatively lightweight and very strong, it made some construction techniques easy. Bill had folded a piece of paper into the rudimentary shape of an airplane and "flown" it across his bedroom. It stood to reason that the same thing could be accomplished if you simply made a bigger one out of plywood and flew it off the roof. It was even better if someone got to ride on it! After some determined persuasion, Bill convinced his little brother that piloting this craft was a great adventure. It was not that Bill was afraid to do it himself; it was that Raymond was so much lighter and his plane might need that advantage. Physics was physics, after all.

Together they coaxed the aircraft up to the roof while their mother was cooking in the kitchen and Dad was at work. The project had taken a lot of effort and planning. They had drawn pictures and projected flight paths. They had laid out a runway. They had clothed Raymond in his winter mittens and tugged on Bill's old Buster Brown hat to act as a helmet. With the nose of the aircraft pointed down slope, Raymond had laid on top of the wings spread eagled, looked up at his big brother, and nodded. Bill gave the pair a push, and they had slid down and off the roof.

The aircraft flew like a bag of wet cement.

Straight down.

The subsequent crash and cries sent shivers up and down Bill's eleven-year-old spine.

The exposed wheels of the two cars unwittingly rubbed into each other. The collective friction and traction forced Wil's car into the air. Cartwheeling end over end, the number "62" seemed to dance upside down and like a cartoon. Arms flailing and head rocking back and forth, Wil's body snapped against the shoulder strap as the car tumbled like a gleaming white egg, the shine and reflection blinking off the chrome roll bar.

The yellow caution flag barely touched the grass where Bill dropped it by the time he crossed the infield making a beeline for Wil's anticipated stopping point. Something primordial grips one's conscience when one is pummeled by the fact that a child is in danger. Pain, discomfort, or concern for self preservation evaporates even faster when it is your child in danger. Sprinting at a dead run, Bill's 5"8" frame established an opaque blur as he came up behind the tumbling car still in motion. Barely coming to rest upside down, eyewitnesses said later that Bill grabbed the roll bar with his right hand, lifted the entire car three feet into the air, twisting his wrist he turned it right side up in mid air and set it down on its wheels. Reaching around the roll bar from behind, he then reached into Wil's lap and unbuckled the seatbelt. Picking his son straight up, he stepped around the body of the car turning Wil and hugging him to his chest.

Saying, "It's OK, kid. I'm here," into his son's ear, Bill patted him gently on the back. Setting him down on his feet, Bill asked, "Are you alright?"

Wil looked up, blinked and nodded.

The sound of the track was a million miles away.

As in most things, neither victory nor success brings people together in a meaningful way. Diversity and setbacks bring out the best in teams. Something ancient and ingrained hurled Bill across the green of the track's infield and an untapped reservoir of paternal strength had picked up the car. It was not magic but it might as well have been.

The Muncey Racing Team went on racing quarter midgets for another season. Bill's weekend availability was ultimately constrained by his hydroplane racing career and Wil's interests went onto perhaps loftier pursuits such as playing cowboys with the other kids in the neighborhood...at least until he was old enough to step into his own race boat.

The third Miss Thriftway Unlimited class hydroplane

Bill's APBA (American Power Boat Association) racing number was 222. Even when he drove in the Unlimited hydroplane class, he kept his reflexes up by participating in the smaller "limited" ranks.

Bill & Kit's business venture, California Marine, in Seattle sending out a shipment of ski boats.

The inboard version of a California Marine ski boat.

The Coast Guard helicopter arrives at the scene of the accide

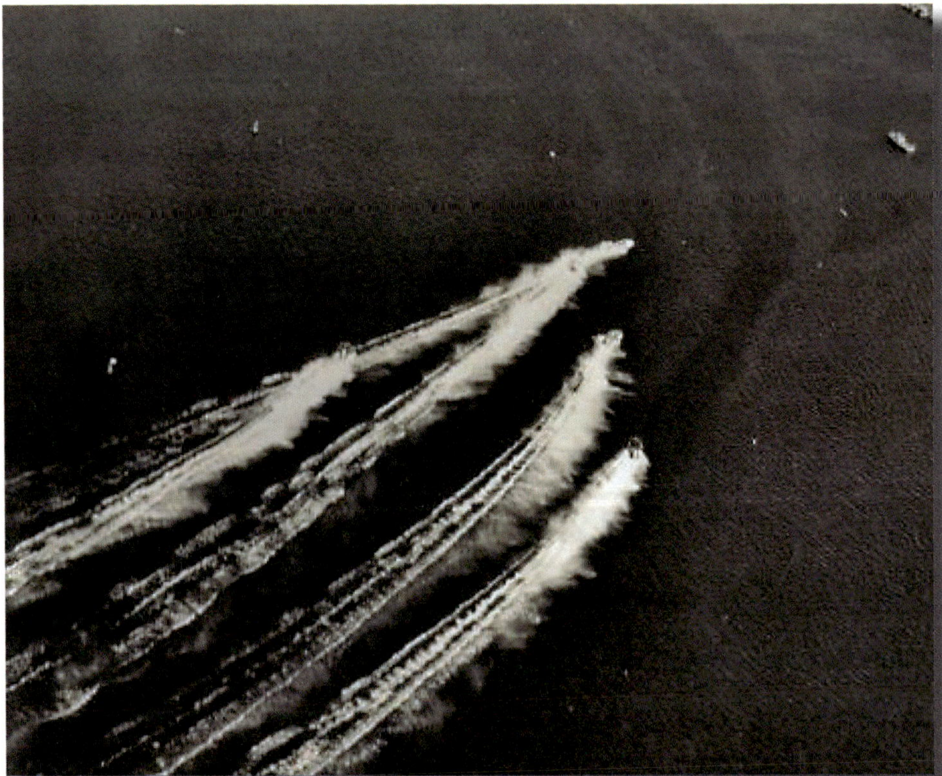

Seconds before impact, Bill crosses in front of the other boats coming down for the start of the race. Note Coast Guard cutter top right corner.

1958. An estimated 500,000 people witnessed the accident.

Bill floats in the water about 100 feet behind the wreckage of his hydroplane knifed into the steel Coast Guard cutter.

Mrs. Bill Muncey with sons, Dorian and Wil

Kit and Bill at shore side in the race pits during Seafair, Seattle, WA

CHAPTER TWELVE

These Boats Turn

The pristine waters of Lake Washington rippled and lapped against Bill's chin as he floated painlessly on his back unrestrained and limp. Both arms extended straight out from his body with palms up. The afternoon sunlight danced against the dimples on the water that pretended to be waves. Opening his eyes to a serenely blue and clear August sky, the distant buzzing that emanated from outboard motors permeated the water and seeped around and into his helmet and ears.

Bill noticed that he was not cold or uncomfortable. The moment was actually quite peaceful. He knew in the back of his mind that this pause of reflective solitude was fleeting and deceptive. As the pleasant fog of shock and denial evaporated, he began to recount the last thirty seconds. Meanwhile, the distant buzzing came closer. He had hurtled over the water at a speed in excess of 150 mph as the Miss Thriftway gracefully rode on a cushion of air compressed between the two pontoons or "sponsons" that she occasionally touched to the water in order to maintain balance. Gently rocking back and forth on each sponson, the race boat proceeded up the furthest straightaway or the "back chute" of the three-mile oval course. She had one more corner to negotiate before coming down for the timed start at an imagined line that crossed the front chute below the judge's stand.

It may be obvious that any time drag or friction is minimized, it is easier to move. Hydroplanes have been doing this for over 100 years. The Greek " hydro" for water coupled with the physics term "plane" implies a vessel that moves over the water instead of through it. The lack of resistance enhances acceleration and dramatically reduces the energy needed for propulsion. This concept, however, does not do anything to alter the mass of the vehicle. As Newton aptly pointed out, a body in motion tends to stay in motion. Once in motion at a high rate of speed, a hydroplane wants to keep going at a high rate of speed.

But then there is the "turning thing".

Most hydroplanes race on a circle course with left hand turns. Ranging in size from one mile to three mile ovals, the intention to turn left places a tremendous amount of stress on all the components that still think that they want to go straight. Encountering the wakes from other boats, tackling naturally occurring waves, and wrestling with the steering wheel to negotiate the corner all conspire to try to throw the driver out of the cockpit. In those days of marine motorsports, a driver rarely used a seatbelt but instead relied upon the steering wheel and his upper body strength to keep himself in the boat and in command of the situation. There had been an unfortunate case where a driver and his riding mechanic had both been killed when their craft had rolled over while they were strapped in. The wisdom of the day indicated that it should be the driver's choice as much as possible when to leave the boat, and if that became necessary, the exit should be clean and unrestricted.

Another aspect of trying to turn is the tremendous stress that it places on the equipment. In the late forties, someone had concluded that the engine could perform better if only the tip of the propeller pierced the surface of the water instead of submerging all the blades or the whole "wheel"" under water. This application enabled the engine to reach its power band more quickly and promptly apply its horsepower and torque. It also accelerated the overall strain and needed an evolving technology to keep up with demand. If an advocate or enthusiast were to break a world record by one or two miles an hour, most would consider that quite an achievement. Media would take note, and the feat would clearly demonstrate to your peers that you obviously knew what you were doing.

By applying this new technology, a hydroplane with the dubious name of Slo Mo Shun shattered the existing straightaway record by twenty miles per hour. As the news of the new record rippled out, shock waves of appreciation and respect from the media, peers and fans around the maritime world echoed back. By essentially grafting aircraft components to marine equipment, a revolution in marine propulsion had been born. This marriage compelled marine and aviation engineers to run to keep up with a whole new set of design challenges undreamed of before and in some cases without any significant points of reference.

Lake Washington is fourteen miles long and lays in a north-south direction next to the city of Seattle in the evergreen State of Washington. Each August, Seattle hosts what would become the fourth

Chapter Twelve

largest festival in the United States called Seafair. This festival flourished around a hydroplane race that started in the early fifties. The race course in those early days was a three-mile oval that facilitated the boats achieving very high speeds. A typical Unlimited hydroplane could weigh well over 5,000 pounds and as much as 8,000 pounds, (or more) constructed primarily out of plywood, aluminum, and stainless steel fasteners, held together and guided by components of cast iron and forged steel. All these elements added up to a substantial mass trying to change direction at previously unheard of speeds when the drivers proceeded to negotiate the required left hand turn.

The load on his 1,650 cubic inch Rolls Royce aircraft engine was steady and even. At 4,000 revolutions per minute, the powerplant was operating well above her intended range when she was initially developed for airplanes in the twenties. Since that time, the development of horsepower- increasing technology had maintained its own even pace. World War II had demanded a dramatic investment of engineering research that doubled those capabilities to the point that not only enabled greater horsepower and torque output, but also increased the overall number of revolutions per minute. It would be conservative to estimate that the Thriftway Racing Team had managed to bring the horsepower of their engine up from the original respectable 950 to almost 2,000. This accomplishment coupled with a surface piercing propeller, created one of the most successful marine motorsport competitors on the race circuit.

The plume of water or "roostertail" that arched up behind her because of the thrust of the surface-piercing propeller could actually have been viewed as a graph of the boat and engines performance. Each swipe of the blade is the depth of purchase and resultant thrust of each cup of water into the air behind the transom is an indicator or "tell" of how well the horsepower and torque was being applied against the load. Often up to 100 feet high, this wall of water could reach back hundreds of feet directly behind the boat and was often used as a defensive tool by the driver in the tactics of competition. Tons of water suspended in the air can create an obstacle of pounding resistance through which another competitor must drive - not something that a driver would want to do without careful consideration of the consequences. At those speeds, that volume of water entering an open cockpit and assailing the driver could cause substantial harm if he was unprotected. A windshield was often not enough protection to stand up to the impact. A driver rendered unconscious from the impact of a roostertail was not unheard of. Additionally, since water generally does not compress, the supercharger of the engine which compresses the air/fuel mixture of the engine on its way to the combustion chamber especially does not embrace the chore of dealing with water. A fistful of water in the wrong place at the wrong time could break an engine. A roostertail was emphatically something to avoid.

As Bill maintained an even load running up the back chute, he counted down to himself the time remaining until the starting gun went off. Although he would not actually hear it, this would technically start the race. Crossing the starting line before the gun would essentially disqualify him from the heat. Bill measured time and distance in two ways. When the time remaining came down to within one minute of the gun, a large orange pie face circle or "clock" started and displayed on the judge's stand. The orange portion would sweep clockwise and turn black as the remaining seconds passed. However, it was not always visible from the cockpit of a race boat at all points on the course. Because of this, the driver needed to continue the acuity of time independent of the clock. Some drivers used a stop watch mounted either on the dash or on their wrist. Bill did neither during this phase of his career.

Having spent thousands of hours playing music to a particular beat relative to a sheet of music gave him a unique and extremely accurate concept of time. Playing a tune to himself in his head gave him all the reference to time that he needed. Some opined that it was a Charlie Parker tune and others the Gene Krupa beat that Bill might have personally played to when he had the opportunity to play in Krupa's band. In either case, Bill had earned a reputation for well-timed starts and this one was shaping up typically.

An added bonus was the fact that he had managed to wrest the inside or number one lane from the rest of the field. This enabled him to take the shortest route around the race course. By the virtue of simple math, the number one lane generally made it possible for a boat to get through the corner a full second sooner than the boat one lane further out. Assuming that his start was competitively timed, it would be very difficult for another driver to get far enough ahead of him to establish the legal distance needed to allow that

Chapter Twelve

driver to move in and take lane one away from him. Racing often came down to the good start, and Bill could sense that time-wise he was in fine shape.

Entering into the corner before the start, Bill pushed against the left footrest to set his hip into the seat and allow precise pressure to be applied by his right foot against the throttle pedal. Contrary to popular belief, there was little adjustment made with the throttle for a corner in a hydroplane. Twisting slightly at the waist, he turned the 22" steering wheel to the left. This act in itself had a tendency to slow the boat down. In addition to the natural resistance to forward motion created by the rudder, the boat also slowed due to the loss of lift and resultant reduction in the cushion of air under her. The sponsons would settle a little deeper into the water, and the cast iron rudder would gain a deeper purchase. A driver would unconsciously compensate for this change as he worked the boat's radius through the arc of the corner and maintain his lane. The boat's overall speed would gradually diminish while much of the load borne by the boat would increase. Often referred to by other drivers as a wrestling match between driver's will to turn and the boats intention to go straight, operating a boat under these conditions could be compared to a cowboy trying to stay on top a bucking bull while trying to guide it through the gate.

The other boats and drivers were all in similar situations off of Bill's right side coming down to the start. Maintaining their lanes and timing their own starts, they were all coming together to conduct what many considered the most spectacular start in motorsports. Over half a dozen boats, up to 30' long and weighing several tons each bounding, leaping, and rocking side-by-side in a waterborne ballet. Tens of thousands of horsepower bellowed out toward the hundreds of thousands of spectators lining the shores or lounging on pleasure boats tied to the mile-long Seafair log boom. The cotton stuffed into the drivers' ears managed to reduce the audio impact, but nothing could minimize the lateral load on the driver and hull as it cavitated in and out of the water. As the hull bucked and bounced, the transom would rotate up and down over the water forcing the propeller and rudder to vary the load against them. The propeller would plunge completely under the surface or completely into the air sending a slapping shock up the propeller shaft through the engine. The rudder would trail three inches under water only to have its blade immersed a foot deeper in less than a second. This load variance could happen to the drive train and control surfaces of an Unlimited hydroplane dozens of times in the corner. The resulting pulse or shock would create tremendous strain, not only on the driver, but on all the equipment, as well.

Flapping back and forth in the cockpit, Bill managed to compensate and apply the proper amount of pressure and adjustment needed to keep the Miss Thriftway in her lane. Passing the apex of the corner, he realized that his timing for the start was very good and he began depressing the throttle deeper, accelerating toward the exit buoy or "pin. " Pulling slightly ahead of the rest of the field, he counted down to himself how many seconds he he had left for his run at the clock.

Ten. The water was smoother at this point of the course, so the overall attitude of the hull settled down and allowed for a more precise correction of the rudder.

Nine. The RPM of the engine began to rise in answer to the command from the foot pedal while the load against the hull peaked. Because the turn began to dissipate and the straightaway began to present itself, the air compacting under the hull came in a more even flow and compelled the hull to start rising higher out of the water.

Eight. Bill is flailing and twisting against the swaying of the boat as boat and driver bend to the task of running at the clock as they start to come out of the corner.

Sev…

The bow of his boat swung violently over to the right while the transom spun to the left. Slamming Bill's head and shoulders back over the seat, his right hand tore off the steering wheel. The forces that had been pressing against the hull in a hard left turn overwhelmed the controls and launched hull and driver into the second lane in front of his nearest competitor. The direct thrust of the roostertail mercilessly washed down the driver that had been next to Bill milliseconds before. Bounding on, they traversed the third lane in a line that was destined to cross the field. Hours spent working out on a punching bag to enhance his upper body strength were translated at this moment in time to an almost herculean effort expended to stay in the cockpit and reach back to the steering wheel. Wrenching on it to the left, while getting his right hand back

Chapter Twelve

on, Bill realized that, for some reason, he had totally lost control of the steering of his boat. Traveling at approximately 145 miles per hour for all intents and purposes, he was merely a passenger on an unguided water bound missile. Sensing more than actually seeing, he knew that the rest of the fleet was rapidly accelerating toward the starting line and were completely unaware of his circumstances. Even a glancing impact with another boat would be catastrophic at these speeds.

"Work the situation," he thought. "Do something regardless of how futile it might seem, because something is better than nothing."

Overcoming every instinct to do otherwise, Bill took both hands off the steering wheel and waved them back and forth over his head as high as he could get them.

"If just one driver notices out of the corner of his eye," he thought, "it might be enough to get his attention."

Although Bill has pulled his right foot off the throttle immediately after the rudder broke, it had taken a moment for the engine to decelerate and his roostertail to drop. The roostertails on the other boats were rising as each driver began accelerating for their own runs at the clock.

All eyes are focused on the starting clock halfway down the front chute up in the judge's stand. No one will be looking next to them for an errant hydroplane swinging and yawing back and forth across and in front of the field. Planting both feet on the floor as wide apart as the space allowed, Bill stood up in the boat waving his arms. In doing so, however, he sacrificed the support and stability of the seat itself and had to try and compensate for the twists and turns of the hull by bending at the waist. Looking over to his right at all the other boats lunging out of the corner toward the start, he observed with relief that the roostertails were dropping and that, for whatever reason, the other drivers were aware of the threat his situation presented.

As his own boat rapidly crossed in front of their path, he could individually read the expressions on the faces of his fellow competitors. They ranged from surprise to legitimately fearful. As he passed by in front of the last one, he felt a momentary respite of peace. The threat had passed, and somehow, they had survived.

Then he looked straight ahead.

Although his speed had diminished some, he was still moving along at about 125 miles per hour when he ran off of the race course. Directly in his path were dozens of spectator boats in the water and thousands of spectators lining the shore.

If, somehow, he were able to manage to avoid hitting one of the pleasure boats, there would still be the crowds to consider. Even if any of them were aware of what was happening, there would be many who would not have time to get out of the way.

"Work the situation," he thought, "I've got to do something."

Reaching down to his right, he completely shut off the fuel to the engine from the fuel pump. Not a spectacular solution by any means but it was something. He then grounded the magneto with his left hand while hanging on to the otherwise unemployed steering wheel with his right.

The spectators and their shoreline were quickly approaching. It had been less than four seconds since he had started this terrifying detour. There was not time to get scared or panic. There was only time to "to do."

From habit, Bill proceeded to shut off the main electrical switch. His mind automatically did the trigonometry to anticipate the actual point on the shore where impact would occur. He knew from a previous accident involving another driver that a hydroplane could make its way remarkably far up the shore. One of Bill's personal heroes, Wild Bill Cantrell, had experienced a similar mishap and ended up in a homeowner's rose garden. With dread, Bill's 20/10 vision enabled him to see the dozens of spectators that would most likely be in his path. It was truly amazing how much thought can be compressed into a few moments. Briefly, he considered what must have been going through Wild Bill's mind at the time.

Then he saw it.

Many would have liked to believe that it was a deliberate act, by either Bill or the skipper of the Coast Guard cutter, but in the end, it was either providence or just dumb luck. A Coast Guard cutter had been assigned patrol duty along the shore a few hundred feet out. It was idling under power and making a modest amount of forward progress. For whatever reason, Bill was able to do the math and correctly anticipate that everything left to itself would bring the Miss Thriftway directly into the path of the cutter. At least one serviceman on the cutter was simultaneously reaching a similar

Chapter Twelve

conclusion. Neither Bill nor the serviceman could be sure. Both considered jumping into the water to avoid the impending impact.

For the first time, Bill emotionally understood that he was in mortal danger. There had not been time to think about it before. He knew that an impact with the cutter would probably kill him. Jumping out at this speed was not especially attractive either, and in spite of the fact that he could not steer, the idea of abandoning his post and just leaving his boat unattended at this speed was abhorrent. If he did miss the cutter, he could stay in the cockpit and continue to wave his arms at the spectators and try and warn them. Maybe get the attention of one or two...

"That's what your life comes down to," he thought, "a few scattered thoughts and a decision. A guess and a commitment. Wait and see."

When the impact with the cutter was about to happen, Bill lifted his right foot out, up, and onto the deck in an effort to jump. Springing on the ball of his left foot, he proceeded to clamber out of the cockpit.

He did not make it.

Kit Muncey was sitting next to Willard Rhodes, Chairman of the Board of Associated Grocers (AG) and primary benefactor for the Miss Thriftway. Named for the stores that represented AG, members of the Miss Thriftway Racing Team could sit in a secluded section of the judge's stand dedicated specifically for crewmembers of any of the teams participating in the Seafair regatta. Although naturally tense, she had looked on with pride and anticipation as her husband had secured the inside lane and was moving up the back chute to the last corner before the start. Although the loudspeakers blasted the countdown from the commentator, she could hear the whirring of the gears synchronizing the pie-faced clock fastened to the judge's stand on the third level next to her.

As the ambient tone of the spectators, media and devoted fans increased in excitement and volume, Kit seemed to withdraw and emotionally detach from the excitement of the imminent start. The flying start of an Unlimited hydroplane race was truly one of the most spectacular moments in motorsports; however, to her it was merely a prelude to the danger represented by the traffic jam of the following corner. Many people counted down out loud in unison with the commentator on the loudspeakers while others chanted words of encouragement to their favorite drivers out on the course.

Due to the line of sight from the judge's stand, all the competitors seemed to come together into one mass as they crossed the apex of the corner coming around for the start. The roostertails formed one enormous rising cascade fanning out behind as the different drivers appeared to break away sliding around to the exit pin. The soft echo and roar of the crowds on shore began to waft up to the highest level of the stand as it mingled with the growing growl of the combined chorus of unmuffled aircraft engines. Kit didn't realize it, but she was holding her breath. Willard was helping her stand up out of her seat and count down with the rest of them. She glanced down and over to the hot pit area as she rose and noticed that not one person was moving. Not even the seagulls were in flight; they sat on the light poles of the Stan Sayers Park in quiet attendance. Then the level of noise dropped, and the birds took flight in natural alarm.

A collection of separate and individual shouts filled the audio vacuum.

"Oh, my God!"

"Oh, no!"

"What is he doing?"

And, "Stop the race!" were the most common refrains exclaimed by the onlookers. Kit quickly looked back to where the field should have been coming out of the corner and saw one boat driving across in front of all the other boats. One by one the roostertails of each boat dropped. The angle of sight exaggerated the speed of the errant craft as it dawned on her who was in it. The profile and paint scheme of the Miss Thriftway was quite distinct and easy to identify even at a great distance. For a brief flicker of an instant, even she wondered what Bill was doing. Then, she understood that something had gone horribly wrong. She had personally witnessed hundreds of hydroplane starts and she instantly knew that her husband, the father of their two young children, was in serious danger. Helplessly she clutched the small handbag she carried. Quietly, she bit her lower lip.

"I must not show excitement or alarm," she thought.

The cheers and calls of encouragement had given way to shouts of alarm. The crowds had then gone silent. Most of the hundreds of thousands of spectators only stood and watched. Even the com-

Chapter Twelve

mentator had stopped speaking. When the Miss Thriftway crossed in front of the last boat occupying the outside lane, even the shouting stopped. Since drivers had slackened their throttles to avoid running into Bill, their unmuffled roars had dropped to a virtually inaudible idling hum.

Kit raised her handbag up in front of her throat below her chin in a natural primordial effort unconsciously to protect her from an oncoming assault. The Thriftway sped on. Out of the corner of her eye, she could make out a tiny speck floating on the water off of the shore. The speck merged with the Miss Thriftway and the Miss Thriftway stopped.

Although sound travels at over 600 miles per hour, it seemed to take an eternity to reach her. The whack of the impact resonated out over the shore and could be heard miles away. It caused Kit involuntarily to jerk in reflex.

The Coast Guard was very proud of their steel hulled cutter but at the speed that the Miss Thriftway was traveling, she penetrated her side like straw through a tree in a tornado.

Kit looked back down from the third level she was standing on over the railing to the pavement below. A new sound began to pervade the silent pit area and judge's stand. The smell of the high octane exhaust mixed with it as the Coast Guard helicopter began to increase its engine speed for take-off from the barge to which it had been secured. A helmeted guardsman in an orange jump suit leaped through the open side door of the aircraft and attached his safety strap to a hard point inside. The pilot and co-pilot were grim faced as they spoke to each other through their microphones and with their eyes. The RPM's of the engine increased. The tail and rotor lifted up, and the aircraft tipped forward into the air. A low conversational murmur of the judge's stand remained after the cyclic chuffing of the Coast Guard helicopter dissipated toward the scene of the accident.

Punctuating the murmur was the hiss and blare of a voice over a radio reporting from a television commentator viewing the carnage on the water. The bow of the Miss Thriftway had sliced through the left side or port forward portion of the cutter. The thrust of impact had driven the pointed edge of the hydroplane deep below decks. The resulting gash had allowed a massive amount of water into the boat, and the weight of the vessel had twisted the Thriftway below the surface. The mass and weight of the Thriftway impaled itself with tremendous power, virtually merging the two vessels into one. The energy produced by the hydroplane fused itself into the pair and caused the duo to spin quickly around in a wide circle sinking in an arc that appeared to be a dance in slow motion. Air and bubbles spewed and sputtered out through broken windows and dipping doorways as the two spun lower into Lake Washington.

As the commentator's voice described the scene to the viewers and listeners, he began to ask, "Where is Bill? What has happened to the driver?"

Willard looked over his shoulder at Kit. If he didn't know her better, he would have thought that she was indifferent. She was wearing a well-pressed blouse and skirt and holding a small purse up in front of her. Her facial expression was blank; the only indication of a failing facade was a slight quiver to her lower lip. She stared out over the railing toward the crash area speechless. From social occasions such as dinners and luncheons, Rhodes had learned that the young wife of the Miss Thriftway's driver was a well educated woman. She was journalism major with a minor in history. Although the Miss Thriftway was a business marketing venture intended toward brand awareness and enhanced esprit d'corp amongst Associated Grocers employees, Willard took a very personal interest in everyone involved with the team. His heart went out to her when he realized that she may have just become a widow. He had no idea how she was able to maintain her composure.

"You either bring your shield back with you or you will be carried back from battle on top of it." The ancient Spartan expression that flickered across her mind represented an attitude she had grudgingly admired. Unfortunately, it did not provide for second thoughts or the shirking and evasion of responsibility. The idea that a warrior's shield could come back to the family that paid for it without its bearer was contemptible. A commitment to the team and a determination to excel independently was what had brought them to this far-off corner of America, coupled with the adventure of a new life together. She knew that this move could have a steep price. The electronically modified voice over the radio was mimicking the same thought that occupied her mind.

"Where is Bill? " She numbly thought about the abstract chal-

CHAPTER TWELVE

lenge of finding his body in the debris on the water. She suddenly and brutally pushed away the concept of his demise.

Kit Muncey was a devoted Episcopalian. From an impressionable age, she had been introduced by her mother to the practice of faith. Kit firmly and irrevocably believed that if she prayed fervently, consistently and often it would keep her loved ones safe. She regularly attended church services and often pressed her husband and two young children to participate also.

This was a test of faith. Her husband was fine. The lip stopped quivering. Willard saw an expression seem to cross Kit's face that he could only describe later as a stoic resolve. She looked at him directly and asked, "Do you have any idea how I can get to the hospital?" The idea that a trip to the hospital would not be required did not appear to cross her mind. The rising backdrop of noise and confused exclamations underscored the quiet but deliberate tone of her voice. She fully hoped that he would have an answer but the truth was that he did not have a clue.

On the other hand, Willard Rhodes was a take charge kind of guy. With a step toward Kit, he gently placed his hand on her elbow and in an equally quiet voice said, "Come with me. "

Pointing toward the stairs with his chin, he instantly recalled that the Thriftway crew chief, Jack Ramsey, had a station wagon parked out by Lake Washington Boulevard in the event that the team needed to make a parts run. The keys were under the driver's seat so that any crew member could take it if needed.

"They will probably take him to the Trauma Center at Harborview Hospital," Willard said, noticing that Kit's optimism was contagious. "It's a good thing the hospital is nearby," he went on. Together they stepped through the railing and went down the stairs in a quiet but hurried shuffle.

Bright red flares crisscrossed over the race course trailing bluish-black smoke, signaling all competitors to stop where they were. Some had resumed their speeds after Bill had passed in front of them. The helicopter was hovering low over the scene of the accident, creating a small field of whitecaps on the water. The mass of the two vessels was still slowly turning in a wide circle as they settled under the water. A Coast Guardsman was seen crawling out from below decks through the gaping hole in the side of the cutter as the rising water had forced him to use whatever exit available.

The bow of the Miss Thriftway had stopped inches from the bridge of his nose as he lay in a berth below decks. A swim suited search and rescue diver was nimbly clambering over the afterdeck trying to find survivors or the driver of the race boat. Other guardsmen had already swum to the security of converging patrol boats.

Law enforcement had promptly responded and attempted the best they could to place their patrol boats in positions around the scene that would get the right people in and keep the bystanders out. No one could find Bill's body or what could tactfully be called his remains.

All the way to impact, he had kept his eyes open. It was not clear until the last second whether the race boat would actually hit the white and orange Coast Guard cutter. In the end, the spring in the ball of his left foot is what saved his life. Using it to push off from the floorboards while climbing on to the deck had brought his left leg just high enough that, when the bow of his boat slammed into the side of the cutter, the inertia of the push carried him up and over the dashboard. Physics did the rest. At 185 pounds, Bill's own body weight had carried him up and over the two boats at about 100 miles per hour into the water on the other side of the accident. Bouncing, tumbling, cartwheeling, and spinning, he had come to a bruised and battered stop relatively intact. His life jacket and helmet had stayed on to do their jobs. Remarkably conscious, he started swimming to the nearest rescue boat to join other survivors but realized that the one he originally intended was already too full. He turned in the water and swam towards another vessel when the helicopter appeared hovering above him. The white caps created by the helicopter ironically obscured and camouflaged his swimming.

A sharp-eyed diver in a black wetsuit standing in the door of the 'copter spotted Bill. He relayed the information to his orange-suited partner, before unhesitatingly stepping into space and rapidly dropping into the water from 50 feet up. Like the professionals that they were, the guardsmen went about the business of dealing with traumatic situations with the lifesaving calm and deliberation required. Once the diver had cleared the doorway, his partner had swung a long, flat open topped metal cage on a hook out beside the aircraft on an overhead steel beam. Depressing an electrical button, the cage was lowered down to the water. Offering adjustments and

Chapter Twelve

instructions to the pilots, the helicopter was guided to where the diver was swimming in Bill's direction.

As the adrenalin level receded, Bill noticed a numbness coming to his face. Bill saw the diver swimming towards him, so he stopped swimming and began to tread water. He remembered his body colliding with something as he had escaped the hydroplane's cockpit. Bill reached under the water to get a sense of the injuries. Cold fingers explored the front of his life jacket which was still intact, and that allayed one great fear. Although internal bleeding from an impact like this was a concern, a ruptured abdomen was one of the the scariest things to a race driver. Boatracing lore has it that your entrails could spill out into the water, and you would not even feel it.

The diver reached Bill just as the stretcher swung into his sight. He helped Bill roll into it while adding reassuring comments. The Guardsman with the orange jumpsuit above them winched the stretcher to the helicopter doorway. While swinging into the aircraft, the helicopter promptly rolled in the air and tipped toward nearby Beacon Hill and Harborview Hospital. The trip would take less than three minutes.

Kit woke up alone and with a start at the Muncey house on Mercer Island at about eleven o'clock the following morning. Disoriented and a little confused, it gradually dawned on her that the events of the previous 24 hours were sequentially correct and not immediately overwhelming. It would be OK. Taken piece by piece and one step at a time, she could deal with them on an emotional level. Taking them as a whole caused her head to ache ferociously.

She had been up most of the night sitting in the waiting room of Harborview Hospital. By the time they had been able to work their way through the spectators, checkpoints and roadblocks leading out of the race pits, it took almost thirty minutes to reach the hospital three miles away. Bill was admitted and remained conscious throughout. The doctors had briefly allowed the couple to talk before taking Bill into seclusion for examination. Kit was comforted in that Bill did not look worried. His face was very puffy, and his speech was starting to slur from the pain medication.

"Bill hates pain medication," Kit said to no one in particular.

She knew this to be true because he had often said drugs made him feel dumb and awkward. He would joke and say, "I don't need any help feeling dumb and awkward."

It was not the first time Mrs. Muncey had seen her husband injured in a race boat. It was not the first night spent in a hospital waiting room. She had earned the dubious distinction of being quoted as saying, "Most boat designing is done in the waiting rooms of hospitals."

Yes, she had said it. No, it was not something she was happy about. The fact was that the sport was evolving so fast that engineers and fabricators were running to catch up. Home of the Boeing Aircraft Company, Seattle was a flying machine town with a concentration of very talented aviation engineers and designers. Seattle also had a deep water port that hosted a respectable naval engineer and construction community. Perhaps the most ideal compilation in the world, but it was still a gallop to stay ahead. A cast iron rudder was more than adequate to deal admirably with the loads…until yesterday.

Kit swung her legs out of bed and onto the floor. A neighbor who also happened to be a nurse had come over to feed the boys. She could hear them downstairs playing in the "rec room". The television was on, of course. She briefly worried if anything about the accident had been mentioned. Had the children seen any news coverage? She and Bill were determined to keep them away from some of the the immediate and intense aspects of racing. They had been home with a sitter over the weekend that had strict instructions not to let them watch the TV. The sitter was also to keep reporters and photographers away from the boys at any cost. Although Kit and Bill discussed the potential wisdom of these precautions, this was the first time that the policy had actually proved its value.

There had a few years back been a kidnapping threat against the children and the police had moved the boys over to a friend's house in protected concealment. That episode had been a wakeup call that notoriety has its price.

This situation was immediate and in her face. Normalcy around the Muncey house would need to be established as soon as possible. Bill's back pain and bruises would keep him in the hospital for several days. The doctors were worried about internal bleeding and had already decided that he had ruptured his spleen, again.

It was amazing that those were the extent of his injuries, she thought. "Count your blessings," she counseled herself. Normalcy

Chapter Twelve

will return one step at a time.

The boys were used to Bill being away on trips. Maybe this could be like that. The first step would maybe do something, the three of them together. Maybe drive into "town" on Mercer Island and do something simple like getting groceries. She thought for a moment about who really needed this therapy; she or the boys?

The boys were happy enough and well behaved in the family station wagon on the trip over the hill and down into the quaint little town. A Chevrolet (of course) and commonly recognized in its two-tone of turquoise and white. The checker at the local grocery store nodded to Kit as she came through the doors. With a half a glance, Kit immediately knew that she knew.

The checker could also tell that Kit was trying to do more than just shop and made a special effort to be engaging, reassuring, and cordial.

"Good morning, Mrs. Muncey," she said. A simple salutation that represented the next step toward normalcy. The boys were oblivious to anything other than the toys and candy.

Kit placed a few random grocery items in her cart and headed to the check-out stand. As the familiar face rang up her purchases, she and the checker exchanged common pleasantries; almost comfortably uninspiring, if not a tad bit forced.

Kit started to relax with a maternal smile in the direction of her boys, when it happened.

"Did you hear the news?" a male patron on the other side of the store shouted out to an acquaintance shopping across the isles, "Bill Muncey got killed yesterday."

The intended recipient responded with, "I thought that he was just hurt real bad? "

"Oh no. He was DOA. They just haven't released the news yet."

Kit's moment of relaxation quickly evaporated. She looked at the checker who returned an expression of stark incredulity. Looking briefly over at the original speaker with a stare that would melt an iceberg, Kit quickly looked to the upturned faces of her two toe-headed boys. They looked at each other in her immediate speechless silence, and she could read the thoughts tumbling through their heads.

"Dad didn't come home last night," she could see William reasoning. Dorian was looking at his older brother for some kind of interpretation or explanation. "If a grownup is saying it, it must be true." Getting no explanation from William, four-year-old Dorian implored of his mother, "Where is Daddy?"

"Your father is just going to be away for a few days," she said.

Oblivious to the family in his midst, and as if on cue, the shopper continued his account, "Oh, they'll announce the funeral sometime today."

Killed and funeral were two words with which her children had not had much experience. The expressions on their faces indicated that they were trying to process information totally foreign to them. They knew that it was important. The concerned look of the checker followed her as she let her original statement stand for the moment and ushered her children out of the store and back into the family station wagon. Her boys were curious and they would continue asking more difficult questions as children are predisposed to do.

Before accepting Bill's marriage proposal, Kit had extended two conditions. She was not going to marry a professional musician, and she was not going to marry a professional soldier. At the time, Bill was a soldier and a musician. He also happened to race boats. Although she felt that her parents had expectations that she would marry a senator, a lawyer, or a doctor, her choice only excluded those two professions. She had nothing in particular against those professions but in the midst of the Korean War being a soldier did not appear to be that secure and the finances of a musician's family were not that stable either. Not extending his military service beyond the required two years was an easy decision for Bill. The music part was tougher because it had real potential, but he loved Kit, and that was that.

As they say, "Be careful what you wish for." Being the wife of a professional boat racer was not exactly what she had planned either. He had a devoted passion and an obvious aptitude for it but making it a profession had seemed so improbable at the time. Nevertheless, they had built a life for themselves out of it and although neither knew exactly how long the ride would last, it was an adventure that they felt fortunate to be on, usually. She was going to have to deal with the surprises as they came. Like two little boys that want to know what "killed" means and why the word is about daddy.

Chapter Twelve

The only way to deal with this was for her children to see their father. Soon. There was extensive film of the accident replayed during the news on the television. The cutter and the Thriftway were still on the bottom of Lake Washington due to be raised shortly. It was big drama and was getting a lot of play on all the local news channels.

Kit had watched the first replay of the coverage. The local news station had panned around the two sinking vessels and watched as the guardsmen below decks had scrambled out of the wreckage with the television commentator asking, "Where is Bill?"

It had not been a particular comfort to know at the time that he was in the examination room nearby. The film was haunting, and she knew it would frighten her children. She was keeping William out of kindergarten that day, but it would be only a matter of time before the news traveled to their tiny ears.

The transplanted Munceys had made a few friends with other young families upon moving to the Northwest. The Lyfords lived relatively nearby and Bill and Kit would often visit them socially. The Lyford children, Chuck, Ginny Lee and their dog Lulu would often look after William and Dorian while the parents visited. The two boys liked riding in Chuck's jeep down the switchbacks leading to Lake Washington on Capitol Hill. Chuck and Ginny Lee were the first teenagers the boys had met and gotten to really know. The Munceys were very impressed with their thoughtful consideration when looking after the boys. The boys were impressed with the teenager's worldly sophistication and freedoms such as driving cars. Their mother, Virginia, happened to work at Harborview Hospital.

In those days, it was hospital policy across the country to restrict visitation in hospital wards to children over the age of twelve. For mutual safety from contagious diseases, the medical profession felt seclusion and rigid separation were the wisest courses. Bill's stay was going to run longer than a few days. If the situation were left to itself, it could actually be quite a while before the children would see their father. Kit Muncey was not the type of woman that was content to leave things to themselves. She was not particularly patient when it came to the welfare of her children either. On the way home from the store, she pulled the station wagon up next to a phone booth and dropped in a dime from her change purse. The information operator from the phone company provided Harborview's number, and Kit was able to get Virginia on the phone. After relaying the situation in the store and her concerns for her children over the next several days, she asked her advice. Then Virginia Lyford went to work on the problem.

While hell may have no fury like a woman scorned, the gates to that nefarious region are no match to a pair of mothers leading children out of it. Virginia lobbied, cajoled, and relentlessly pursued permission first and then the proactive cooperation second, of the hospital's administrative staff in bending policy to allow two young boys to briefly visit their father. Initially, well intended resistance was ruthlessly subdued with bulldog persistence and pitilessly set aside. Then she coordinated the containment of the other patients on the entire wing of the hospital with the aid and assistance of the doctors and the nurses. As an adolescent during WW II, Kit had become a qualified practical nurse and was appreciative and overwhelmed with the attention to detail that Virginia addressed. A simple walk down the corridor was a daunting and substantial undertaking in these circumstances and the Munceys would speak of Virginia's determination for decades.

At the prescribed hour, Kit led her two children by the hand down to their father's room. Half a century later, the offspring vividly recall that their father looked as if he had been in a prize fight. His face was black and blue, and his speech was slow and deep from the pain medication. Nevertheless, unquestionably that was Dad, lying in bed under white sheets in a room that smelled of disinfectants. While Kit and Bill exchanged glances, he spoke with his kids about the importance of helping their mother around the house because he was going to have to lie in this hospital for a while. He extracted an individual promise from each that they would be the men of the house. The visit was necessarily brief but conclusive. The conversation short but deliberate.

Immediately after that, Kit led her two small blonde charges by their hands out the door out of the smelly room and back down the corridor. And for a moment, everything was as it should be.

The Racing Team. Left to right: Stan Adsit, Joe Langer, Ray Ballard, Lorrie Aumsager, Jack Ramsey, and Spanky Allen.

Preparing for the mile record attempt

Flashy even on land, Bill's Corvette took him to speaking engagements across the Pacific Northwest.

The collaboration between the designer, Ted Jones, and the driver, Bill Muncey, set the standards of racing performance for several years.

CHAPTER THIRTEEN

The Mile

"Sure, why not?"

In the exuberance of the moment, groups often share the optimism and the enthusiasm for ambitious projects, challenging undertakings or innovative ideas. Often fueled by a legitimate confidence earned from the successful completion of tasks and trials, a team coalesces into a driving force unto itself. After a series of seasons together, the Miss Thriftway Hydroplane Racing Team had become such a group.

Therefore, when Willard Rhodes, the owner, asked Bill Muncey, the driver, if their boat could set the world record for top speed over a sustained mile, his response was predictable. After all, the Thriftway team had earned a commendable record on circular race courses around the country capably led by their crew chief, Jack Ramsey. How difficult could it be in a straight line?

Bill's respect and admiration for Rhodes were such that there wasn't much Bill would not at least attempt to do for him. It had been Ted Jones's recommendation with a nod from Willard Rhodes that gave Bill the opportunity to race the Miss Thriftway in the first place. Bill felt he had essentially been plucked from obscurity, and placed into the cockpit over the heads of more qualified drivers. He shouldered his portion of the team responsibilities with a high degree of respect and sincerely felt that most of his efforts on the race course were merely a reflection of the combined focus of the ten-man Thriftway team. If asked, he would have confided that most of the success he had enjoyed the first few seasons was attributable to his ability to conserve the equipment rather than push it to its limit. It was truly a team effort, and he was grateful to be a part of it.

The challenge of "The Mile" might not take on definable features until one contemplates the concept of the straight line. Point A to point B seems simple enough on a piece of paper or a chalkboard, but if the pressures holding the chalk and the shape of the chalk changes the faster it goes, maintaining that straight line becomes increasingly challenging. Airborne turbulence buffets the top and bottom of the boat and batters the deck and control surfaces.

A dramatic example had occurred during time trials at the Seafair hydroplane race on Lake Washington. The pressure of air traveling under the hull between the sponsons, or pontoons, had built to a level that pushed the nose of the boat into the air. Moving over the water at a speed in excess of 150 mph accelerated the diminishing control of the driver so quickly that the higher the bow lifted, the faster it compacted the air, forcing it straight up into a complete somersault. With no straps or seatbelts, the driver fell out of the airborne, inverted cockpit and was seriously injured. Though he survived the initial impact, Bill believed the driver's death sometime later was a delayed but direct result of those injuries.

The entire episode was caught on camera and had been studied by fascinated fans and earnest engineers alike. Both audiences had walked away from the viewing with virtually identical conclusions. At these new speeds, a lot of unanticipated factors involved with marine motorsports were still to be learned and understood. The driver had not made any discernable error in operation, and the crew had not configured the hull in any unusual way. It was a mystery that could have fatal consequences. Although Seattle, Washington was an aircraft burg with some of the best and brightest aerodynamic and hydrodynamic authorities in the world in residence, the fact of the matter was that sustained flight close over the water was a recent and high-tech phenomenon. Add to this experience, the independent development of components relative in their own peculiar way to hydroplane racing, and you have a recipe for cutting edge disasters.

Then there was the water. The nature of a varying surface that is unreliable and difficult to view caused racers to pause. Decades before, on Loch Ness in Scotland, another group of dedicated teammates had attempted the record. Film footage existed that showed a relatively modest wave cross in front of the boat at speed and caused a chain reaction in the loss of control that ultimately ended in catastrophe. The source of the errant wave was never determined and sardonically attributed to the Loch Ness monster. Regardless, the fact that unpredictable water surfaces represented a threat should not be underestimated.

Whether it was the whispered word or the clarion of the media, the news that the Thriftway was going to make an attempt on the measured mile spread quickly. Bill often said that there were no secrets in boat racing and this was no exception. He kept whatever trepidations he had to himself. Any apprehensions Bill had, he shared only with his wife, Kit. Quietly and with deliberation, he did his part in the preparation by setting his affairs in order and making sure his life insurance payments with New York Life were current. Twice a week Bill spent his evenings at the boat shop inside Associated Grocers warehouses to offer his help. The crew treated his attendance as a curious novelty. His input as the driver was pivotal but, as a working hand on the boat, his contributions were relegated to swinging a brush of varnish or sanding a secondary surface somewhere on the hull. On more than one occasion, Bill grabbed a broom and swept the concrete floors while the crew worked on the boat.

On some evenings, Bill would bring his phonograph player so he could share the latest recordings of Shelley Berman jokes or the comedy act of Bob Newhart. Muncey was proud to be part of this dedicated team whose collective effort was volunteer hours, for the most part. When Bill was able to come in on the weekend during daylight hours, he accepted the task of running to Dag's Drive-In for Beefy Boy burgers, or a parts run to the local hardware store. There was very little he would not do to show support. Muncey felt the successful chemistry of the team was a compilation of orchestrated intentions applied to a common cause. Every effort counted. He also knew that some drivers had a tendency to develop an overconfidence that could be misunderstood as condescending or dismissive when it came to the substantial sacrifices his teammates made. He was determined not to be misunderstood.

Rarely is it possible for a group of people to apply themselves to a common goal and have the opportunity to step back and see the results of their efforts in so spectacular a form. It has been suggested that hydroplane racing is the most spectacular sport. With roostertails thrusting tons of water high into the air trailing behind the boat hundreds of feet as it hurtles over the water at three times the speed of the average automobile, it is easy to see this viewpoint. The fact that so graceful a craft can represent the application of thousands of horsepower is never lost on the team that makes it look easy. A couple of turns on a liquid race course can convey the quiet exultation of success. A mature teammate must be satisfied with the knowledge that they contributed their part for that may be all the compensation they acquire for the effort. When asked what his contribution was, Bill would only say, "I stab it and turn left."

This particular endeavor for the record mile attempt did not even require that he do any turning to speak of. The regional media inquired about the meticulous preparation going into the Mile attempt and Bill and Willard treated the journalists with a shared round of golf at a local course. A certain degree of theatrics didn't hurt as Bill got down on his knees to complete a putt by using his golf club like a pool room cue stick to sink the golf ball into the hole. Public appearances and public speaking was a large portion of Bill's role representing the Public Relations Department of Associated Grocers and he took the responsibility wholeheartedly.

Often Bill would rehearse an upcoming speech in front of the mirror on his master bedroom door. From an appearance point of view, Bill was the primary face that the general public got to see representing the popular Thriftway grocery stores that dotted the growing suburban landscape of the Pacific Northwest. Marine motorsports had done a lot to put Seattle on the map - literally, as many of the Washington State maps available through the corner gas stations in the country showed the dotted line, representing the oval hydroplane race course on Lake Washington. Specifically, hydroplane racing had become an integral part of how the Pacific Northwest perceived itself. Rain, water, and race boats were becoming the local heritage.

It seemed that, at any opportunity, Bill would find himself dispatched to some corner of the state to speak at a luncheon or dinner about marine motorsports and the Associated Grocers organization. The public interest and support were infectious. Whether it was the annual Christmas dinner for Bekin's Moving and Storage in Tacoma or a fundraiser at the Rainier Club in downtown Seattle, Willard Rhodes did not hesitate to send his company's ambassador. As Chairman of the Board, Willard knew that an interested public would reciprocate at the check-out stands. It was good business.

A popular historic personality of the 1950's was the young outlaw of cowboy fame known as Bill Bonnie and commonly referred to as Billy the Kid. Some local newsman anointed Bill Muncey with the moniker and for a while it stuck. Although he personally did not care for the nickname "Billy", he was astute enough to know a fun PR idea when he heard it. A local cartoonist, named Bob Hale, created the image of a short, helmeted child pulling a model race

Chapter Thirteen

boat behind him on a string. Hale's character appeared in the local newspapers, on the TV stations and even the Muncey family's Christmas cards. Although a transplanted Detroiter, the Northwest community at large embraced Bill as their own.

It looked like a campfire in the middle of the road. Coming back from a speaking engagement in the middle of the night, Bill was cruising down the highway across the Olympic Peninsula in his two-seater sports car by himself. Kit rarely attended these functions since there were two young boys to tend to and the family budget didn't allow for sitters often. Actually, Bill liked the solitude of travel and used the opportunities to sip a cup of coffee and organize his thoughts. Sometimes he would speak out loud to hear a given phrase considered for a speech or he would compose a checklist of things to do or draft music scores. Sometimes the radio playing music was enough. In any case, on this night, the flickering of light on the highway disrupted the solitude created by the absence of traffic and the close confines of country darkness. It was ten at night, and the cloudy overcast had shielded the fields and forests from starlight or the glow of the moon. Depth and distance were deceptive, and Bill came upon the scene sooner than he expected. Clicking the radio dial to the off position, Bill pulled his car onto the shoulder and stopped.

A four door sedan was facing him, tipped over on its side and straddling the white line that ran down the middle of the road. The wheels were still turning, and the body of the vehicle rocked subtly back and forth, as Bill heard pieces of glass dropping onto the pavement in small spatters from the back window. Further ahead about two hundred feet was a pickup truck turned partly facing the opposite direction, right side up, but with a small fire emanating from under the mashed hood. Although the road was not blocked, Bill pulled on the parking brake and quickly got out of his car. He held his hand up and squinted to peer through the glare of the headlights from the canted car that were still beaming askance into the darkness. The sound of dripping water and the smell of radiator fluid greeted his nostrils as he walked toward the sedan. The ticking sound of a quickly cooling exhaust manifold exposed to the cold night air emanating from the bottom of the car with soft folds of steam furling into the darkness. Bill had taken three steps before he heard it.

The Mile

At first, his initial appraisal was the sound of a cat or kitten mewing. Ridiculous but that was the only reference he had. A moment's concentration and focus reached a different conclusion. Someone was groaning or crying from inside the tipped vehicle. Quickly he sprinted around to look inside the windshield which was remarkably unbroken. He could see through it a woman pressed against the passenger side of the glass. She was slowly trying to get to a sitting position relative to the disoriented confines of the bench seat. The sound Bill had heard was the moaning that was involuntarily uttered in her efforts.

His own headlights had helped illuminate the car's interior. He could see she had a broken nose and bloody lower lip. She probably could not see him due to the glare from the headlights. Bill hopped up on the driver's door and spoke down through the broken window. He recalled that his mother in law had survived a similar crash back in the days of plate glass for windshields and door windows and had been terribly disfigured. Although it would be small comfort now, the safety glass that had apparently impacted the drivers head had done its job. Mandatory seatbelts, however, were a decade in the future. She had apparently tumbled around inside as the car had slid on the pavement to a stop.

"Can you reach my hand?" Bill asked as he extended his arm down through the door. She looked up, startled at the shadow of his face for a moment. Moving her legs under her and nodding uncertainly in his direction, she reached up and grasped his forearm. Bill clasped hers in return and gently pulled her into a standing position on the inside of the passenger door. Bill moved to the side to allow her to extend her head through the opening in the driver's door.

The highway extended on in a straight line into the dark for several miles. Although there did not appear to be any dwellings in sight, he could discern a solitary pair of headlights coming their direction.

"How do you feel?" Bill asked. "Take a moment to get your bearings," he suggested. "Do you feel any broken bones?" he asked. He could still feel the heat escaping from the interior of the car into the night.

A soft cool breeze fluttered across her forehead as she came up through the door that further tangled her shoulder length auburn

CHAPTER THIRTEEN

hair. She still could not see his face clearly but looked his direction and said in a trembling voice, "I think I'm ok. " She steadied herself by clutching the window frame she was standing in. Her gaze wandered back over the side of her car toward the pickup truck.

Bill followed her gaze and noticed that the fire under it had gone out. Looking back at her face, he asked, "Why don't you wait here a moment and catch your breath?" She nodded quietly as Bill slid off onto the blacktop and hurried over to the passenger's door of the other vehicle.

By contrast, the pickup was remarkably intact. The front end was obviously smashed, but the engine was quietly idling at a low purr. Bill peered through the passenger window and could see the driver leaned over the steering wheel. His hands were still in the one o'clock and eleven o'clock positions. If Bill did not know any better, he would have thought that the driver was merely asleep. Knocking on the glass of the passenger door, the driver looked up and straight ahead over the mangled hood. Turning, he looked straight at Bill and stared blankly. Obviously dazed, Bill raised his voice and asked if he were ok. The driver seemed to pause and think for what seemed like a long time. Looking directly at Bill, he only nodded. Bill waited for him to say something, but nothing came. Opening the passenger's unlocked door, Bill swung it open and set one foot on the running board to lean into the cab.

"What day is it? " Bill asked.

"Why its Friday, "the driver said. " What a silly thing to ask." He went on. Bill determined that the driver's attitude was a testament to his well-being. Then the driver said, "They crossed right over the center line!"

Now, Bill was not particularly concerned with how the accident had happened or even who was at fault. In the end, it did not really matter much.

The oncoming car pulled up next to him as Bill looked back over to the woman standing with her head peeking out of her driver's window. A young man of teenage years leaned across and asked through his rolled down passenger window, "Should I get to a phone and call an ambulance?" Bill nodded at him and simply said, "I think that that would be a good idea. " The teenager quickly drove on into the night. Bill silently marveled that no other cars had appeared. It had seemed like a very long time had passed since he first came upon the scene.

The driver of the pickup had appeared to have gathered his thoughts and reached up to turn off the ignition. Getting out, he had walked around to the front of the truck to survey the damage to his vehicle. Bill stepped off of the running board and quickly walked back over to the woman. Taking out a clean handkerchief that he always kept in his back pocket, he handed it to her and suggested that she use it to keep pressure against her lip and contain the bleeding. She accepted it and did so. Bill then said, "Let's see what we can do about getting you out of there. That young man is going to the nearest phone to call for help." The woman seemed reassured at the news and looked on expectantly as Bill climbed back up on the side of her car. Reaching down, he helped lift her up and out of the car as she stepped on the steering wheel. He noticed that she was light, like Kit. It occurred to him that this was the first time that he had felt the weight of another woman since he had been married, and he was curiously relieved to notice that the hand he grabbed had a wedding ring on it.

After leading her over to his car, he opened the door and helped her sit in his passenger seat, encouraging her to keep the handkerchief pressed against her lip. After starting the car and turning up the heater, he turned the radio back on to create a comfortable distraction and said, "Why don't you try to keep warm, and I will go check on our friend in the pickup?" She nodded while she stared straight ahead out into the dark. As he walked away, he noticed out of the corner of his eye that she had turned his rear view mirror to look at her hair and was trying to brush and pat it back into place. Bill thought, "I may not be a doctor, but that's a good sign."

The driver of the pickup was hunched down in front of it with his hands on his knees looking directly at the radiator. Shaking his head, he straightened up as Bill approached and said, "It doesn't seem to be leaking. I just might be able to drive her home." Bill nodded silently and then suggested, "There's an ambulance on the way. You might want to wait and let them check you out. "Going on he said, "You look like you might have a nasty bruise on your forehead. It might be wise to give yourself a few minutes." The driver laughed and seemed to say more to himself than to Bill, "Well it's a cinch that I don't need to be in any kind of hurry."

Bill picked up the thread of the joke and offered, "Yeah, you

Chapter Thirteen

might say that it seems to be your lucky day." They smiled at each other, and Bill looked up to notice a pair of flashing red lights off in the distance. That must be the ambulance; he thought.

Bill had not had a drink of any alcoholic beverage in several years, which made him sensitive to its scent on other people's breath. He had not smelled anything of the kind from either of the drivers. After giving a brief statement to the Washington State patrol officer that eventually arrived, he went on his way and arrived home a couple of hours later. Kit was already asleep but lifted her head to ask what had taken him so long. "I stopped to help some people on the way," was all Bill said.

Sunrises in the Pacific Northwest in the winter months can be particularly spectacular. The view across Puget Sound of the Olympic Mountains as the sun painted them in bright reds and yellows was one of the main reasons that the Muncey's had chosen this particular lot to build on. A Saturday morning was usually a relatively quiet affair at the Muncey house without the daily urgency of getting to work or school. Kit liked to take her time to create a memorable breakfast and Bill liked to contemplate the newspaper along with the first cup of coffee of the day. Therefore, it was somewhat of a family surprise when that newspaper went sailing across the living room, turning into a flutter of print and paper as it settled harmlessly against the large living room picture window.

"Those reporters never get anything right!" Bill bellowed.

Kit looked up alarmed from the stove in the kitchen and asked out to Bill through the dining room, "What are you talking about? " The children looked up from the Living room carpet at their father for the answer.

Bill picked up the paper and walked over to show it to his wife. Reading the relevant headline out loud Kit said, "BILL MUNCEY INVOLVED IN AUTO ACCIDENT.."

After quickly continuing with the text of the story, she realized that the editor had manipulated the facts to create the type of headline that would compel someone to read on. The balance of the article merely described vehicles and circumstances and went on to mention that Bill had stopped to render aid after the fact. Journalistically dishonest, perhaps but not illegal or libelous. With a look that only couples can share, they acknowledged that it was not a good development but there was not really anything anyone could do about it. Both knew how it looked and how it had happened. Someone had talked to someone who talked to a reporter who made a story. It sold newspapers. It went with the territory. They hoped that the people that mattered to them would know the difference and the inevitable rumors that would follow would be short lived.

From the carpeted floor of the Living room, one of the children assured his parents, "But reporters can draw pictures."

Bill looked down at his child, chuckled briefly, and then laughed out loud. Nodding vigorously he said, "Yeah, they can sure do that."

Bill looked back at Kit as she smiled and said "Breakfast is ready."

The day of the Mile attempt was a typical overcast February day. It was anticipated to be cold and gray with a soft drizzle in the air that Bob Hale, the cartooning weatherman on the local television station predicted would clear up by the afternoon. The streets were pasty and wet as Bill drove in the predawn down to the Associated Grocers warehouse and the shop that was home to the Thriftway Racing Team. It sounded similar to the sound of tearing paper as his tires rolled over the pavement in the dark across the world famous floating bridge on Lake Washington.

The soft yellow glow of the shop lights pushed out into the damp darkness through the snuggly closed bay doors as Bill pulled up in front to park his car. Guiltily he realized that he was one of the last of the team to show up. Most of the crew were moving about the shop and he could hear the banter of their exchanges as he walked up to open the door. The preparations of the boat for the Mile attempt had been much more meticulous than Bill had anticipated.

A boat that accelerates out of the corner and ultimately turns hard left is balanced very differently than a boat that goes in a fundamentally never ending straight line. Some of the adjustments were straight forward while others were theoretical in the anticipation of what was going to happen when the boat reached such a high and sustained speed. Questions came up that could only be addressed from a drawing board such as" Would the dissipating weight of the gasoline being exhausted overboard affect the balance of the boat?" The quantity of fuel consumed is of a volume one can imagine if a garden hose is turned on full. At eight pounds

Chapter Thirteen

per gallon, the weight changes could be significant. The only control surfaces that Bill would really have would be the rudder that hung down from the center of the transom. There would be little he could do from an adjustment point of view. Any modifications to the throttle to compensate would defeat the purpose of their efforts. The crew had labored to move the weight, such as the heavy batteries to locations centralized to the Miss Thriftway's center of gravity. Although every conceivable expense in energy, planning and funding had been applied to prepare the boat for the ambitious effort, Bill knew that, in the end, it would still be a roll of the dice.

He had done what little he could do by regularly applying his relatively vigorous workout schedule to maintain his physical fitness. Even though many drivers alluded to the need to be in tough and resilient shape, many of them would admit that Bill took it more seriously than most. Every evening Bill stood in front of the punching bag that hung down in his carport and practiced his rhythm and balance while working out his upper body. The neighbors on either side of the Muncey home were used to the curious pattering that would trickle out from the top of the driveway every day. Other than that, there wasn't a lot that he could provide to the team effort. He had tried to be available for pushing a broom or run an errand, but that had been the extent of his contributions.

He had to admit to himself that there was an odd sense of foreboding in the pit of his stomach. He could not put his finger on it, but a sense of apprehension had grown as this day had approached. It was dramatically different from any kind of race day jitters or prerace butterflies. The last time he had tried anything like this had been back on the Detroit River when he drove the Miss Great Lakes in the Silver Cup competition. In an effort to be competitive, he had taken that boat to speeds she had never gone before. It had not ended well. He had nearly drowned in the process. As he reached for the doorknob to step into the shop he bluntly recalled that back then he did not seem to have a lot to lose. He knew that sometimes ignorance was a blessing. Back then, he had no real idea that someday he would have a wife and two children to love and care for. The sense of community and investment was not even a vague factor for that young man. A house in the suburbs and the life he and his wife had built 3,000 miles from where he grew up starkly represented the dramatic change in his life and the tangible value of what he had accomplished and what he had to lose. On the other hand, no one was holding a gun to his head.

He stepped through the door.

The heat in the shop was dishonestly reassuring. Clearly, someone had gotten there long before him or maybe had been there all night. The salutations extended from the crew were sincere, and he reciprocated with a glib and feigned casualness of "So are we going to do this today? Or what?"

Winking at Joe Lewis who was crouched under the port sponson Bill asked, "What are you up to, Joe? " The tall lanky Lewis was pressing a standard screw driver against a slotted wood screw that helped hold the aluminum running surfaces against the bottom of the sponson. "A few of these had backed off a turn or two during that cold snap last week. " Joe offered." I'm just keeping them tight." He quickly went on, "Nothing to worry about though." Bill nodded and stood up from his own crouch to walk over to the coffee percolator.

Jack Ramsey, the Crew Chief, was standing next to the table holding his perennial pipe in his left hand. Nodding to Bill as he walked up, he sidestepped any salutation and said, " We spun the magneto up to forty eight hundred RPM over at the Boeing wire shop last night. " Biting on the end of the pipe and bringing a match to the bowl Jack went on," Straight and steady from zero to the top." The last was mumbled as he drew the flame through the tobacco, but Bill had been speaking with Jack for years through the pipe and his message was easily understood. The quiet confidence of his chief was represented in the blue smoke he exhaled when he went on to say," We had our tallest propeller magna fluxed, too. No indication of cracks or stress."

Bill knew that the magna fluxing process was expensive but was definitely reassured with the information. The worst thing that can happen to a a hydroplane is to break a propeller while under load. The result is often catastrophic for the boat and driver. Bill had been under Jacks wing for several seasons now. He was grateful and honored to have someone as capable and conscientious as Jack as a crew chief. Not only was he a master of detail, but he had the intense loyalty of the crew. This latter was perhaps the most difficult for a crew chief to acquire. Bill knew that there were other chief's in the business that exuded more energy and camaraderie,

Chapter Thirteen

but Bill wouldn't trade places with any other driver in the sport. As a driver, he was well aware of the secret that you are only as good as your crew chief.

Like a drum roll, the massive doors to the boat shop were rolled aside as the tow truck backed up to the tongue of the boat's trailer. The smell of the gasoline exhaust replaced the heat that spilled out into the fading darkness. Bill and Jack quietly looked on as the crew routinely went about preparing the rolling entourage for its trip over to Ted Jones combination home and shop on the shore of the east channel of Lake Washington. Eventually, without fanfare they rolled into the dawn.

The waters on Lake Washington were calmest in the morning. The initial run was scheduled for ten o'clock. When the team arrived at the home of the Ted Jones family, on the shore facing Mercer Island they were met by the positive but reserved attitude of the boats designer. Ted Jones was not only a respected Boeing engineer, but also he had been an instrumental figure in the development of the three point 'prop riding' concept in a hydroplane. Although technically a French invention dating back to the last century, it took the application of various industrial technologies and the creative innovation of many engineering perspectives to bring the concept through its ensuing evolutions. Often by education and sometimes by intuition, Ted Jones had nudged these high speed motorboats through the latest hurdles of performance. Over six feet tall with dark hair and Hollywood good looks, he exemplified the image of the quiet commitment to excellence projected by the Thriftway Team. This record attempt would nevertheless be a gamble. He knew there was nothing certain about the outcome of the day.

Handshakes and rising sunshine seemed to conspire to expel the damp residue from the rain overnight. The sun tipping over the top of the Cascade mountain range spilled its winter heat against the east side forests and country homes of Mercer Island across the part of Lake Washington called the East Channel. The prevalent mist on the water caught that heat and gradually rose in luminous sheets into the crisp morning air. The channel was essentially half a mile wide for about seven miles of the lake and provided a controllable and stable environment for the record attempt. The only substantial drawback was that the channel had a significant dogleg in it halfway down its length. A layman might suppose that half a mile should be more than enough room to negotiate a gentle turn except that it occurred in the only place where the channel pinched to a quarter mile. At a speed in excess of 170 mph, the driver would definitely have to be on his game. To compound that challenge, a bridge spanned the channel precisely at that point with concrete abutments that restricted the opening to several hundred feet. He would most definitely have to be on his game.

Representatives of the media began to show up as the crew fired up the engine and warmed up its oil. The record attempt had never been a secret, and the public was keenly aware that an attempt at world caliber level was about to occur. Small puffs of white smoke occasionally appeared in the exhaust from the aircraft engine as the individual valves seated and assumed the appropriate shapes determined at operating temperature. Walking about the deck with fire extinguishers in hand, each member sternly searched his portion of responsibility in the engine compartment for telltale fuel, oil, or water leaks. Literally looking for trouble the entire team took this aspect very seriously. Egos totally submerged it would not be uncommon for one member to ask another to QC his work and double check his craftsmanship. Quality control was a collective accomplishment. Each team member took pride in his ability to set his ego aside for the sake of the team's success. Somber faces, nodding heads and complete conversations conducted entirely with eye contact and facial expressions concluded that the Miss Thriftway unlimited type hydroplane was as ready as she would ever be for her Mile attempt.

The quiet was palpable as Bill took his seat in the cockpit of the boat as she was gently held to the dock by two crew members. No instructions to witnesses, media, crew or spectators were needed. This was a special moment. With his left hand resting on the switches on the dash and his right palming the knob of the fuel control lever attached to the right side engine stringer, Bills head looked down in the bilge. As if almost in prayer, his total focus was on the sounds and vibrations coming from the engine as he went through the procedure for starting the 1650 cubic inch Rolls Royce powerplant.

With a frumph and a roar, the driver and his boat lurched away from the dock as the two crew members casually pulled in their

Chapter Thirteen

lines. Quickly attaining 125 mph, Bill carefully watched his gauges for any discrepancies or irregularities. Driving past the buoys that represented the measured mile he took his boat under the East Channel Bridge down past the north tip of Mercer Island to turn her around gradually for his first run. Bringing her back around and pointing her south toward the tiny opening in the bridge four miles away he began to bring up the RPM of the engine. He never liked to take the Rolls Royce over 4,000 RPM. It was said that the V-12 aircraft engine can "get pretty windy" down in the crankcase at that point. This alluded to the clearances of the bearings and the twisting and torsion characteristics of the massive aluminum engine block. The engine was originally designed to exceed 3,000 RPM for only short periods of time; Bill also knew that this effort would require much, much more. As his boat would hop and free wind through a corner in competition, it would commonly but temporarily spike to 4500 RPM.

So far so good.

Attaining a steady 4500 RPM, he noticed that the unique gearbox ratio for this attempt put him at almost 175 mph. As he looked over at the Luther Burbank Reformatory, which was located on the northeast shore of Mercer Island, an unusual thing started to happen. Although he had achieved this speed many times before, it had always been for a relatively short duration. The corner would come up, and the resultant drag of the left hand turn would cause the boats speed to drop. With the sustained speed, the aerodynamics of the boat was able to develop in a way never encountered before.

Although there were many choices for eyewear available, most drivers used some variation of the type used in the operation of aircraft. Some goggle styles actually had plate type glass in angled sections that could easily withstand rain, should an open cockpit situation demand that. On the other hand, a bombardier had to be able to continue seeing his localized bombsight regardless of distractions, and this called for a different design. A fighter pilot had to be able to twist and turn in his cockpit, deal with severe g-forces and contend with the potential of an open cockpit situation. The later style was made out of plastic lenses that were sealed within a rubber rim that would press snugly against Bill's face by way of an elastic strap. He would put them on so tight that often there would be pressed rings into the skin of his face immediately after a heat.

Apparently, the aerodynamic flow over the deck of the Miss Thriftway would ebb and tumble as it tried to get over the cowling and past the windshield and it created an extremely low pressure area around Bill's head. At the speed that he was now maintaining, the effect of this turbulence was such that it literally pulled the goggles straight out in front of his face. By floating out and away from his eyes, the goggles allowed his eyes to water profusely.

A small opening in the span of the East Channel Bridge was blurring and waving, and Bill had to blink repeatedly to get an accurate distance reading. The image wavered constantly, and Bill finally realized that he would have to back off of the throttle in order to let the goggles settle back onto his face. Gripping the steering wheel tightly with his left hand, he reached up with his right and guided the goggles back in place. A spectator up on the sidewalk on the bridge might have thought that he was waving back or maybe saluting in a friendly gesture when, in fact, he was just trying to avoid slamming into the bridge that the fan was standing on.

Clarity prevailed just in time for him to accurately gauge where he needed to be in order to avoid the cement and I beam supports of the bridge.

As he pointed his boat back toward Ted Jones's dock, Bill was thinking of two things. The first was somewhat frustrating. He knew that since his goggle strap was uncomfortably tight that the forces he was dealing with from an aerodynamic point of view must have been substantial. Jack Regas and the Hawaii Kai had just recently set the world's record in the tall 170's and Jack hadn't had this particular problem. This kind of problem can be particularly demoralizing to the crew in that there is not any easy answer and the whole issue is completely unanticipated and especially time consuming. It could take hours of research, discussion, and analysis before a possible solution to the peculiar aerodynamic problem was agreed upon, and subsequent weeks before that solution could be designed, fabricated, and installed. He was sure the answer was there; it could simply take way too long for this attempt.

Then there was that other point about which no one wanted to talk.

February was partly considered a good month for making the Mile attempt in for the primary reason that if a catastrophe occurred, there would be time to effect repair before the start of the

CHAPTER THIRTEEN

race season. That may not be a practical consideration if a cure for the aerodynamic factor took any appreciable time to address. In further thought, this problem could be especially demoralizing to the crew. Although he did not exactly know how, he had to try to avoid that. Bill realized and appreciated that they had worked so hard to get ready for this.

His thoughts went onto another crew. Back in the fall, he and Kit had sat down at the dining room table with six-year old William and four-year old Dorian and had a rare family meeting. The parents had asked the children how they felt about the possibility of having a new little sister or brother. After much discussion it was decided that having a much younger sibling to care for and play with would be a good idea and the Muncey team had decided that it would be ok to "go get one".

Kit had wrestled with the news and debated about whether to tell Bill before today or not. He already had apprehensions about the record attempt. He had gone to considerable effort to make sure that his affairs were in order and that his life insurance was paid up. His Last Will and Testament had even been updated. In the end, she had relented and told him that she was two months pregnant. The stark reality was the risk factor involved with this record attempt was enormous.

A somber face greeted the crew as he pulled up to the dock. Getting out, Bill looked directly at Jack and Ted and motioned toward the shop up from the gantry. They knew immediately that something was up. The three stepped through the door without conversation. Once isolated away from the earshot of the media and the rest of the crew, Bill explained the situation. Jack quietly puffed on his pipe while Ted stared off into a dark corner of his shop deep in thought.

Bill really liked Ted's shop. It had a lot of the traditional wood working tools but it also had an enviable supply of the latest fasteners and specialized equipment for working with aluminum. Bill's shop at home did not have half the capabilities and Bill scanned the walls and counters lost in thought. Then it hit him.

Two words. Simple and crude, but perhaps effective.

"Masking tape," he said out loud.

Like three kids building a tree fort, they plunged into the simple and mutually obvious exercise of taping Bill's goggles directly onto his head. Jack Ramsey, one of the most successful crew chiefs of one of the fastest hydroplanes in the world, Ted Jones, one of the most intelligent and innovative aerodynamic engineers in the world and Bill Muncey, recognized as one of the most capable hydroplane drivers in the world were laughing and joking like twelve year olds as they strapped and slapped the 18 cents worth of painters masking tape onto Bill's face.

Even though Bill quickly pulled his helmet on as the trio walked out into the sunlight, his change in appearance did not discourage the jaws that dropped or the buzz that emanated from fans, crew, and media. Promptly walking back down the dock and into the cockpit, the crew spun the Miss Thriftway around. Bill restarted and gradually drove back into the channel.

This time his approach to the bridge was anticlimactic. Granted, he had to slow a modest amount to negotiate the right hand corner needed to line up and move through, but overall it was a pretty straight forward affair. The goggles did not budge.

Slipping through the span, Bill picked the landmark of the Boeing hangers at the south end of Lake Washington in Renton as an aiming point. Bringing the RPM of the powerful Rolls Royce engine up to 4800, he felt the boat speed increase dramatically. The speedometer climbed into the 180's. The sponsons touched down to the water less frequently. The thunder of the exhaust spewing past the edges of his windshield seeped past the cotton in his ears. Sitting on bare plywood with the padding deliberately removed, Bill could feel the crankshaft harmonics vibrate up through his tailbone.

As he applied a modest amount of pressure against the steering wheel to compensate for the torque, tending to push the nose over to the side Bill felt a soft tapping. He began to realize that what he had thought was a hum coming from the wind vibrating against the cowling was actually coming up from the bilge between his legs. Curiously, the hum seemed to be in concert with the tapping that was growing in severity as his speed increased. Somehow, he knew that it was not coming from the engine. It continued to purr dominantly without the slightest sense of complaint. This was something else.

As the speed climbed closer to 190 on the Keller speedometer, the tapping became more of a knocking. A collateral vibration began

Chapter Thirteen

to shimmy the steering wheel in his hands. Then the nose began to "hunt". Hunting was an expression drivers used to describe the phenomenon a boat sometimes had when it seemed to swing or yaw back and forth apparently "hunting" for a lane in which to to travel. Many boats will do this particularly at the end of the chute, but it lasts briefly and after the driver is aware of it, he can anticipate and compensate. This was not the end of the chute. This was the beginning of the chute with a mile to go. The swing was becoming more pronounced and the shaking of the steering wheel was becoming more violent. The tapping had become knocking. The idea of a linkage failure and total loss of control fluttered across his mind. Careening from sponson to sponson with the rudder rocking limply and impotently back and forth took on a distinct image in his mind. Reflexes and training kicked in and Bill brought the boat speed down to a manageable level. After going through the measured mile or "the Traps", as they were called, the overall speed was negligible compared to the Kai's record of 170 MPH. He brought the boat back to the dock again.

Bill debriefed with his crew. They lifted the boat out of the water and brought her over to where they could inspect the rudder. Jack verified that there wasn't anything obviously wrong with the linkage or the steering. This wasn't going to get fixed with a roll of masking tape. As Ted contemplated the issues, Bill spoke with the media. Downplaying the situation, he assured them that the Thriftway team was the best in the world and that he had all the faith a driver could have that they would attain the record. He did, however, go on to admit to a TV reporter that he was not at all interested in doing this again.

Leaning up against the door jamb of his shop, Ted thoughtfully stroked his chin. The load of the water traveling past the forged steel rudder must be causing some kind of oscillation or vibration as it dissipates and spills past the trailing edge, he thought. He recalled that a dramatic amount of time and expense had gone into making the rudder very straight and very well balanced. Machined and polished, the resistance to the load against it had to have been minimized to the point that the water hardly knew it was there. The common engineers' joke about the water's knowledge took on a real dimension.

"What if the turbulence created by the water as it left the trailing edge of the rudder was alternating back and forth forcing the load to do likewise?" he asked himself. There simply wasn't any data to consider at this level of performance. There was not even anything within the aircraft community with which to compare.

"Maybe some hydrodynamic physicists over at the Hanford nuclear plant might have an idea about vanes and flow that would apply?" he thought. Unfortunately, there was no time for that. He had to come up with something – now!

He knew that he couldn't remove the load or subsequent turbulence. Although… maybe, he could move it? Quietly but with deliberation, Ted Jones walked over to his toolbox and picked up a fifteen inch crescent wrench. Walking over to the transom of the Miss Thriftway still hanging in the air, he squatted down on his haunches and took hold of the bottom of the rudder with his left hand. Looking carefully at the gleaming blade-like surface of the rudder, he verified that the surface was perfect, with no bends or blemishes. Jack Ramsey happened to look over casually in Ted's direction. What he saw next caused him to drop his pipe.

With a strong, lateral, and well-aimed swing, Ted brought the side of the wrench against the side of the rudder. With a clang that would have rivaled the cracking of the Liberty Bell, Jones caused a small dent to appear midway up the length of the rudder. Standing up, he studied and considered his work. Jack walked over and looked down at the newly blemished rudder. Immediately understanding the intent, Jack straight-faced asked, "So, are we ready to try again?"

Ted somberly nodded. Crude, simple, but effective.

Whether that loud clang at the back of the boat was ever explained adequately to Bill is uncertain. The Miss Thriftway was set back in the water and the masking tape reapplied.

A television camera aimed down on the East Channel from the Kennydale Hill near Ted Jones' shop couldn't record the apprehensions Bill had as he pointed his bow toward the north end of the lake. Bringing her up to a comfortable 125 MPH, he was determined to get this done but realized that he would be less than honest if he said that he was confident of the outcome. He had tried to keep any apprehensions he had from showing to the crew. To the fans and the media, he had presented his usual and expected boisterous and optimistic attitude. However, internally, the reality

Chapter Thirteen

of the situation was something different.

Bringing her around and aiming once again at the tiny portal in the East Channel Bridge three miles away he brought the cruising speed up to 150 MPH. Turning right under the bridge the speed increased to 170. The goggles stayed stuck. Carefully glancing down at the dashboard, he saw the speed increase to 185 MPH. The humming started again.

He pressed the foot throttle to the floor and flashed past the first trap marker, and the steering wheel began to vibrate in his hands. Bill focused intently on the huge doors of the Boeing hangers at the south shore of the lake. For the flicker of an instant, he recalled the accident in Madison, Indiana where the Miss Thriftway had bounded from sponson to sponson, torn off its left side, and disintegrated into a flurry of splinters and parts. The cartwheeling blackness following that incident still haunted him today. He forcefully banished the thought and brought his eyes across to stare at the last trap marker.

The entire hull was vibrating as the speedometer blurred around 190 MPH.

"If I'm going to do this," Bill thought, "I'm going to put some serious distance between Jack's record and mine."

A recollection of a hazy, foggy, fluorescent light filling the room when he had regained consciousness in the little hospital in Madison, Indiana flashed through Bill's mind. Mira Slovak had been sitting in his room at the time. Kit was out in the waiting room. "A curious thing to think about at a time like this," Bill thought. "Maybe Mira should be the baby's Godfather. I think Kit would like that."

Mira had been the first Unlimited driver to come to Bill's aid as he floated down the Ohio River. He had not known it at the time, of course, but Bill was deeply touched when he learned that Mira had turned his own race boat around and sped back to the scene of the Bill's accident. In retrospect, Mira's actions of leaping off of his own boat into the water to get to "Billy" were considered by some to be melodramatic. These detractors had obviously never floated unconscious down the Ohio River.

In considerably less than a minute, the exit marker flashed past the Miss Thriftway.

Gently lifting up on the throttle, the vibration began to dissipate.

The Mile

He brought the boat down to a more manageable speed in order to turn her around. The Union of International Motorboating (UIM) required that the same course be traversed within a short time after the initial run in the opposite direction.

The exit marker was now the entrance marker. As it whipped by, Bill's confidence flooded back. Looking over to his right, he noticed an air sock floating over Ted Jones' shop and realized that he was heading into a slight breeze. This might help his speed a bit.

On the return trip, the vibration resumed. The apprehension that attended it before was gone now. The second leg of the effort yielded a speed of 192.513 MPH. Following the Union of International Motorboating regulations, the averaging of the two legs resulted in the official new World Record of 190.001 MPH – a considerable distance from the previous record, indeed.

CHAPTER FOURTEEN

A Simple Tulip

Different people take different things away from success. In some cases, public acclaim and recognition as an accomplished leader within one's community or someone of apparent ability is a redemption of commitment or reassuring proof of competence. For Bill Muncey, he would have been first to highlight the fact that he had been exceptionally fortunate. It was often a case of being in the right place at the right time. Although later in life he would be quoted as saying, "There is no such thing as luck; only God, thorough preparation and follow through", he would also be the first to say that he had often been at a fortunate point in history through no prowess or special attribute of his own. He had often survived shattering accidents without so much as a broken bone, only to see fellows within his sport die from seemingly less traumatic situations. Success and good fortune to him were byproducts of a determined commitment that was extremely susceptible to chance. As an example, he was outspoken in his praise and recognition of his friend Ron Musson as a better driver than he was, and he had said that Ron's fatal accident had only been a case of wrong place at the wrong time. To Bill, success was a very humbling experience.

The 1960's brought the chapter of his accomplishments with the *Miss Thriftway* Racing Team to a spectacular end. Although somewhat sobering during the last season, the team had left a trail of victories that few would ever imitate. Within his community, Bill Muncey had become a household name. This level of notoriety could be a parental challenge when it came to conveying to your offspring realistic expectations and benefits for a commitment to hard work and responsible social behavior. He made a conscious effort to impart on his children the same lessons his parents had conveyed to him. Bill recalled what it was like to be a child in the house of E. L. Muncey. Bill's father had also earned a substantial degree of notoriety in their community and Bill was often referred to not by his own name, but simply as "E. L.'s son."

In spite of acquiring no more than a sixth grade education, Ed Muncey had been nominated for president of General Motors at one time during the 1930's. Bill's uncle and namesake had gone on to be a senator. All of this attention could easily have been head swelling, and Ed was quick to remind his children that half of good fortune is really left to chance.

Perhaps the best example of Bill's humble attitude was conveyed to his children during the rare occurrence when the young family could find time to go on a camping trip. Sitting on log stools around a campfire at the end of a Pacific Northwest spring day, they roasted marshmallows on pointed sticks. Kit would caution her sons about being careful with fire, reminisce about the time when she as a small girl doing the same thing with her parents along Long Island Sound, and relate the tale of the burning marshmallow that had stuck to her forehead. Gathered together next to a borrowed tent and their station wagon, it was obvious that this special family moment was comprised of some very simple but important elements. The sense of satisfaction and accomplishment would settle over the parents as they realized how little it had taken to bring their family together and truly enjoy some of the finer things in life. All the boys were excited to be doing something outdoors and exotic while both Kit and Bill appreciated the fact that this type of situation could be accomplished less than twenty minutes from home. Not expensive or difficult, just fortunate. Yet, it had all the attributes of wealth and success. Bill realized that moments with his family could hardly get better, and he would say out loud, accompanied by the usual crackle of the fire, "I wonder what the poor people are doing tonight?"

At first, this was a puzzle to his children. "Anyone could start a fire, get a stick, and roast a marshmallow," they thought. It didn't take much money. They were not rich. After all, they had to borrow the camping tent.

"What was Dad talking about?" they asked. It wasn't for years that the lesson actually did the job. He spoke the expression only a few more times during the course of raising his family, and each occasion was a simple but sublime situation. The best things in life are usually inexpensive.

At first, it looked like a small flower. A simple tulip, perhaps. In this case, the observers were two families sitting around a fire pit, eating potato salad and sandwiches on paper plates, preparing marshmallows and watching one of the patriarchs preparing to start a fire. There had not been a fire in the pit since the day before

CHAPTER FOURTEEN

and Bill had carefully built a small stick house of fire wood and kindling over the ashes and filled it with compressed newspaper. Over that structure, he had carefully laid a substantial log that would be the intended recipient of the heat generated once the fire got going. Harkening back to his hunting days in the northern forests of Michigan, Bill had learned that a campfire was a classic example of you got out of the project what you put in. The more time and thought invested, the better the fire.

After building this transient structure for the fire, he stepped away to the nearby shore and retrieved a plastic five-gallon container of gas set aside for the outboard engines of the small boats the families had been using. The San Juan Islands in the Pacific Northwest provided many coves and bays to vacation at, and the two young families had created a rendezvous at a cabin on one of the islands. Secluded and only accessible by boat, it provided a respite from the impending demands of the racing season about to start. Each family had three children of comparative ages with the eldest of each able to look after the younger members. All had watched attentively with quiet anticipation as Bill had carefully constructed and prepared the elements of what undoubtedly would be a first rate marshmallow roasting fire.

Unscrewing the cap on the neck of the spout, Bill walked up to the edge of the fire pit and planted his feet about three feet apart. Carefully tipping the gas container toward the center of the pit he allowed a small stream to pour onto the structure he had created. None of the children had ever seen a fire started like this before and had been instructed to sit back until Bill had established the fire. Bill had done such a meticulous job building his little house of sticks and kindling that it seemed almost a shame to burn it down.

As the stream glanced off of the side of the stick house, a small flower grew out of its base. With petals that looked like hands reaching up, the flower innocently began to "grow" up the stream.

Bill instantly realized that coals from the fire the day before had apparently been still smoldering. They quickly lit the base of his structure and that fire continued its ignition along the stream of gasoline being poured from the fuel can. Spinning on the ball of his left foot, Bill turned with the fuel container under his arm down the hill toward the shore. Being a short distance away, he sprinted in an effort to separate the stream from the spout. However, the flower of flame had grown into an arrow that leaped through the air and fastened itself onto the mouth of the spout. Flaring out like a blow torch from the opening, the fire grew as its heat intensity caused the fuel inside to vaporize faster. Leaping down the small hill toward the water, Bill strove to separate himself and his flammable appendage from the families seated around the pit. He shifted the weight of the container to his right hand by its built-in handle. He knew that he had very little time to deal with the issue before it turned into an exploding bomb. Bill felt the intense heat as the spout began to melt and the quantity of the fuel being made available for the fire grew exponentially. Letting the weight of the container carry itself behind him as he leapt toward the water, he let his right arm fall back, and his body weight in motion become the fulcrum that could send the explosive away from the shore into Puget Sound. Swinging it like a discus in high school, he hurled the growing fireball high into the air from the water's edge.

Arcing through the air, the bundle of fire left a trail of sooty billowing smoke that described its path. A surprising distance from shore, the fiery package landed with a pronounced plop on the water and burst into a spreading pool of burning gasoline hurling heat back toward the shore. While the kids made comments from the pebbled shore like, "Cool!" and "Neato!", Bill watched with growing apprehension as the circle of flames widened.

He correctly anticipated the expanding path of growth and bolted into the water. Bill sprinted through the knee-deep waves toward the bow of one of the tethered boats. The water level quickly rose to his hips as he plunged toward the oncoming flames and the dinghy. Racing for the bowline, he secured it in his hand and spun in place. As he lunged back toward the shore, flames licked at the boat's transom. With his legs churning through the sea water, in a burst of adrenalin, determination, and commitment to the task at hand, Bill did not stop dragging the boat until he was several feet up from the water's edge and the boat was completely out of the water. The fire had given brief chase but was unable to keep up, leaving the boat only modestly singed.

Although the time from the first appearance of the simple yellow tulip in the fire pit to the launching of the gas can rocket had taken less than four seconds, everyone in the camp area had risen to his or her feet in silent apprehension. There had barely been time to

Chapter Fourteen

realize what was happening - much less react. All that was left at that point was for the two families to watch as the fire on the water harmlessly but dramatically burned itself out.

In a manner that would do special effects in a James Bond movie proud, the entertainment had been unintended but remarkable. Bill's quick reflexes and the ability to sprint had neutralized the risk of harm, leaving the episode to provide the unquestionable, but dramatic form of entertainment that would give birth to a camping yarn that would evolve into embellished legend for years to come.

A Simple Tulip

Moving a hydroplane on and off the water can be a complicated process.

The alliance between O.H. Frisbie of Atlas Van Lines and racer Bill Muncey produced one of the most formidable hydroplane teams in the history of the sport.

The "Blue Blaster" at near record performance on Lake Washington in Seattle

CHAPTER FIFTEEN

Ice Cream

Bill liked ice cream! His mother had been what some might call an Ice Cream heiress. Hailing from New Orleans, her parents had owned and operated an ice cream company that specialized in the manufacture of gourmet ice cream. On special occasions, like when dignitaries came to town, her parents were contracted to produce fruit flavored ice creams in the shapes of those fruits. Small purple balls of ice cream tasted like frozen grapes. A large red ice cream big enough to fill your palm would taste of apple while a yellow tubular crescent would conjure up the flavor of a banana.

As a young adult, Bill had resolved that alcohol would never be a factor in his life. Although he continued to smoke cigarettes and occasionally enjoyed a good cigar, his personal favorite indulgence was his unabashed love of ice cream. Many times after a day of racing, he would treat his crew to ice cream at a local parlor. A drive into town with his family could be merely a whim for ice cream. Although, on rare occasion, he would suffer through something offered on a stick, he was mostly a banana split man. After all, his grandparents had been successful ice cream aficionados. He had a standard to maintain.

Bill was determined to pursue success in business. He had earned a Bachelor of Arts degree from the General Motors Institute of Business and felt a certain obligation to put the education his parents had paid for to use. He was certain he could not drive race boats forever. His major in marketing could apply the high profile of his racing career to further just about any business he wanted to enter, especially if it was related in some way. He liked to work with his hands particularly in woodworking. The forests of northern Michigan had provided an abundant resource for creative endeavors, and the more recent development of plywood and its cousin, fiberglass, opened up new frontiers in design flexibility. The marine applications of these technologies were still fresh and exciting. Technicians proficient in the use of fiberglass were revered in a similar way to society's reverence for scientists. This was warranted because this new technology would render a product on the "cutting edge" of popular science. Like plywood, fiberglass-reinforced plastic, or FRP, was primarily a product catapulted into society by World War II. Plastic was new, hip and very marketable.

Another development common with Bill's generation was the pastime of waterskiing. Anything that featured people scantily clad, physically active and enjoying the outdoors would be of interest to a consumer-based market raised on Swing music and dancing. The idea of a boat dedicated primarily to skiing was gaining a devoted following. After much soul searching, Bill and Kit rented a small wood shop in Ballard, Washington and under the name of California Marine they started building 16' plywood ski boats. "California" because that state was commonly perceived as a haven for bikinis, bathing suits and sunshine and activities like water skiing. Although Bill kept his full time public relations job with Associated Grocers, he helped promote his California Marine brand to the public at every opportunity. After work at his AG job, he would put in his hours at the California Marine shop like any of the other employees.

An opportunity came up to promote his products at a local boat race on Lake Washington near Kirkland. The spectator crowd would be substantial, and the media would be there. The boats from California Marine were not designed for circle course competition, but he could legitimately enter one of the American Power Boat Association classes that raced under the auspices of the Seattle Inboard Racing Association. The idea that a family boat could actually participate on the race course had some marketing appeal and the media seemed amused at the idea that a successful Unlimited driver would be out there attempting to compete in one.

One of Bill's newest crew members was a young man from Ballard, Washington named Dave Seefeldt. Seefeldt had volunteered to help on the Limited-class inboard hydroplanes that Bill raced on the Northwest circuit. It would be ordinary for a Limited inboard team to attend more than twenty-plus such races a year. David Seefeldt had been both an outboard and inboard driver himself and had proved to be an avid and determined crew member in his own right. For this particular race, Dave was not only tasked with getting the primary race boat ready, but helping with the ski boat also. Bill had come to appreciate the attention to detail David demonstrated. The intelligence of his new friend was remarkable, and Bill came to rely on him often.

Chapter Fifteen

The California Marine ski boat chosen was 16 feet long, constructed out of plywood and fiberglass, and powered with an inline six cylinder Volvo engine. The powerplant did not develop a tremendous amount of horsepower, but it did create a very respectable amount of torque. Torque was the primary element needed to pull a skier out of the water. Attached to the transom was an outboard lower unit that held the propeller and acted as a rudder with which to steer. Very high-tech for its day.

The family version featured a thickly upholstered bench type seat that spanned the beam of the boat and was located directly across and in front of the covered engine. Next to the steering wheel located on the left side of the boat was a conventional style ignition switch that required a key. Unlike a race boat, the key was turned to start the engine just like an automobile. Also unlike a race boat, it had a handle that controlled whether the boat was in neutral, forward or reverse gear.

It has been said with some authority that it takes twenty four man-hours for a race boat to run one minute. In other words, 24 hours preparing, maintaining, building, and/or rebuilding a race boat and its systems for it to run for one minute on the race course. The unique nature of hydroplanes complete with exclusive vocabulary, customized parts, and unique procedures requires attention to a myriad of facts and details unfamiliar to the average motorsport competitor. In addition to that, there is always Murphy's Law, which says that "anything that can go wrong – will go wrong". Boat racing was well acquainted with this law.

On the morning of the regatta at Juanita Beach near Kirkland, Washington, Bill had personally trailered his new California Marine ski boat to the Lake Washington boat launch at a public park. The event was to be held in front of the park. Unlike many race boats, this one did not require a crane to be launched into the water. In fact, Bill had gone to a lot of trouble to make it family-friendly and easy to handle. Seefeldt had assumed the responsibility of getting the actual race boat to the secured area referred to as the "hot pits" and getting it situated for the event.

After floating the ski boat off the trailer and securing it to a nearby dock, Bill parked his car and the trailer in the nearby parking lot. He noticed an ice cream parlor right across the street.

After returning to the ski boat, Bill attempted to start it. That would be the first time Murphy showed up. Turning the switch to the start position accomplished nothing. Although this particular powerplant had always been considered slow to start and get running or "cold blooded", as mariners would call it, this was an obvious case of ignition switch failure. A quick consultation with Dave verified that they did not have any extra ignition switches with the racing supplies. They would have to "hot wire" it. Quickly cutting the wires leading to the ignition switch located on the dashboard, the pair decided to wrap the power lead wire to the ignition wire and then, when the time was appropriate, touch the starter wire to this "wrap" which would allow electrical current to be temporarily diverted down to the starter. Once the engine started, the appropriate wire could be left hanging loose while the "wrap" would continue to direct electricity to the ignition system in order to run the boat. Pretty simple. The pair was pleased with their fix. Not particularly high-tech, but effective.

The start of the first heat was quickly approaching, and they decided Dave would idle the ski boat out of gear at the designated area near the beach where the race boats could be staged prior to the the five minute starting gun. The ski boat was still characteristically slow to start. Once warmed up, Dave unwrapped the ignition wires to stop the engine. While Dave tended to other needs of the boat, Bill went to the public restroom and changed into his driver's suit. This was a one-piece coverall garment manufactured out of a special fire resistant fabric. With helmet and life jacket in hand, he then walked down to the beach near where the ski boat was staged. In the meantime, Dave had donned a pair of rubberized pants that fisherman often used when standing in a river to fish. Held in place with suspenders, this garb enabled crew members to hold the boat in position in the lake while waiting for the five minute gun.

Once the two men met at the shoreline, they proceeded with an odd-looking maneuver particular to boat racing even to this day. It is more difficult than it may seem for a race boat driver to get from the shore to the driver's seat without getting wet. Anything that adds weight to the race boat is to be avoided, including a water-drenched driver. The boat itself cannot be backed up too close to the shore without chancing damage to the propeller, so it becomes necessary for the crew member to transport the driver to the boat on a crew member's back, piggy-back style. Not only is this ungainly, but a slippery rock, lake algae, or misstep occasionally launches both men into the water. Nevertheless, the duo managed to sidestep Murphy, minimize the drama of the moment and successfully get Bill planted on the bench seat behind the steering wheel without incident.

Yet, as is the norm with boat racing, both Murphy and his attendant drama prevailed. Here was an accomplished Unlimited hydroplane driver about to answer the call of the five minute gun and ride his steed out on to the race course. Every onlooker and fan knew that the ski boat would place poorly by virtue of the fact that it was not configured for competition. Yet public curiosity was piqued with the thought that if it could do anything at all, Bill was the driver to do it. Media had anticipated its appearance and were on hand to chronicle the event. Some knew that the boat was his personal creation, but most were just amused to see the effort.

"One-to-the-five" was the call that blared out over the public address system, announcing one minute until the five-minute gun would be fired. Bill firmly wrapped the ignition wires together and held them in his left hand. Grabbing the starter wire in his right hand, he poised the stripped end over the bundled wrap.

"Five, four, three, two, one." "Bang!" went the five minute gun. Dave gave the boat a gentle push away from shore so that the propeller would not dig into the shore when she started to spin.

When Bill touched the starter wire to the ignition wrap, it did indeed perform the task of turning the engine over and gaining ignition. Dave later said, "That engine was always cold to start and slow to accelerate, but not that day. Oh no. That day she fired right up and started making power."

Bill moved the gear lever into the forward position and quickly applied full throttle in order to move the boat to a planing attitude as fast as possible. The inboard – outboard drive system for a boat was a relatively new idea. New technology, new parts, new theories. It was never determined when the mistake was made, but it was later apparent that one could purchase a propeller that would rotate the wrong way. Instead of digging down and gaining traction, the transom of the ski boat rose up as full power from the Volvo Penta engine was applied, and it's remarkable torque proceeded to reverse the boat up onto the beach, pulling the sixteen foot hull and its unwitting driver past the shoreline and completely out of the water. Bill realized the problem but could not get his hands off of the steering wheel and grab onto the wires now bouncing around in the bilge. The hull bucked back and forth pivoting on the now fully exposed lower unit with the nose dragging in the beach sand. After a great deal of fumbling, Bill finally wrested the wires apart, and the engine stopped. With the hull unceremoniously tipped resting on its side, Bill rolled out onto the beach on his hands.

The sound of the other boats motoring onto the race course was somehow drowned out by the silence of the crowd watching Bill and Dave and their beached boat. Bill stood up with sand pasted all over his pant legs and with a quick, almost violent flick of the wrist undid the chin strap of his helmet. Bill later said, almost convincingly, to a TV reporter, "I believe I delicately placed my helmet in the bilge of the boat. I don't think that helmet will work again," Bill finished.

With his hands at his side and a pursed lip, he turned to Dave.

Both knew that Dave had ordered the propeller and installed it. Dave had unquestionably made a mistake that was as apparent as could be. Ordering the wrong part was one thing. Installing it and not noticing the wrong rotation was another. Dave felt awful, responsible, and vulnerable in the first place. In the second place, he had unwittingly formulated this to happen to someone he truly cared for and admired.

Rage, fear, and frustration evaporated when Bill saw the rueful expression on Dave's face.

Muncey took a deep breath, looked Dave straight in the eye and said, "Oh hell, Slim, let's go get some ice cream."

Together they walked out of the park and across the street.

Dave Seefeldt preparing equipment for competition, May 1962

Front row left to right: Kit Muncey, Bill Muncey, George Simon, and Penny Simon. Back row left to right: unknown, Commander Cooper, Dave Seefeldt, Ricky Iglasius, unknown, unknown, unknown.

The Miss U.S. Unlimited hydroplane, prior to its renovation.

The Miss U.S. Unlimited hydroplane, after renovation.

CHAPTER SIXTEEN

Testing

Graceful and elegant. Two words not commonly associated with a motorsport and definitely not with something that is hurtling over the water at high speeds. Nevertheless, when a hydroplane twists into a corner the rising arc of its roostertail seems to gently bend and flow behind it like ice from the blades of an Olympic skater. Steady, seamless at a height majestic and surreal. The observer feels a sense that this is an imagined transient image. It can't be real. A curtain of water weighing thousands of pounds is being lifted into the air by a comparatively small vessel with the tip of a propeller smaller than your hand? An apparently effortless act that deems the two words appropriate. Nimble and deft would be two other unlikely but applicable words. If a driver were in a separate boat on either side of that roostertail, or better yet in between two roostertails, they would find themselves occupying a truly transient and ethereal space. A curving, cavernous channel where the end may be out of sight. Depth, speed, and distance are distorted by virtue of towering, cascading walls that flicker out the sun and cause shadows to strobe across the cockpit. If the temperature is just right, misty vapor raised by the propellers cavitations will drift slowly over your bending path of travel. Since so much of the hull is out of the water, the resistance at the steering wheel is nominal. With a remarkable sensitivity to command, a competent driver can usually put the sponson of his boat within six inches of where he wants it

Ungainly and cumbersome is the kindest way to put it. An unlimited-type hydroplane is perhaps the most ungainly creation ever placed on dry land. Even an airplane has the ability to travel on land over short distances in preparation for takeoff or landing. Other marine craft of similar length usually has a trailer which was designed specifically for transport and to look unassuming as it goes. Any effort to try and approach this result with a hydroplane would be like rearranging the deck chairs on the Titanic - a total waste of time.

The development of the "air trap" or the space between the sponsons that helps create the lift for the boat has become so

Testing

spread apart that the hydroplane is too wide to go down the road legally in most countries because it takes up more than one lane of a roadway. The answer was to place the craft on a cradle or set of "bunks "on the trailer, then with the assistance of hydraulics, the hydroplane is tilted approximately 45 degrees so that it is confined within the legal width limits needed for transport. On one hand, this looks particularly unstable as if it is about to tip over. On the other hand, drawing attention to a sponsor's name emblazoned across the deck and cowling can be a good thing. In either case, it most certainly does attract attention.

Usually, with an unlimited type hydroplane, it takes a crane just to get it on and off the trailer. Two or three people are needed to ensure that it is set properly on the bunks since improper placement as it goes down the road can warp the shape of the whole boat. All in all, a lot of time and care goes into just getting the race boat from point A to point B; just one more reason that it has been authoritatively opined that it takes about twenty four man-hours to run the hydroplane on the water for one minute.

Part of that statistic is the amount of testing that goes into preparing for competition. Testing is a big part of racing and hydroplane competition is no exception. The attention to detail and the collective intellect needed to campaign is often obscured in lap times and race results. Managing the team's resources into an orchestrated effort that could produce a world champion is a full time job. Simply put, the more testing time, the better you run.

George Simon had earned his place in an Unlimited cockpit back in the fifties. Named for the Detroit-based U.S. Equipment Company he had built post World War II, Simon had jockeyed the Miss U.S. around many race courses competently. However, his wife, Penny Simon, made a good argument that it might be more sensible for George to help tend to the raising, health and welfare of their ten children than the care and feeding of a hydroplane flying over the waves of the Detroit River.

George had already had a profound influence on motorsports, as an owner when he single- handedly contested the Internal Revenue Service assertion that motorsports was merely a disguised hobby and not a true marketing business expense. Still generating benefit for businesses and fans today, the decision arrived at in court set the precedent that motorsports was a legitimate marketing/adver-

Chapter Sixteen

tising expense that did, in fact, generate sales. Although obvious and constantly proven by today's standards, Simon's stance was by no means certain and constituted a substantial personal and financial risk at the time.

The compromise between Penny Simon and her husband had focused George's talents in search of a driver who could also act as Team Manager year round. He ultimately found that combination in Bill Muncey. While the Miss U.S. had all the right equipment, it was in the wrong state of the Union for Bill to manage it during the non-racing season. The team and its equipment was relocated to Seattle, Washington with Bill attending to all the administrative details including the team headquarters, personnel, local business relationships, and maintenance of the equipment.

Bill immediately enlisted the support and the enthusiastic participation of Dave Seefeldt. Together with future Budweiser crew chief Dave Culley, who had been an employee of Ted Jones and volunteers they toiled through that winter refreshing and refurbishing the V-12 powerplants. If the engines were rebuilt and assembled according to military specifications, it would take up to 1500 man-hours each. Learning what corners to cut and where to apply later technologies that would speed up the process was a daunting task. The concept of an inboard skid fin was gaining greater acceptance for helping the boat get through corners and was top on their list for this hull.

The tail section directly behind the driver was completely redesigned and rebuilt. Sporting a dipping shape configured and designed by Bill, it created a unique profile of which he was proud. Friends would tease him about the fact that the form was reminiscent of a D.A. haircut that had been popular in the fifties. Bill would laugh it off and say," Yeah, that's probably where I got the idea."

The day to test the Miss U.S. Equipment Company on Lake Washington arrived. While all the engines that would travel over the road with the tools and other equipment were kept in a forty foot covered trailer, the boat itself was transported by a flatbed truck dedicated solely to that purpose. After checking of lists, double and triple inspections, and any other quality control feature or procedure the crew could think of, they meandered away from the South Park part of Seattle where the team was headquartered,

Testing

up over Beacon Hill and down to the marina on Lake Washington. All systems had run well in the shop, and the team was eager to test some new propellers.

Lake Washington lays in a north-south direction directly to the east of Seattle. Fourteen miles long and relatively deep, it provides ideal conditions for testing an unlimited-type hydroplane for one special reason. There is no speed limit 100 yards off shore. As long as the driver keeps the boat out in the lake away from shore, he can go as fast as he likes, but he is still subject to the standard maritime rules and regulations. This was one of the main reasons that the Miss Thriftway was able to set the mile record; lots of room and no top-end limits. Bill was excited.

Muncey also had a lot on the line. He had not driven a boat with this kind of potential in years, not since the Thriftway days. That was a very well-financed team with a large crew, a first-rate hull, and one of the best crew chiefs in the history of the sport, the legendary Jack Ramsey. It was not that the Miss U.S. was underfinanced. It was that he and David had never been responsible for the actual set-up and operation of an unlimited-type hydroplane before. Nevertheless, Bill was optimistic.

The marina they chose had a crane in place. The chase boat which would be on the water in case of trouble had been brought over earlier in the day. A sixteen foot "baby" Donzi, her six-cylinder engine, had plenty of torque in the event that it needed to pull the Miss U.S. back to the dock. Maximum running time on the water was the goal and anything that helped avoid taking the boat out of the water for minor adjustments was a bonus. The little Donzi "chase boat" had plenty of speed should a crew member need to get to the hydroplane and make tweaks or corrections.

As the crane swung the Miss U.S. up, off her trailer, and set her back down in Lake Washington, Dave Culley warmed up the chase boat and idled at the dock. Dave Seefeldt tended the bow line while another volunteer looked after the stern. Bill climbed into the cockpit, settled into the seat and looked toward Seefeldt. The pair exchanged two short nods, and Bill stared down into the bilge, focusing his senses on hearing the cycles of the engine as he began the starting sequence. The unique squeaking, squealing, and thunk that the aircraft starter normally makes when turning the engine over disappears once the unmuffled exhaust of the Rolls

Chapter Sixteen

Royce roars to unbridled life. World War II surplus engines now powered virtually all Unlimited-type hydroplanes (with very few exceptions). The British Rolls Royce Merlin V-12 engine had one distinct advantage over its American counterpart, the Allison engine. Although slightly smaller with 1,650 cubic inches, the Rolls had a two-stage supercharger or "altitude compensator" that allowed quicker acceleration. The Miss Thriftway hydroplane that Bill had driven several years before established the British creation as highly competitive, and he was intent on reasserting that standard with the Miss U.S. team.

Reaching a planing attitude at about 75 MPH, the bow dipped down, and the Miss U.S. made her way out toward the middle of the south end of Lake Washington. Mentally imprinting an imaginary course, Bill alternated his gaze from the dashboard and the myriad of gauges there to the ripples and swells on the water in front of him. After verifying that the vital systems to the engine signaled healthy numbers, he put the foot pedal down and proceeded to put the Miss U.S. through her paces.

Gently leading her through the first corner, he was pleasantly surprised at her response to the helm and the fact that the new inboard skid fin was working as hoped. The tendency for the hull to tip out of the corner and try to keep going straight was dramatically less than the last boat he had driven and the new propeller was maintaining its purchase very consistently. Coming out of the corner in front of Seward Park, the roostertail arcing behind rose dramatically as they accelerated up the imaginary " front chute " 300 yards off shore.

Other than the chase boat, there were no other boats in the area. The fact that they had chosen later in the day toward dinner time to run the test had paid off. Taking her through the next corner went equally well as Bill maintained the same level of load while asking her to decrease the radius at the apex. Holding the revolutions per minute steady, he cut through the "infield" and headed back to the dock.

Fortunately, the chase boat was also able to return promptly to signal the crane operator and prepare to lift the boat out of the water for a propeller change. Bill was excited. The crew was very upbeat. Hundreds of winter man-hours were showing definitive progress in the performance of their boat. They were well aware that it was very early to make any definitive judgments, but it was difficult to minimize their exuberance. Even Bill blurted to a crew member, "That sled is coming out of the corners at a hundred and forty five miles per hour! I haven't seen that since the Miss Thriftway."

With the propeller changed, and the boat refueled; Bill hopped back into the cockpit. Nodding again to the crew tending the lines, they cast off, and Bill restarted. As the Miss U.S. pulled away from the dock, the crew scrambled into the chase boat and hurried out on to the course. They brought the boat back down to idle prior to actually getting into the infield and were able to position themselves well between the course and the dock.

Early evening in the spring in the Pacific Northwest is a study in fading light and varying temperatures. Clouds drifting in front of a lowering sun can create contrasts that are the envy of professional photographers and long shadows encourage residents to wear layered clothing. Shadows from the trees in Seward Park stretched out over the lake up to a quarter of a mile in spikes and valleys punctuated by pinks and yellows from a sun descending toward the Olympic Mountains.

The crew did not notice it at first, but a police boat had motored into the middle of the course. Since all the required notices and permits had been posted, they presumed that law enforcement was there to help keep any spectators out of harm's way. No one on board gave it another thought. After all, it is very difficult to alter the course of an unlimited type hydroplane if a spectator boat unwittingly drives into its path at the wrong time.

Bill noticed the police boat right away. Sitting in the middle of the course toward the Seward Park side, he mentally computed its rate of travel and logical course. "Shouldn't be a problem," he thought. As he turned the Miss U.S. into the north turn, he decided that he did not particularly like the way that this "wheel" planted itself with the shifting load. He decreased the throttle in order to keep the boat on track. Bringing her past the apex of the corner and up to where the exit pin would be he looked down toward the other end of the course.

Sitting on the padded seat of the chase boat, Dave Seefeldt's jaw slowly lowered. He had immediately noticed a drop in the roostertail as she went through the corner. That was not a concern. What

Chapter Sixteen

was a concern was what the police boat was doing. As Bill was heading out of the corner, the police boat was accelerating into the path of the race boat. Throwing out a substantial wake, the officer had pointed his vessel out from the center of the course and headed directly toward Seward Park. "What the heck is he trying to do?" Dave asked himself. Then it occurred to him with the impact of a wrecking ball. Out loud, he answered the same question that was on the faces of the other crew members. "He's going to try and pull Bill over!"

From Bill's cockpit things started to happen fast. He quickly noticed that the police boat had changed from an idle to a faster speed. That fact in itself was not a threat. What was a threat was the enormous wake that the police boat had just hurled onto the course. At the speed that Bill was going, unless carefully negotiated it could cause his boat to leap out of control. Rapidly calculating the rate of travel he determined that if he maintained his own speed the roller would probably pass behind him out of harm's way. On the other hand, the police boat itself was doing just the opposite.

The police officer had deployed his boat directly in the path of the race boat which was still traveling at over a 130 miles per hour. "What is this guy thinking?" Bill asked himself.

The answer was spontaneous. The red lights on the police boat came on. Bill suddenly realized that this particular officer had absolutely no idea of two important facts. One: there was no way that the Miss U.S. or any other hydroplane could stop before reaching his boat. Two: at the rate of closure between the two boats Bill only had milliseconds to make a decision on how to avoid impact.

Choice one was to drive in front of the police boat into the safety zone in front of Seward Park. This was not desirable because he honestly did not know if anyone was there, and he did not know if he could correct soon enough to avoid running up over the beach and into the trees. The other choice was to turn into the rolling wake behind the police boat and deal with an uncertain landing.

The same choices were simultaneously occurring to his crew chief. The crew had stood up in the boat speechless. Dave Culley's right hand absent mindedly traveled up to the top of his head and rested its palm there. Dave Seefeldt mumbled, "What the ... is Bill going to do?"

Then Bill thought of a third choice.

Somehow, he had to signal the severity of the situation to the police officer. There simply was not time.

Bill pushed the throttle down. The officer had the only card left to play that could avoid an accident.

Every mouth on every crew member grimaced, biting lips in tense anticipation as they watched the roostertail of the Miss U.S. sparkle and catapult another twenty feet into the air. The sound of the increased power of the Rolls Royce engine thundered over the lake at 600 miles per hour. Twenty eight feet of race boat immediately rocked with the increased load. The sun reflected off of the deck in flashes as she galloped from shadow to shadow. Bill spread his knees apart against the sides of the cockpit in a vain attempt to brace for impact.

The police officer stared in disbelief as this plywood missile made an obvious and unignorable statement that it wasn't going to slow down. For the flicker of an instant, it occurred to him that he was a target. Regardless of the conclusion, he had to pull ahead, or it was going to be bad. Slamming the throttle full forward and staring straight ahead, the young officer hurled his boat toward Seward Park. Quickly turning to look back, all he saw was an elongated bright red blur flash past his transom missing by inches. The roar was deafening, and the deluge from the roostertail doused his boat from stem to stern. Understandably frightened and furious that the driver had not stopped he turned his patrol boat after the race boat and gave pursuit with red lights flashing and siren blaring.

Simultaneously, Bill still had his hands full. Although he had not had to contend with a full blown wake, the hole in the water temporarily created by the leaping police boat had provided a cavity into which his right sponson could drop. This caused the left side of the boat to rise. When the right sponson bounded up out of the hole, it started a chain reaction causing the hull to rock back and forth from side to side. Whipping Bill's body like a rag doll, he tried to maintain control by averaging the amount of time that the rudder was violently dipping in and out of the water. The Rolls Royce free spun crazily over its redline as the 28-foot, 5500 pound hydroplane twisted and bucked. The two-blades of the propeller alternately stabbed the surface of the water, sending a shock wave up the drive train through the engine that caused the entire shape of the hull to distort and flex. The back brace that Bill always wore

Chapter Sixteen

under his driving suit dug deeply into his ribs.

Plunging up and down, the rudder jerked and twisted with the alternating load. Swaying left and right; Bill was able to average out the corrections at the steering wheeling while resisting the natural temptation to pull his foot off of the throttle. He knew that doing so would have exaggerated the bucking bow to stern. Slowly, the violent gyrations of the Miss U.S. began to subside.

Some people say that it is a learned phenomenon. Others contend that it is a kind of paranormal activity or a form of ESP. Still others suggest that it is just another example of deductive reasoning. Regardless of which, the relationship and thought processes between a driver and his crew chief often resemble an uncanny common stream. Dave Seefeldt not only knew exactly what his driver was thinking but also exactly what needed to happen next. First, with all the damage done to the engine and other equipment that he just saw and heard he knew that they were done for the day. The dips and valleys the crew witnessed in the fluctuating rooster-tail across the lake told him that there would be magna-fluxing to a rudder and propeller in the impending future. Second, now that Bill had regained control of his craft, he also would recognize that they were done for the day. Bill was returning to the dock so there was no reason for the chase boat to be idly sitting in the water. Thirdly, considering the speed with which the police boat was also heading toward the marina, it appeared to Dave inevitable that his driver and the law enforcement officer were going to have a discussion.

"William is not going to be happy," Dave said to the crew as they also anticipated the next sequence of events. He knew with certainty that the sooner he could get that boat back on the trailer, the better for all concerned. As he pulled the Donzi up next to the dock, he signaled the crane operator that they would be lifting the hull out with the universal hand signal of the index finger pointed skyward rotating in a circle. The operator responded with a deep nod, puffed on the cigarette projecting from the corner of his mouth and fired up his diesel engine. With a rumble and a belch, a perfectly round black circle of smoke rippled up out of the crane's exhaust pipe mimicking the smoke from its operator's mouth. As its boom swung out over the water, the crew scrambled out of the chase boat and took up their appropriate stations on the dock.

Bill had covered thirty times the same distance in almost the same time it took the chase boat to get there. He shut down his systems and drifted the Miss U.S. gently into the dock. Crisply he said to his team, "Let's take her home." As he took his helmet off, he looked up at his crew chief's face and saw Dave's gaze focused out on the water behind him and before Bill even turned around, he already discerned this day wasn't quite wrapped up yet. Turning, Bill saw the police boat coming on them at full speed. Looking back at his crew chief, he said, "David, we might want to hurry this along."

The crew made a deliberate effort not to make eye contact. It was obvious and understandable their driver was cross. They tried to focus exclusively on the effort of setting the boat on the trailer and bolting her down until they overheard conversation between the police officer and Bill. Initially the officer was outspoken and brusque but his demeanor changed when Muncey pointed out the fact that there was no speed limit on the lake 100 yards offshore - a distinction of which the young officer was unaware. Bill tried very hard, with limited success, to contain his anger as he pointed out the dangerous experience they had just shared. Describing the basic physics involved when attempting to stop a hydroplane operating at a very high rate of speed was equally educational to the officer.

The last thing that the crew heard as they pulled the Miss U.S. out of the marina was Bill saying to the chastised officer, "Running lights? What do you mean running lights? It's not even sundown yet!"

CHAPTER SEVENTEEN

In the Saddle

If you stood up in the stirrups with the reins in your hand and leaned forward over the withers or shoulders of the steed as it galloped along, the feeling of power and speed would reflect the feeling of driving a hydroplane. Maybe standing up on the foot pegs of a motorcycle and leaning over the headlight as the wheels bumped over some modestly lumpy terrain, or some have likened the sensation to sitting on a piece of plywood (which is closer to the truth) and hovering over the water with little directional control. The most telling aspect that is usually experienced is the surprise of the dramatic speed the craft can reach compared to what the driver's senses suggest. It is common for a rookie driver to bring the vessel up on plane for the first time and feel a sense of sluggish response to the controls, lack of acceleration, and an anxious need for more speed when a glance at the speedometer reveals the boat is literally flying along at 125 mph.

Twenty-six to thirty feet of boat, 12 – 14' wide, gliding over the water with anywhere from 1500 to 3000 horsepower. Sailing around a 1200-foot diameter corner, one end of the boat twists and flexes slightly as it dissipates the tremendous forces pressing against it. Since it doesn't have any substantial shock absorbing system like an automobile and must address these forces much like the wing of an aircraft which merely bends with the load, a hydroplane truly has more in common with an airplane than a boat.

The boat had felt good to Bill that week during the pre-race qualifying attempts. Not great, but good. She had set a string of victories over the course of the season that was truly enviable. Almost from its debut, she had set standards that essentially raised the bar for the entire sport. Designed, built and crew chiefed by Jim Lucero, design refinements constantly upgraded her performance at each race during her initial season. The enhanced performance had the team dominating the circuit.

Many felt that when Jim Lucero left the team to be crew chief for the rival Pay and Pack Racing Team it would end the performance curve of the "Blue Blaster" as the Atlas Van Lines team's boat had come to be known. There was some solid foundation for this opinion. Jim had come to demonstrate that not only was he a capable boat designer, but also some felt that he was perhaps the best crew chief, or at least team manager, the sport had ever seen. Although he probably would have pinned that distinction on Jack Ramsey of Thriftway fame, Lucero had definitely shown an aptitude for fine-tuning the performance of his team and equipment to suit the needs of each regatta and the specific race courses. That hands-on leadership had driven the team to raise the bar for the sport's standards.

Lucero's replacement, Dave Seefeldt, had just come out of retirement after spending several years away from the sport. Many doubted that he could get any more out of a boat that had already attained a pinnacle of sorts. Although from years of racing together he had developed that unique relationship with his driver that is indispensable, he never had the benefit of a front running team as a crew chief. His time as crew chief of the Miss U.S. had exposed him to some essential experience, but the finances backing that program were lesser and the resulting performance mirrored the team's checkbook.

The biggest difference between Jim Lucero and Dave Seefeldt was leadership style. Anyone who ever met Jim Lucero knew that they were talking to an intelligent, eloquent, and forceful person. His attention to detail was ruthless and efficient. Six-foot tall, clean shaven and dark hair, he could be charming and thoughtful. He did not, however, suffer fools well. His crew was intensely loyal, because he reciprocated and was not afraid to get his hands dirty. He could do this primarily because there really was not much that there was to be done in the sport of Unlimited hydroplane racing that Jim had not done. From designing and building a boat to rebuilding an engine, from maintaining team morale in the face of disappointment to personally slapping a coat of varnish on a sponson's running surface, Jim was a passionate scholar of the sport and had occupied just about every possible station on a racing team.

Dave Seefeldt's leadership style was a stark contrast. Although the experience level was comparable, the style of interface with the crew was dramatically dissimilar. Any passion on his face effectively hid behind a beard that would rival that of a Civil War general. Shorter than Jim and slightly balding, Dave did not come across as an intense individual. In fact, he had a natural aptitude

Chapter Seventeen

to make a new acquaintance comfortable and at ease. He seemed to project commitment to his teammates that said, "You're here because you want to be, I don't need to push you the rest of the way." His capacity for patience seemed limitless.

Perhaps that was Seefeldt's greatest strength because it would take tremendous patience to get anything more out of equipment that many had felt had already peaked. First, he had had to start with rebuilding a team.

Second was the equipment. The Budweiser Racing Team was the nearest competition and was aptly chiefed by a former Miss U.S. teammate, Dave Culley. Budweiser Team Owner, Bernie Little, was a formidable opponent and his team would not be sitting idle during the off-season.

Upon review, Dave determined that the most effective way to increase performance for the Atlas was not to focus on the engine first, but to upgrade the propeller. Often an overlooked aspect to the performance of a hydroplane, experienced competitors might argue that propeller design can account for twenty percent of the boat's performance. Although Seefeldt legitimately had design ideas of his own, he called upon the counsel of the legendary Jack Ramsey for advice. The collaboration led them to a Northwest builder, and a new design was born. Muncey was skeptical at first. He too knew how important the propeller is, and he was leery about changing something that already worked well. Bill had invested heavily in a large inventory of propellers but in Dave's opinion, their design was outdated. Not happy news, nevertheless, Bill backed his chief and supported the collaboration.

Thirdly, review the engine program. Jim Lucero was a meticulous builder of Rolls Royce engines. There was not going to be a lot that you could do with the existing program that had not already been done without a radical departure from the norm. Any student of the internal combustion engine would attest that the Rolls Royce Merlin V-12 engine was a work of art in motion to begin with. Displacing 1650 cubic inches, its strength was the "upper half" or induction system that featured a two-stage supercharger or altitude compensator. The air/gas mixture would be compressed twice before it arrived at the combustion chamber. This, by itself, constituted a substantial departure from its American brother, the Allison engine, which stood at 1710 cubic inches. Although the

Allison only had a single stage supercharger, it did have a superior feature of its own. Its lower end or crankshaft assembly was clearly superior to the Rolls Royce. The components such as the piston connecting rods were of better strength and design enabling them to deal with higher load and torque. Perhaps more important, they were able to deal with the horrendous varying loads that were commonplace in hydroplane applications.

Automotive engine manufacturers often underestimated this factor and optimistically entered the hydroplane arena with substantial horsepower and torque-rated powerplants only to find that the pulverizing load pulses sent up through the propeller shaft as the boat bounced through a corner were disguised nudges toward the scrap heap.

These aircraft powerplants were not impervious to the mechanical abuse, shocks demanded by combat, so the standard and quality demanded by that type of aircraft service enabled them to live longer on a brutal hydroplane race course. The shortest distance to a better powerplant for the Atlas team was to integrate the best features of both aircraft engines. This would take additional funding beyond the current operating budget of the Atlas team.

O.H. Frisbee was the chairman of the board of the Atlas Van Lines furniture moving corporation. Frisbee was from Detroit, Michigan, which was one of the most dynamic boat racing towns in America. The story was that O.H. helped found the Atlas Van Lines company with one truck and a pair of ice tongs back in 1947, when the delivery of ice for the family ice box was a very competitive business in high demand.

O.H. was acquainted with the need for attention to detail in any competitive effort and was not afraid to get personally involved. Although Bill already had one of the most lucrative contracts in the marine motorsport world, he realized that he would have to do something to enhance the performance of the team if he were going to answer to the threat of the Budweiser's ongoing development of the huge Rolls Royce Griffon engine with its additional 600 cubic inches.

The Miss Budweiser hull was the first Unlimited-type hydroplane designed and built around a particular model and kind of engine. Bernie Little had enlisted the considerable talent of designer Ron Jones, Sr. to create a craft literally around the particular dimensions

CHAPTER SEVENTEEN

and specifications of the British powerplant that displaced well over 2,000 cubic inches. Parent company, Anhaueser-Busch, made a financial commitment to the project that was substantial.

Bill consulted at length with his crew chief on the subject of where they could get more power out of their engine. Once determined, it was now his responsibility as the owner to go find the resources to attain that goal. Fortunately, for Muncey and the Atlas Van Lines Racing Team, O.H. Frisbee was a competitive individual. By outlining the plan and presenting the cost, Bill convinced him to help acquire the additional funding.

With the assistance of fellow teammates Glen Davis and Tim Tafil, they had managed to take the better connecting rods of an Allison aircraft engine and graft them onto a Rolls Royce aircraft engine crankshaft. Additionally, they remanufactured the Rolls Royce pistons so that the piston ring was machined at a higher point on the piston creating more compression and therefore, more power.

After countless hours of studious research and meticulous assembly, the Atlas team was able to fund, create, and prepare two complete powerplants of this exotic configuration. The horsepower output was most likely near the 3,000 mark, and no one could offer any kind of guarantee of its life span. The Rolls Royce engine was originally rated to perform between 2500 and 3500 revolutions per minute under constant load. In competition on an Unlimited race course, these engines would see 5,000 RPM under varying loads.

The game plan was ambitious.

As Bill brought the Blue Blaster down off of a plane from the Seattle race course, he guided his boat over to the dock where his team stood with lines and boat hooks. Dave Seefeldt was standing on the dock with his arms crossed over his chest and a straight face. His signature straw cowboy hat was tipped forward over his face. The qualifying run had felt fast, but not that fast. Bill was eager to learn the results in lap average speeds. The engine that he had just used was not one of their new exotic powerplants. Those engines would be conserved for ideal circumstances, and the Seattle race course had some inherent challenges that rendered it less than ideal.

First, the log boom that paralleled the race course had proven over the years to be ineffective in dispersing the wakes that rolled up to it from either direction. The majority of the wakes and rollers spilled over from the spectator traffic between the log boom and Mercer Island. Hundreds of boats carrying thousands of fans and festive spectators would troll back and forth in the qualifying periods during the week leading up to the Seafair Regatta. Especially at slow speeds, their wakes would be significant.

Then there was the "Genesee Cut." The Stan Sayers pit area was located off the Seattle shoreline on Lake Washington at what would best be described as the base of a bowl. The geographic bowl was dissected by Genesee Avenue which inadvertently caused the wind to funnel through it, out onto the race course directly next to the pit area. This created a depression in the adjacent water that was indiscernible to the naked eye, but when traveling at speeds over 100 mph, the equivalent of a thirty foot wide ditch in the water. This ditch often unsettled a high speed boat traveling and could contribute to accidents and blow-overs. Over the years, several accidents were initiated by this depression when either a driver failed to anticipate its presence or the wind came up unexpectedly. Conditions like these were not what records were made of.

Nevertheless, the propeller had felt good.

Stepping off the boat, Bill removed his helmet and placed his combination goggles/glasses in it by force of habit. Taking Dave's proffered hand, he swung up onto the dock and immediately asked what his time had been.

"I don't know David," he said. "She didn't feel that strong to me out there." The prop seems to be doing its job, but she doesn't seem that fast."

After years of racing together, they would often feign formality in calling each other by their full names. Dave would sometimes be David, and sometimes Bill would be William. Not many people could call Bill 'William'. It was a term of endearment that few ever earned.

"Well, I don't know about that, William. Your time was around 137 mph," Dave replied in a matter of fact, monotone voice, letting his words sink in slowly.

Bill's jaw dropped slightly. He looked up and noticed crowds of people were looking at them. Apparently, the loudspeakers of the public address system had been drawing attention to the near lap average record run as the Atlas was on the course. The speed

A happy moment at home.

Left to right: Bill Muncey, Tim Ramsey, and Dave Seefeldt.

Going through the sophisticated starting sequence of the Rolls Royce engine demanded focus and concentration. Note the tongue sticking out

The 'Blue Blaster' Crew Chief, Dave Seefeldt, during a reflective moment in the racing pits. (Above). Tim Tafil (Left)

Bill Muncey as the driver of the Atlas Van Lines Unlimited Hydroplane.

Chapter Seventeen

Dave stated constituted a lap average approaching World records. Moreover, that had not been with one of the special powerplants.

Although Dave Seefeldt had set the world record at seventeen minutes for an engine change in a hydroplane during his Miss U.S. years, Bill quickly dismissed the idea of swapping the engines today. There was not time, and this was not the place. And David wasn't suggesting it. He also knew that the potential may be there, but the Seattle course was not the best place to try the record. It may be possible with this team, but it would not be prudent.

"Well what do you think, David? Do you think that we should make a concerted run at the record? "Bill asked.

"It's pretty much up to you, Bill. You are the one that actually has to go out and do it. What do you think?" Dave replied.

"I'm actually surprised at the times." Bill said and then repeated, "She didn't feel that fast. I think that we need some more time with this gearbox and wheel combination."

Dave realized that this translated into Bill wanting more time in the cockpit. There was not any real "we" about it.

"Fair enough," Dave thought to himself and then said out loud, "Like I said, you are the one who has to do it."

Bill mentally revisited and confirmed the factors detracting from a concerted record attempt. Nevertheless, the anticipation mounted throughout the regatta as the Atlas continued to demonstrate its growing potential. Every time Bill took the boat out onto the course, crew members from other teams and attentive fans and spectators would watch and ask each other, "Is he going to do it? Is he going for the record?" The fact that the record was in jeopardy was the buzz across the sport. The Miss Budweiser was also showing potential. Its massive Griffon engine was coming of age.

Although the qualifying speed of the Atlas at 137.195 was not a record, it definitely constituted a challenge and a speed to beat. Dean Chenoweth jockeyed the Miss Budweiser around the race course in an effort to answer the Atlas challenge. In a rare systems failure, the rudder came off of the boat during the effort, causing a crash that sent Dean to the hospital and knocked the Bud's hull out of the regatta.

Ultimately, Bill was poised to set a new record and David was indifferent. When the last opportunity to set a record during the qualifying period passed, the general optimism amongst the enthusiasts persisted. The record was going to fall.

With the Miss Budweiser absent from the scene, the Atlas team encountered substantially lesser resistance to another victory. Winning all three heats and the race was particularly rewarding because O.H. was on hand in the pits with the team. As the Atlas glided gently into the dock after the first heat, Bill walked up onto its bow to receive the bow line from his crew. O.H. was standing in the crowd. There was a throng of fans and spectators teeming around the edges of the dock area.

Sea change: a Shakespearean poetic or informal term meaning a gradual transformation in which the form is retained, but the substance is replaced.

As the bow line landed across his extended arms, Bill heard something that he had not before. Coming in from a victory, encountering a few "way to go's" or "nice job" from the fans was commonplace. It had almost become part of the racing ambience or complexion. The victory that he had just accomplished had been assured, resounding and without controversy. He had come a long way to develop his team and his personal performance to this point of competence. He knew that, but for the first time in his career, he noticed the booing.

Maybe it was because O.H., a man that Bill had a profound respect for, was in the crowd. Maybe the particular enthusiasts were especially loud or articulate. In either case, the overall attitude of a portion of the crowd had changed. If he had committed some sort of foul or made a controversial move on the race course he could understand, but he knew that was not the case here. He had gotten out in front and stayed there without contention. He began to realize that something important had changed in the eyes of the average fan. The Atlas team had reached a level of competitive proficiency where they were not being regarded as the struggling underdog anymore. With more wins than any other driver in the history of the sport, his victories were old news.

Overcoming substantial adversity and challenge was not the apparent issue. The sea change in attitude had evolved from the point where some of the fans resented the fact that they were guessing who would come in second. Bill had prided himself on taking the time to get to know his fans. He always tried to take more than a moment to scribble an autograph or acknowledge a wave. Maybe

Chapter Seventeen

what he was hearing was an exception and not the rule but he had to admit that it bothered him. They were booing him because he had won.

The most recent source of pride for Seattle as a community was the 1976 construction of a sports stadium capable of hosting national competition for football and baseball on par with any other major metropolitan community. Commonly referred to as the "Kingdome" (officially King County Multipurpose Domed Stadium) was located in downtown Seattle, a few miles from the Lake Washington race course. Nothing approaching this size of facility existed when Bill had lived in Seattle, and he enthusiastically accepted an invitation to speak to the fans of the newly formed Seattle Mariners, during opening ceremonies for the baseball game. He was sharing the podium with Senator John Spellman, a key proponent of the Kingdome's construction.

Bill accepted the microphone immediately after Spellman. With the mention of the fact that he no longer lived in Seattle and now resided in San Diego, the booing began. He did his best to banter with the crowd, but the overall experience was a wake-up call to the fact that not everyone likes a winner.

It bothered Bill... a lot.

When he mentioned his feelings about the episode to his family, one of them relayed a story where John Wayne was booed when he visited a hospital ward in Oahu during World War II. Here was somebody that Bill respected and had done so much to promote the heroism and sacrifice of America's troops being scorned by those same short sighted troops. Bill was genuinely surprised to hear that and seemed to take some comfort in the fact. Still, he sincerely cared what the fans thought.

The next race course on the circuit was on Mission Bay in San Diego, California and was reputed to be the fastest in the world. It had earned this distinction primarily for two reasons: salt water is denser and therefore provides a better purchase for the propeller, and the course was positioned in a way that minimized wake interference and wind effect. That was not to say that the wind couldn't be a factor to consider, but this particular race course in San Diego could be very fast to run on, especially in the morning.

In all, the Atlas team had two specially prepared engines designed, assembled and capable of record setting performance. The special pistons and rods created substantially greater strength and power than in previous models. The team had yet to run them except to test fire them in the engine well. As the team set up their pit area on the back stretch side of the San Diego race course, even the stolid Dave Seefeldt was a little anxious to apply them to a run at the record. The talk within the sport was still prevalent that the Blue Blaster was capable. Would she make the effort?

Neither Bill nor David actually discussed the topic while setting up in the San Diego pits. Some might argue with conviction and more than a little justification that this particular conversation was unnecessary between the crew chief and his driver. The team would go as fast as it could....period. It literally went without saying. Some that were superstitious might say that to talk about it could jinx it. In either case, Bill asked David to drop one of the special engines into the boat for its initial qualifying run.

The team promptly complied, and the anticipation grew.

Curiously, the Atlas Van Lines' Blue Blaster had always had a problem getting up on a plane. Getting from zero to 100 was infinitely more challenging than performing on the other side of the century mark. Once she attained a certain hovering attitude, she would behave well, but getting there was an unusually demanding proposition. In the beginning of its development, it had other substantial handling problems, as well. Bill had said during its maiden run on Lake Washington, home of the world famous "Floating Bridge" that she had wanted to fly over the bridge more than beside it. Jim Lucero had been able to quickly minimize that particular tendency but Bill continued to need to use maximum power in order to get the boat on a plane at the beginning of each run.

This particular practice was the reverse to everything in Bill's nature. "Conserve your equipment," was a practice that he preached to any novice. To apply maximum power to a cold engine at the start was against the grain and practice of any operator of mechanized equipment. Nevertheless, that was what it took to get the Atlas on a plane. In the beginning, not even that was adequate for the task. The application of nitrous oxide, which enabled the injection of an inordinate amount of fuel into the combustion chamber, was needed to get the job done. Although nitrous was commonly used on the course during competition, this particular use was somewhat of a trade secret. Furthermore, the orifice size for the nitrous/

fuel was fifty percent larger than commonly used in this practice.

The results of all this development created a resounding roar and leap anytime the Atlas would leave the pits. She could go fast; she just did not go slowly well.

As Bill hurled his boat onto the race course that particular morning, the crew stood on the dock coiling their lines or fidgeting with their boat hooks. Dave stood quietly up on the bank with his arms akimbo gazing out on the course. He knew the potential was there but ultimately it was up to Bill to get the feel of the course and boat to put it all together. The Budweiser team had paid a terrible price to learn that there were distinct limitations to men and equipment and Dave did not want to relearn the same lesson for a record run

The conditions that September morning were ideal for a record run - a quiet subtropical breeze of five mph with a moderate ripple on the water that actually helped the boat get up on top and stay there.

"It couldn't be better," Bill thought.

One of the crew members looked up at Seefeldt and asked, "Do you think he's going to do it?"

David just shrugged.

A few other fans looked on, sensing the gravity of the moment. The pits were generally quiet and unpopulated this early in the morning. Somehow, it seemed quieter.

As he crossed the starting line on the front chute, flew past the island in the middle of the race course, and approached the first corner, Bill knew that he had a lot more power on his hands. Although he rarely looked very carefully at the tachometer on the dashboard during competition, he could see enough to realize that, at the speed he was going, the needle on the gauge should be further over.

"More power at less RPM," he thought. After laying down a conservative first lap that provided all the systems to warm up, he decided to make a concerted effort to run as hard as he could.

Flying past the starting line a second time, the tachometer continued to climb. Tearing into the first corner, the hull rocked onto its starboard or right sponson and settled there. Without the wakes from other boats to overcome or any other substantial whitewater, the load on the engine and propeller was even and balanced. Instead of the traditional pulsating blare that was an auditory signature of the sport, the Atlas was able to broadcast an evenly balanced roar. Bolting from the exit pin, she galloped down the back chute toward the Hot Pits or second corner.

Then the tachometer dropped.

Midway up the chute, the RPM perceptively dropped off. It may not have been discernible to anyone on shore, but Bill noticed it immediately. He knew better than to push the equipment when he also knew something was wrong. Gradually dropping the RPM further, he swung the Atlas off of the course and back toward the pits.

Dave met him on the dock when he stepped off of the boat.

"I don't know, David. The power just seemed to go away," Bill said.

David knew that there was not any time to inspect the engine in detail. Unless it was something obvious, it could take a substantial amount of probing and trailer testing to determine the cause.

David turned to Tim Tafil and said, "Let's take a peek under the hood."

There was not anything Bill could contribute at this point, other than to get in the way. He turned, with his helmet which contained his goggles, under his arm and walked down the dock, up the ramp and into his motor home.

At the same time, David and Tim stepped onto the hull and stood on either side of the fiberglass engine cowling. "Looking under the hood," as Dave called it, involved unstrapping the rubber tie-downs that held the cowling in place, carrying the surprisingly light shell up and off the boat, and setting it on the dock. Hopping back onto the deck, they stood on either side of the engine well and studied the Rolls Royce powerplant and attendant lines, wires, and systems that made it run. No discernible splash of oil or scent of high octane fuel provided a clue, nor were there any loose wires dangling in the bilge. Quickly checking each sparkplug wire, they verified attachment and eliminated them as candidates for problems. At that point, both stood up from a bent over position on either side of the bright red engine and looked at each other. Seefeldt briefly looked at the morning sun.

There would only be time to swap and run the other powerplant.

Without saying a word, he looked up at the crane operator, gave a thumbs-up signal, and nodded toward the crew to begin getting the boat on the trailer.

Chapter Seventeen

As the September morning sun rose higher in the Southern California sky, the running conditions for setting a world record on Mission Bay sank lower. The team knew it. The fans knew it. Even the vendors knew it. As one crew member steadied the hull lying next to the dock, another met the hook from the crane as it swung over and attached it to the spreader bar used for lifting the hull out of the water. Immediately swinging back up and into the air accompanied by a diesel rev and smoky belch from the crane, the spreader was carried over the Atlas, guided into the appropriate position by another crew member whose eager hands steadied it, and connected the clevises to the aluminum lifting straps projecting out of the baby blue deck of the Atlas.

While one crew member kept tension on the rope or line secured to the transom of the boat, another maintained eye contact with the crane operator and gave specific instructions. Lifting it too quickly could actually damage the boat, so the first few feet off of the water were acquired slowly. The signal to do this was conveyed to the crane operator by the crew member with a hand signal that resembled the thumb and index fingers held over crew members head rubbing together as if feeling the texture of some oil or foreign substance. Once completely detached from the water's surface tension, the hand signal instruction to the crane operator changed to an index finger pointed skyward and twirling in a circular fashion followed by the universal thumbs up that acknowledged a thank you and a job well done. Settled onto the specially shaped hull cradles, or bunks, attached to the trailer, the crew scrambled onto the deck to detach the aluminum spreader with its steel cables from the boat. There were other boats that wanted to run, and it was a universal courtesy to release the crane's use as soon as possible. The Atlas crew always did this with alacrity by force of habit.

From the sultry and humid banks of the Ohio River to the dry heat of the desert in Eastern Washington, the Atlas team had worked together in the crucible of competition. Not kids, the average age was somewhere in the thirties, and they had become a contending unit performing under the most severe of circumstances. This situation called for an engine change involving dozens of lines and wires, a ton of equipment and nuts and bolts ranging in size and configuration from American threads to British Standard in Whitworth configuration. Each crew member was responsible for his particular area, and each other crew member relied upon him to dispatch his job in the fastest time possible without a mistake or set back. Furthermore, cross training allowed each member to appreciate the areas of expertise the other had while preparing for the possibility of absence or diversion.

There is no room for immature egos that would cause a member to take offense if someone were to double check a teammate's work. Actually, the contrary would often occur. One crew member might seek out another to come and check his work to verify its quality, or another might supervise without request and without conveying offense. The only thing that mattered was getting the job done right. Insecurities and fragile psychology had no place on the Atlas team.

This particular morning called for a seamless transition of one powerplant to another. Each engine had already demanded over 1,000 man hours to assemble, in addition to the time spent, for any special applications of parts or unusual preparations.

Quietly and with a minimum of conversation, each crew member went about the task. They had performed it dozens of times that season. With an economy of motion and a deliberation and focus often only seen on a Broadway stage or a NASCAR pit stop, the Atlas team rotated the powerplants and promptly swung the Blue Blaster back into the water. A virtual duplication of the twin brother it had just replaced, the Rolls Royce Merlin V-12 powerplant currently in the Atlas was possibly the most powerful engine of its size ever placed in a hydroplane. The potential for performance was truly remarkable, but no one spoke an unnecessary word. Dave Seefeldt was not the kind of crew chief to brag nor were his teammates the type of people prone to boisterous outbursts. This was a concerted effort to overcome the tides of chance and misfortune. Everything had to work as planned in order to achieve the planned pinnacle of performance. Focus, preparation and a little bit of good fortune would be required to pull this off.

The conversation between Bill and his chief was minimal as he stepped onto the baby blue deck and into the cockpit. There wasn't much to say. Wiggling down through the thick padding of the seat sides and sitting on the bare plywood bottom, Bill nodded to David as the latter stepped off of the boat. The plywood of the seat was deliberately bare in order to convey that extra amount of

Chapter Seventeen

sensitivity to Bill as he drove. Every bump, swerve, and vibration needed to be sensed and evaluated. To take his boat to a record level of performance, this personal preference was born of years of experience and would be even more appropriate this morning. Time was passing, and the ideal conditions for record performance were rapidly diminishing.

By this time, hundreds of spectators and fans had convened into the Hot Pit area for the day's activities. The whole area which was about the size of a football field was becoming a mass of teams, sponsors, media, and general enthusiasts. The weather was picture perfect. If there had been any pretense of secrecy or even discretion about the attempt on the world record, it had evaporated with the morning mist. Dozens of fans ringed the shore and dock area around the Atlas camp.

The salty water of Mission Bay roiled, bubbled, and cascaded into the air behind the Atlas as she lurched out onto the race course that would someday be named after her driver. Quickly gathering speed, she warmed up and settled into a comfortable drone running up the front chute past the hundreds of motor homes parked along the sandy shore. Annually migrating from across North America, these avid fans were intent on witnessing world class performance in the final regatta of the circuit. They were not usually disappointed.

Coming out of the first corner, Bill raised the engine's RPM and headed down the back chute or straightaway toward the SeaWorld end of the race course which was named after the internationally renowned aquatic facility located within walking distance of the pit area. All gauges and systems read fine. The hull flew effortlessly down the course and through lane two as it pulled around the second corner. Bringing the engine RPM up as loud as his ears told him that he dare, Bill pointed the front forks of his boat back down the front chute and focused intently on reading the water a quarter mile ahead. At that speed, anything happening any closer than that would be humanly unavoidable. Briefly, he glanced at the tachometer that was fast becoming a vibrating blur and determined that the RPM of the engine was quickly approaching a new increment.

Rocketing past the imaginary starting line, Bill took mental note that he was now on the clock. The timers and scorers sitting in the judges' stand adjacent to that imaginary line that ran across

In The Saddle

the front chute in front of them would be carefully recording his performance. The hull did not argue or buck as she slid through the upcoming corner and maintained the lane. Bill knew that the shortest way around the race course was often the fastest and was determined to use the lanes closest to the buoy line. As if from a slingshot, he and his steed bolted back down toward the SeaWorld corner.

Then it happened again.

The engine's performance perceptively dropped. Disappointed but disciplined, Bill gradually brought the speed of the boat down to cruising level and guided himself off the course directly back into the pit area. Trying to get world record performance out of an ailing engine would have been irresponsible and dangerous. Sliding up next to the dock, the disappointment was palpable on the crews' faces. Bill unsuccessfully tried to mask his own. There was no reason to think that they would be any more successful in finding the cause of the problem in time.

Once the boat was back on the trailer, David continued to ponder in frustration. For no particularly good reason, he instructed his crew to grab their individual fire bottles and man their positions on the deck for trailer running. Bill stood off to the side near the security fence line discussing his appreciation of his team's efforts with the media essentially maintaining media damage control. He didn't really have anything hopeful to say.

Placing himself in the driver's seat, David proceeded to restart the engine. While doing so, he called to his team and encouraged all of them to look for anything out of the ordinary. Anything at all.

Having recently been run, the Rolls started easily, and David brought it up to the aircraft cruising RPM of 2500. Every crew member peered intently into the bowels and confines of the engine compartment. Sometimes squatting down on their haunches, they would tip their heads or turn their ears in order to discern the slightest deviation from the norm.

Straightening up with his hand on his hip and his fire bottle dangling by his thigh, Glen Davis stared across the polished silver aluminum valve covers of the powerplant at his teammate Tim Tafil. Their eyes met, and Glen shook his head from side to side.

Then Tim's jaw dropped and he pointed at Glen's head while looking at Glen's ear. Glen reached his hand up to touch his ear and

Chapter Seventeen

then looked at his hand. Blood?

David happened to be looking at Tim and realized that he was seeing an expression he had never seen before. After working together for as long as they had, volumes could be spoken with a mere expression. This compelled him to look over at Glen and see him blankly staring at bloody fingers. Promptly going through the shut down sequence, David correctly deduced that the engine was spitting out pieces of piston ring. Under power, it was not particularly dangerous but it would immediately compromise the performance of the engine. For whatever reason that was most likely the cause of the power loss.

The silence that followed was somber and sobering. While the crew helped Glen tend to the nick on his ear, David climbed down from the deck to the ground and went over to Bill with the estimate of the situation. Dave felt responsible, but Bill took the news quietly. There wasn't much to say.

"Well, let's swap the motors back to one of our racing engines and get ready for competition," was all Bill could muster.

The attending crowd seemed to sense the disappointment and quietly dispersed.

As the crew was putting the finishing touches on the engine install, both Bill and David found themselves looking out over the race course. Predictably, the pace of the team had slackened to the yeoman stride of competence, and it was afternoon by the time the fuel system was retested and verified for the impending contest. Also predictable was the fact that the conditions for a record run had deteriorated, and while Mission Bay continued to be an excellent race track, it assumed a more rugged posture.

Nevertheless, a wistful expression passed over David's face as he walked over to his driver who was standing on a shore side boulder common to the man-made facility. Almost as an afterthought he said, "You know, William, you still have a perfectly good racing engine that can make that boat go pretty fast…" and let the sentence finish itself.

"…and it is a pretty fast race boat…" Bill went on. They looked at each other as if both were on the same side of a window looking outside on a cold, snowy, winter day. Almost as if he were saying, "The sledding could be pretty awesome…"

Bill looked at David and perceptively nodded. Without any further statement or commitment of purpose Bill said, "Let's throw her in the creek and feel out the course."

David only nodded and went over to instruct the crew. Whether the running conditions could accommodate a record run was not only unlikely, but something only a driver could determine in the saddle on the course. Changing tides, cross currents, cat's paws or bursts of wind skipping unreliably over the surface of the bay could all detract from the necessary ingredients. Bill went through the usual warm up sequence as he took the Atlas down, away from the Hot Pit area, and down the front chute past the Judges Stand. Coming out of the first corner, there was nothing noticeable indicated in the arc of his roostertail which would be the first sign that he was building speed for something special. As he came down the back chute and approached the second corner, Tim Ramsey looked up from the dock to David and excitedly asked, "Do you think he's going to try again?"

David did not take his eyes off the race course. He refused to anticipate or publicly predict what Bill was going to do on a race course. Part of his driver's strength was his flexibility and ability to adapt quickly to opportunities. He continued to look on as Tim waited expectantly for some kind of response. They noticed Bill slide the boat over the water as it approached the second corner from lane two into lane four for a wider turn around the course buoys.

Then David knew.

The only reason that a driver would make a move like that would be to use air pressure under his boat longer to enable quicker acceleration off of the corner, and the only reason for that would be to reach the maximum speed while crossing the starting line. In addition, there was only one practical reason for that. David glanced at Tim and finally gave him the nod he had been waiting for. That was all the response Tim would get from Seefeldt. If David had any sense of anticipation on his face, it was hidden deep beneath that extensive beard.

The Atlas powered out of the corner and thundered down past the judge's stand. Someone in the stand must have said something via radio to his counterpart in the Hot Pits, because immediately upon passing, the loud speakers of the P.A. system crackled to life and an announcer scratched out a statement that the radar was

Chapter Seventeen

suggesting that Bill was apparently putting the Atlas through her paces.

Fans and spectators stopped in midstride. Something was happening.

Others teams stopped working from the decks of their own boats and stood up in place looking past the cranes down toward the race course.

Canting through the first corner, the arc of the roostertail stayed tall and steady. With the grace of a ballerina performing a pirouette, the Atlas transformed from a turning creature into a drag boat as she assumed what resembled a lineman's stance and hurled herself onto the back chute straightaway. The roostertail grew higher as she came on down the course, reaching a level never seen before. Steady, growing and building the ascending roar projecting ahead of her at 700 MPH caused mouths to open and conversations to halt.

Something special was happening.

The singular roar of the Rolls Royce rolled over the crowd assembled at the shore line as the Blue Blaster tipped and turned through the SeaWorld corner. Unbroken and unwavering, it was trumpeting a different kind of a sea change. Everyone but the driver knew it. While it may not last, they were truly witnessing world class performance. It could be argued that every minute invested by every man on the Atlas team that season was reaching a culmination of effort at that moment. Articulate attention to detail, hours of extra labor to make sure that the job was done right regardless of notice or appreciation, countless meals missed, checklists checked, and parts carefully balanced and cared for were being applied at that moment. The skid fin flexed and held, the rudder stretched and twisted, yet the Atlas flew on out of the corner maintaining its lane.

The unbroken arc of her roostertail continued to describe a height never seen before on Mission Bay. Tim Tafil's hands clenched and pumped up and down. "Go, go, go!" could be heard emanating from several throats across the pit area as the Blue Blaster sailed over the starting line.

Immediately upon finishing his run, Bill decelerated and began cooling down the engine. He had no real idea whether he had accomplished anything with the lap he had just driven other than to have subjected his equipment to a substantial amount of strain. "Conserve the equipment," was the chant he recited to himself. Bringing the boat back into the docks, he carefully throttled down shutting off the fuel and electronic systems. The Atlas glided into the appropriate dock, and the crew casually grabbed and secured her with lines and boat hooks. Bill stood up in the cockpit and looked over at David. Pulling the helmet off of his head, his mouth held a frown, and he looked directly at his crew chief whose arms were folded akimbo as he stood at the edge of the dock.

When their eyes met, Bill subtly shook his head from side to side and quietly said, "I don't think so."

As if on cue, the P.A. system announced, "Ladies and Gentlemen. A new world's record has just been confirmed. The Atlas Van Lines just completed a lap with an average speed of 140.625 miles per hour..."

Although the announcer went on with more detail, his voice was drowned out by an overwhelming wave of cheering from fans and spectators across the pits. A modest smile grew on Bill's face to a broad-faced beam that clearly displayed the famous gap between his two front teeth as he stepped onto the dock.

Hugging his chief and personally shaking hands with every crew member it occurred to Bill that:
on that day,
on that race course ...
and in that place in time...
he had inarguably driven the fastest boat in the world
to a world record
with the best team in the world.

As an owner and a driver, he realized he had come a long way from Bogie Lake.

Less than 100 yards from where he was standing at that moment, a monument would be erected in his name shortly after his death.

Beneath a bronze relief of his face, would be engraved the words, "Just playing, like all the other kids I know."

The Atlas Van Lines race team probably developed the Rolls Royce powerplant as far as it could go in racing applications.

Bill putting the Blue Blaster through her paces.

The Bill Muncey Memorial on Mission Bay in San Diego.

CHAPTER EIGHTEEN

The Legacy

It was a classic spring morning in the Pacific Northwest. The sun was out; there were hardly any clouds in the bright blue sky, and the chill of the morning was ebbing away with the rise in baseball chatter amongst the boys as they donned their uniforms. Parents were spreading modest blankets on well-worn bleacher seats as the coaches gave last minute instructions to their gathered charges.

Several baseball diamonds were laid out over many acres, and the whistles of the umpires punctuated them each as they officially directed the players to assume their positions of play. Coaches stepped behind backstops; parents raised binoculars to their eyes to view their favorite players, and some players nervously tucked their shirts into their waistbands.

It was hardball, a different breed of play to those involved in the sport. Competition commanded that each player pay greater attention because there was a higher degree of risk. Play was a little faster than softball just by the virtue of physics. Americans seem to love to go fast. Whether it is on the playing field or race track, they truly embrace the challenge demanded by speed. Moreover, they happen to be good at it.

The pitcher and the catcher had limbered up through a couple of practice pitches before the umpire announced, "Let's play ball."

With that statement, a batter stepped up to home plate, and the competition formally began. Regardless of the ultimate outcome, for that brief moment both teams were equal. The competition was balanced. The result of the contest was anything but certain. The elusive pursuit of fair play and sportsmanship was about to begin. These concepts have been bred into the societal consciousness since the country's inception. Sometimes without realizing it, parents carry on this tradition of hope in a real and personal way with a determination that supersedes the Manifest Destiny or the perpetuation of the First Amendment.

Profound in its simplicity, most Americans sincerely believe that everyone has a chance.

Play that day was going to be different for at least one parent and son. For the first time, the eldest son of Bill Muncey, Wil, was going

The Legacy (unfinished)

to watch his son, William Edward Muncey III, play baseball. Bill's grandson had been given the nickname "Cruzer" by his parents who optimistically envisioned him "cruisin' for burgers" just as they had as teenagers.

The exclusivity of the moment had been greatly affected by the divorce of Cruzer's parents at an early age, and the ensuing relationship of the parents had strained. Careers, other relationships and interests, and a multitude of impotent excuses had prevented a more healthy exchange.

It was a special day and the first time that the two had been together since Bill's death during competition at the World Championship in Acapulco, Mexico on October 18th, 1981. The youngest was nervous, and his father sensed it. Wil had made an effort to emphasize to his son recognition of the nobility of his effort to compete rather than the result of the outcome. Being the namesake grandson of a sports celebrity carried with it an unreasonable level of responsibility in the public eye and today's activities heightened that further with the rare presence of Cruzer's father to watch him play. It did not ease his tension either knowing that his grandfather and father had both been earnest sportsmen.

In classic high drama fashion that could only have been conjured by a Hollywood screenwriter, Cruzer came up to bat at that critical point in a baseball game where his team was behind by a point, at the bottom of the ninth inning with the bases loaded and two outs. Up to that point, the contest between the two teams had been lively and equalized clearly demonstrating that, for Cruzer's part, he could hold his own.

He was not big for twelve years old. The regulation size bat balanced back over his shoulder accentuated his slight build. He kept the blond hair that he had inherited from both parents at average length which was barely discernible beneath the blue plastic batter's helmet he wore while standing in the batter's box. He was at that point in life where boys become young men and begin to take things more seriously. Cruzer fully realized that the pressure to perform was on him, and he was determined to extend every effort. Locking his gaze on the pitcher's eyes, he waited for the pitch.

His teammates were quiet while the opposing team heckled and cajoled from all quarters attempting to break the batter's concentration. The first pitch was a fastball low and to his outside. Cruzer

Chapter Eighteen

pushed off with his right foot and swung the bat into the ball with every ounce of power that his 99 pounds could muster. The ensuing crack of contact between the leather covered hardball and his Louisville Slugger could be heard two baseball diamonds over. The ball rocketed away from the batter's box.

It went straight into the first baseman's glove with a decisive, "whap!"

Cruzer was out, and the game was over before he laid his bat on the ground.

Blanketed by the din and cheers that tumbled out of the opposing team, Cruzer wished at that moment that he could be anywhere, any place but the place where he was.

Quietly, he looked up and saw his father walking over from the small set of bleachers where he had been sitting. With downcast head, Cruzer moved to meet him. When they were just a few feet apart, almost as if on signal, both stopped in their tracks. Cruzer looked up expectantly.

"Did you know," Wil asked, "that your Grandfather Muncey was the winningest hydroplane driver in history?"

Cruzer hung his head, biting his lip and nodded. The weight of the family fact seemed immense.

"Did you know," Wil went on "that he was also the losingest hydroplane driver in history?"

Cruzer slowly looked up, and his eyes seemed to get bigger. His jaw dropped slightly as he contemplated the point. He blurted out the question, "How did he do that!?"

"Your grandfather was a very determined and competitive person." Wil said, "All his life he tried to be the best at whatever he did, just like you just did. Whether he was going to be a musician, a soldier, a grocer, or a politician, he put everything he had into it in an effort to be the best there ever was at it. Once he decided that he was going to be a professional driver, he gave it 110 percent regardless of how each race worked out or how often he won. The only real difference between a winner and a loser is that a winner knows when he is winning. He told me that there were more second- and third-place finishes that he was proud of than first-places. Anyone can be a gracious winner. Sometimes a win reflects more on the team than the driver, but it takes a true champion to get up from the mat after he has been knocked down or do well with a situation

THE LEGACY (UNFINISHED)

where others might falter. A true champion is born by overcoming adversity and setbacks. By giving it 110 per cent, you stand a better chance of winning, but some days it works out and some days it does not matter what you do, Cruzer, the ball just does not bounce your way. Persistence is a talent!"

With that explanation, Cruzer became very quiet and thought for a moment about what his father had said.

Smiling, he looked up and asked, "Can we just go get ice cream?"

"Sure," Wil said.

Almost twenty-five years after Bill Muncey's death, the Hydroplane and Raceboat Museum in the United States conducted a survey of fans and racing enthusiasts, asking them to name their favorite hydroplane driver.

Bill was still number one.

Acknowledgements

The first person that I would like to acknowledge, without whose support this book wouldn't have been possible, is my wife, Debi. This tome was years in the making and required a substantial amount of patience, effort and understanding on her part.

After that I would be lost without the editorial support and services of Fred Farley and Holly Zynda. Any errors in fact or grammar are purely my own through obstinate determination or deliberate ignorance of good advice.

Individuals that contributed their time, encouragement and memories would include but not be limited to Marc Connelly, Stan Fitts, Gina Funes, Steve Garey, Ron Harsin, Dennis Johnson, Ron Jones Sr., John Lynch, Laurie Mercadante, Steve Muncey, Fred Radke, Dave Seefeldt, Joy Seefeldt, Brendan Shriane, Mira Slovak, Tim Tafil, Cruzer Webster, Dave Williams, and Randy Milligan.

For more information, pictures, author's blog and news about upcoming sequels, please log on:
www.BillMunceyChronicles.com